MOM'S LAST MOVE

A MEMOIR

ARLEEN WILLIAMS

United States, 2018

Cover Design by Loretta Matson
Interior Layout by Adam Bodendieck

:

ALSO BY ARLEEN WILLIAMS

MEMOIR

The Thirty-Ninth Victim

FICTION

Running Secrets
Biking Uphill
Walking Home

In Loving Memory of
Marcella Adeline Huber Feeney
September 21, 1924 – February 22, 2013

AUTHOR'S NOTE

This work is a memoir based on the personal recollections and perceptions of the author. All dialogue is reconstructed from memory. Some names have been changed or omitted.

PROLOGUE

THE THIRTY-NINTH VICTIM

THE HORROR BEGAN in 1984. The backstory began earlier, much earlier. A lifetime of backstory. In 1984 I was living in Mexico City, married to a Mexican national and eager for my youngest sister's second visit. Maureen had visited the year before. We connected for the first time since I left home at seventeen when she was still a Camp Fire Girl. Now at eighteen she was the troubled youngest of nine children carrying a whole load of baggage. But she came and fell in love with Mexico just as I had done years prior. We were both eager for her return.

It never happened. What happened instead is a horror no young woman, no parent, no family, no friends should have to endure. But we did endure and we still endure and we will continue to endure because that is the nature of horror.

My sister never returned to Mexico. Instead she fell in love for the first – and last – time with a man we later learned had a lifetime record, a family history – fathers, uncles, brothers – of drugs, extortion, and prostitution. Maureen was easy prey. The youngest of overprotective parents who grew up in rural isolation, she knew nothing of city life. She disappeared a week after she moved into her first Seattle apartment.

Missing. That's the word my mother used when she wrote to explain why Maureen hadn't answered my letters, hadn't sent her travel plans. Missing.

My parents tried to report Maureen's disappearance the day it happened, perhaps the day after. That close they were. Another sister, Doreen, was scheduled to pick Maureen up at her new apartment for their regular Sunday dinner with Mom and Dad.

That dinner never happened. A search began instead. The cops waited three days because Maureen was nineteen. The family started immediately. They called friends, posted signs, contacted Maureen's landlord and employer.

Maureen was missing. For three years she was missing. In those three years I returned to the United States, my marriage ended, and I fell apart bit by bit, scattered, lost, confused. But still there was hope. Maureen could be alive. Despite what the cops said, despite the fact that her case had been turned over to the newly formed Green River Taskforce, despite the chokehold the Green River Killer had on the city of Seattle, I still had hope.

Then on a beautiful sunny afternoon I was met on my doorstep by a woman who told me Maureen was dead.

My sister's remains were found in a triangular area of land created by the intersection of Highway 18 and Interstate 90, a spot halfway between our family home and my mother's workplace. Maureen's scattered bones were found in an area where those of two other Green River victims were found.

Those facts, the name of her first love and the location of her remains, were enough to label my baby sister a Green River victim and a prostitute, one of society's throwaways. In today's world she'd be recognized as an innocent, naïve victim of sex trafficking who had likely been drugged, raped, beaten, and forced onto the street. There was evidence to support this. But not then, not at a time when the entire investigation could be summed up by heel-dragging, inefficiency, and incompetence.

Maureen was branded, and my family was destroyed. For twenty years, Dave Reichert and the Green River Taskforce were unable to solve the worst serial murder case in the country. The taskforce was dismantled, and it felt as though my sister's killer, the man who was eventually convicted of forty-eight murders but suspected of twice that number, would never be captured. For twenty years I lived half a life, a life dimmed, blinded, suffocated by questions, anger and pain. I got pregnant, re-married, was blessed by a man and a daughter who stuck by me, though I was only half a mother and half a wife because the horror of what happened to my sister had torn me apart and left me emotionally ravaged.

In late 2001 the sole detective still working the Green River case ran a DNA test and identified the perpetrator. Maureen's killer was arrested on November 30, 2001, our father's eightieth birthday.

I spent the next half decade trying to make sense of what had happened to my sister, my family, my world. Under the guidance of two of the greatest teachers and most generous souls I have ever met, Robert Ray and Jack Remick, I gathered truths and wrote my way through the confusion and pain. The story became a manuscript, the manuscript became a book, and *The Thirty-Ninth Victim* was published in 2008.

But the story was not over.

I

SEVEN YEARS AND SIX DAYS

2002

DAD HAD BEEN sick since Christmas, but we didn't know how serious it was. Each time I called, Mom told me not to visit, Dad didn't want anyone in the house. But with each refusal she sounded more exhausted, so after weeks of being turned away, my sister, Doreen, and I decided to visit anyway.

We should've gone sooner. During that long drive to the Pacific Coast we learned Dad had died. Paramedics had rushed to the house, broken down his heavy gate with the hand-cut decorative wooden slats, and been unable to resuscitate him. We met Mom at the Aberdeen Hospital where she believed Dad died, unable, unwilling to believe it happened at home.

For the next week the family congregated. Then, after Dad's funeral, Mom's house was empty. All the siblings had returned to their various homes and jobs. My husband, Tom, and daughter, Erin, caught a ride back to Seattle with Doreen and her husband, and I remained alone with Mom.

I didn't want to go home. I didn't want to leave my mother in the tiny beach house. I didn't want to abandon her on the Washington coast in the gray dampness of early February, in the dampness that permeated the heart and soul even in times of joy. At times of loss, the dampness was suffocating. I tried to convince Mom to come to Seattle with me, to stay with my husband and daughter for a while. I assured her that Casey, my father's dog, now her dog, could come too. Our house was small, but we'd make it work.

"Or you can stay with Doreen for a few days," I told her. "She's got that pretty spare bedroom."

But she refused. When I left on Monday evening, Mom was alone with her pain, and I felt there was nothing I could do to make

it easier. I promised to return on Thursday, Valentine's Day and
drove home, my stomach in knots and tears tracking my face.

I'd been away from home for almost two weeks and knew I'd be
leaving again in three days. I touched base with Tom and made sure
that Erin was keeping up with her school work and dance classes,
that friends were thanked for their support, and that future
transportation arrangements to and from school and after school
activities were set in place.

I met with the substitute instructor who had been filling in for
me during my abrupt absence and collected the piles of papers that
needed grading. I taught my classes for a few days and provided the
sub with another batch of lesson plans.

On Valentine's Day, I taught my early morning classes and
headed back to Grayland to check on my mother. I didn't know how
to talk to my mother. Even after my sister, Maureen, was murdered,
I hadn't learned how to talk about loss. Now, I didn't know what to
say to Mom about Dad's death. Maybe we didn't have to talk at all.
Maybe I just needed to be with her.

The traffic to Grayland was light, and I made the trip in two hours.
As I pulled to a stop at the gate, I saw Mom at the front window peering
through the slats of the venetian blinds. I fussed with the latch and
struggled to open the old gate. The small metal wheels no longer rested
in the metal track beneath it. Apparently the paramedics hadn't realized
the gate rolled open and forced it to swing like a door.

As I drove up the short driveway to the house, Mom poked her
head around the edge of the front entry. She stood with her body at
an angle, the door opened only enough for a good view of the
driveway, but not enough to allow a much needed blast of cold,
Pacific air to freshen her tiny beach house. She didn't know my car,
never seemed to remember what I drove, but as soon as she saw my
face, she stepped out to greet me.

"Happy Valentine's Day, Mom. How are you and Casey? Do I
get a hug?"

"Of course," she said. "Are you alone?"

"Yup. Tom's working, and Erin's got Erin plans."

"What's all this?" she asked as I pulled bags from the backseat.

"Just a few things for the weekend."

"Weekend?"

"Yeah, if it's okay with you and Casey, I'll stay until Sunday. What do you think Casey? Will that work for you?"

Mom's house stood on one side of a large, fenced lot. Within this lot, a smaller fenced front yard lined the driveway. Behind this fence, a dirty, hairy golden retriever wriggled around, wagging his tail and barking his fool head off.

"Casey wants you to say hello," Mom said. "She hasn't even said hello, has she, Casey?"

"Hello, Casey." I stuck my hand through the gate to receive the slobber Casey never learned to keep to himself. "I'm not opening this gate, you stinky mutt. Just hold your horses, and we'll go out soon. What do you think? You want to go to the beach, don't you?"

"We go to the beach every day," Mom said. "Arleen's here, Casey. Do you want to go for another walk?" The barking and wriggling and wagging continued.

"Let's get this stuff into the house, Mom. Casey, we'll be right back."

"Oh, you can come in too," Mom assured the dog. Or maybe she was assuring me.

We headed into the house, and Casey raced in the opposed direction. He came in through the sunroom door on the south side of the house and stood at the open slider between the sunroom and the living room his tail still wagging.

"Look at Casey. He's such a good dog," Mom said. "And good company, too."

I dropped a couple of grocery bags on the kitchen table, and Mom sifted through them, lining up fruits, vegetables, cereal, and frozen dinners on the counter. "What's all this? We don't need anything, do we, Casey?"

"I know, Mom," I said. "But I saw a sale at TOP Foods when I stopped to use the restroom and had to take advantage of it. You always taught me to take advantage of sales. I couldn't pass up a good discount, could I? Here, let's get this stuff into the freezer."

"Well, we can have two of these for dinner tonight." She held up a couple of the frozen dinners I'd bought to stock her freezer.

"Not a chance. We're going out for dinner tonight."

"Casey can come too," Mom said.

"No way. This is girls' night out. He's a boy. No Tom. No Casey." I bit my tongue before blurting it out. No Dad.

As I nosed around Mom's house, putting things away, I noticed signs of change. Already the house was no longer "Dad and Mom's house." Photographs I didn't know existed were now stuck into the corners of frames that had long cluttered every flat surface of the living room. Unframed photographs of Maureen, my youngest sister, murdered at nineteen. Others of Laureen, an older sister who my father had disowned and refused to see for over thirty years. I was happy to see these photographs, but I didn't have the words to ask my mother about them or about her feelings. I was, in fact, acting just like her, acting the way I'd been raised to act. I was leaving the pain unspoken.

For years Tom and I wondered how Mom would respond when it happened. There was never a doubt in my mind that Dad would pass before Mom. He didn't have Mom's physical health. Instead, I wondered if she would honor Dad's choices and stick to his rules after his death just as she had done in their fifty years together, or if she would follow her own heart.

The first sign Mom might break from Dad's rules came when I asked her permission to invite Laureen and her daughters to the funeral and she didn't object. Laureen was teaching overseas and couldn't make it, but her daughters came to pay their respects to the grandfather they never knew. I watched in silence as my mother held her two adult granddaughters in a tight embrace for the first time.

I'd always believed my mother had a deeper, stronger love for my father than for any of her nine children. How else could I explain away her acceptance of his behavior toward my older sister and her daughters? So on Valentine's Day when I saw those photographs stuck up around the house, I believed I was seeing signs of my mother coming into her own, somehow returning to the woman I imagined her to be before she married my father.

It was midafternoon. Mom had put away the groceries, and I'd unpacked my overnight bag. There was still plenty of daylight on the beach. "What do you think, Mom? Should we go for a walk before we head up town?" I asked.

"Oh, we go to the beach every day."

"I know, but how about going with me?" I paused. "Unless you don't want to share your beach with me."

"Let's go," she said.

"Great. Are you dressed warm enough? Tights under those pants?"

"I'll be fine," she said.

But I knew she wouldn't be. I knew we'd climb the dunes between the house and the beach and be slammed by the winter wind off the Pacific Ocean. I knew we'd walk the short distance through the loose sand and by the time we reached the water's edge, she'd be cold.

"Do you think Mom's going to be warm enough, Casey?"

"Of course I'll be warm enough."

"I don't know. What do you think, Casey? Did she put tights on under those pants this morning? You were here. Did you look in through that bathroom window?"

"Arleen!"

"Okay, Mom. Hand me the leash."

"I'll do it."

"It's okay, Mom. Let me. Casey, you want me to do it, don't you old boy?" The dog wriggled and circled and jumped and slobbered. Mom handed me the leash and disappeared to the bathroom at the back of the house.

"Okay, you miserable mutt, we're going for a walk. Now behave yourself," I said when I knew Mom was out of earshot.

We made our way down the deadend street toward the neighborhood access trail that led across the dunes to the beach. "Stay off the road, Casey," Mom said.

I didn't say a word. I'd heard Mom repeat the same thing so many times I'd given up trying to convince her it was silly to walk in the rough gravel at the side of the road given only a few cars passed by each day and usually at about twenty miles per hour. I moved into the gravel, and Casey plunged into the weeds and overgrowth, tugging me along with him, in search of scents only a dog could enjoy.

"Tea?" I asked after we took off our sandy beach shoes and hung our damp jackets.

"Yes. That would be nice," she said. "Can you stay?"

"All weekend, if you'll have me." From the kitchen window, I watched Casey walk the fence line, sniffing for intruders.

"And your husband?"

"Tom and Erin will be fine. They can take care of themselves."

"That's good." She sat at the kitchen table and fingered the pink ribbon on the small gift I'd set there before leaving on our walk. "What's this?" she asked.

"Just a little Valentine's Day surprise. Go ahead and open it."

"For me?"

"Yes, for you, Mom. Happy Valentine's Day." I watched her open the gift, rolling the ribbon into a careful ball and smoothing the paper flat. She took the white ceramic dish from the box and removed the cellophane wrapping from the red heart-shaped soap. Then, she brought the soap to her nose and took a deep breath.

"Does it smell good?" I asked.

"Oh yes," she said. "It's very special. Thank you."

Years later, when I was emptying the house, I found that soap and soap dish still unused in a bathroom cabinet, saved for guests she never had.

"Here's your tea, Mom." I handed her the cup and walked over to the dining room table. "How's the puzzle coming along?"

"Oh, that thing," she scoffed. "Larry works on it sometimes. I'm bad."

"Larry?"

"You know Larry. The neighbor. He visits sometimes."

"That's nice," I said. "Come on. Let's see if we can put a few pieces together. Larry hasn't done all of this by himself."

We sat at the dining table fitting together pieces of two golden retriever puppies, sweet faces and chubby paws hanging over the edge of a wicker basket.

"Hey, Casey, is this a picture of you and your sister?" He perked up his ears where he now lay at the threshold between the sunroom and the living room. That was his limit. He knew he wasn't allowed into the rest of the house. Only the sunroom. From the time I was a child living on the farm in the Issaquah Valley, dogs were "outside animals." I'm not sure whose rule it was – Mom's or Dad's – but it was one rule that held after Dad's death. At least in the beginning. As the years folded onto each other, Casey found his way into the living room, the hallway, maybe even Mom's bedroom, though if asked she'd deny he ever came into the house at all. Already there were dog-hair laced dust bunnies in the corners and telltale dog hairs on the blue carpet.

I sat to work on the puzzle thinking of Larry, the neighbor down the street. Dad's friend though several decades his junior, a man who checked in on Mom, had tea and did jigsaw puzzles with her to keep her company. I was glad for the extra set of eyes, grateful that in this remote beach community there was one friend who lived year-round like Mom who would call us if there were a problem. Yet it felt odd, unfair, to be dependent on the goodwill of a neighbor I knew only by name.

"Shhhh, quiet, Casey," I whispered the following morning as I pulled open the sliding glass door to the sunroom. I patted him on the head with one hand and grabbed his tail to stop the thumping with the other. "Let's not wake Mom, you stinky old mutt. Now lie down and be quiet."

I tiptoed across the living room to the kitchen and switched on the coffee maker I'd set up the night before. When I pulled open the kitchen blinds, inching them up without a sound, I found the world beyond the tiny kitchen covered by a blanket of deep Pacific fog, blocking even the two-story blue house just across the road. I itched to be outside, to go for a fast walk on the long, lonely beach. Instead, I poured a cup of steaming black coffee made from grounds I'd carried from Seattle knowing the local market wouldn't have the fragrant, dark roast I craved every morning.

A folder of student essays lay on the kitchen table where I'd left it the night before, and I was determined to get some work done before Mom got up. This sleeping in was new. The mother I remembered was an early riser.

I worked for several hours, my pile of papers becoming more manageable, before I heard the sound of running water from the back of the house. Moments later the bedroom door opened.

"You ate without me?"

I heard the hurt in her voice.

"No, of course not. Good morning. Did you sleep well?"

She looked at me, at the kitchen table, at my cup. Unconvinced.

"I just had my coffee. That's all."

"I don't drink coffee," she said.

"I know. That's why I had mine. Alone."

"Okay. That's good." She wandered over to the sunroom door. "Hello, Casey. Let's let you out, okay?" Then she returned to the kitchen and pulled a box of Cheerios from a cupboard, milk, bread, and jam from the refrigerator. I gathered my papers – both graded and ungraded – into the folder and set it aside. The workday was done. The remaining hours were for Mom.

"How about I make some eggs or French toast?"

"Cereal's okay. And bananas." She stood at the kitchen sink gazing into the side yard. "Where's Casey?" she asked.

"He's out there, probably around back. You just let him out."

"Are you sure?" She went to the sunroom and opened the back door. "Casey. Casey. Come, Casey," she called.

I looked out the side window where Mom had stood just moments before and saw Casey under the large beach pines along the far fence line. "Mom," I called. "Come here. I see him. It's okay."

"Oh, I know that," she said. She scooped a cup of dry dog food into his dish, the first of many that day, and joined me in the kitchen.

"What should we do today, Mom?" I asked. She shrugged.

As I sat at the tiny kitchen table that filled the narrow space between stove and sink and watched my mother pull breakfast together, I marveled at her ability to get herself out of bed each morning, splash water on her face, and put on the same clothes she'd shed the night before. Only two weeks had passed since her husband, her life partner of fifty years, had died. How did she cope with her losses, with this pain so intense it took my breath away?

My father died of pneumonia in his recliner, refusing medical attention. Two months and three days before Dad's death, the police had arrested Gary Ridgway for murders committed twenty years earlier. The Green River Killer, who remained on the loose and continued killing for those twenty years, was arrested during my father's eightieth birthday party. After the party, Dad caught a cold, retreated to his recliner, and allowed pneumonia to take his life. I believe he chose not to live through the investigation, the new round of publicity, the confession, the sentencing.

My sister, Maureen, was murdered on September 23, 1983 when she was nineteen. At twenty-eight, I lost my position as the middle child. My daughter, Erin, was born five years and eight months later on a beautiful day in May when I was thirty-five and my mother was sixty-five. With Erin's birth, I was again in the middle. Now, instead of holding the middle slot in a string of nine siblings, I took ownership of that generational position between my daughter and her grandmother.

Mom was seventy-seven, I was forty-seven, and Erin was twelve when the earth again shifted beneath us, when we had to discover a new compass to direct our lives. Dad was dead.

Maureen had been gone for twenty years, but with no arrest there had been no letting go. With the arrest, Dad died leaving Mom alone to pick up the pieces of their shattered life. My mother hid her emotions, but her red puffy morning eyes told another story. Silent tears filled her lonely nights, and pain blurred her memory. She began to slip away, but lost in my own pain, I didn't see it coming.

We walked the beach again on the second day of my Valentine's visit with Casey tugging at his leash. I was desperate to free him so he could run the beach until he was exhausted.

"Sorry, Casey," I said. "Mom says no, so stop pulling. My shoulder hurts."

"Here Casey," Mom said. She reached for the leash to take it from me.

"No way, Mom. I don't want to watch you dragged down the beach. Casey, it's my turn. Now slow down."

"Okay," Mom said. "Casey, we have to take turns." That's the way it was. In a family of eleven, we all learned to take turns. Even Mom.

My mother and I shared our love of the Grayland beach. And maybe Maureen and Dad did as well, but I never took long beach walks with Maureen. I'd already moved away by the time Dad built this home. And I didn't walk much with Dad either. As he aged, the pain in his knees limited the walks he was able to take in the soft beach sand. Now with Mom it was different. We walked, and we gathered. Sometimes I searched for sand dollars. Other times I was on the lookout for agates or small beach rocks, worn smooth by the waves and sand.

"What are we looking for?" Mom asked that morning when we headed out after breakfast.

"I don't know. Sand dollars, I guess."

"Here's a good one," she said with the excitement of a child at an Easter egg hunt. When she handed it to me, I flipped it over only to find that the underside was broken. The search continued. Other days, when it was beach rocks, she'd ask me what color I wanted. We'd walk along the shore scoping out treasures, eyes glued to the ground in front of us, open to whatever showed up, whatever caught our attention.

"Look at this one. Do you think it's an agate?" I held it up to the light to see if there was enough translucence to call it an agate and add it to one of our various collections.

We walked the beach, pulled forward by Casey, pushed along by the stiff wind. Still, there were stops. Mom saw another sand dollar. Perfection. We filled our pockets because once again we'd forgotten a plastic bag for our sandy treasures. And we filled our lungs with salty, cold sea air. We made the one-mile loop. I was exhilarated. I wanted more but Mom was slowing down and Casey no longer pulled at the leash, his limp more pronounced. We returned to the house.

As I write these words it saddens me that Erin didn't share these walks. When she was young, until five or six, she loved the beach, but she never loved her grandmother's concerns, corrections, scolds, nags, or whatever they were. Erin just wanted to get wet and dirty and have fun. Mom worried about her going into the water – the undertow would get her. Mom fussed about her getting cold – she'd get sick. Mom scolded about how sandy she was getting – it would track into the house. The nagging was constant, and soon Erin lost interest in the beach and in visiting Nana. She got bored with the long walks and the collections of beach rocks and agates, sand dollars and shells.

When Erin was very young, three or four maybe, we used to wander Alki Beach near our West Seattle home and gather beach glass – broken pieces of glass in various tones of blue, green and brown tumbled smooth by years of tossing and churning in the ocean waters. Erin learned to check for points. If the glass was sharp, she gave it to me to throw in the garbage. If it was as smooth as stone, we added it to our collection.

Years later when Erin was a pre-teen and our walks together along Alki Beach were a thing of the past, she asked if we could give the beach glass collection to a friend's mom who did arts and crafts. The problem with collections is I never know what to do with them. I hadn't found just the perfect container for the beach glass so it was stashed away in the attic. I gave away that collection. Like a fool, I said okay.

Now when I walk Alki Beach, I realize the beach glass is gone. More collectors? More plastic bottles? I don't know. I just know I've gone to the beach several times thinking I'd start a new collection of beach glass only to be disappointed. But then what difference would it make? Even if I were to replace the entire collection with new pieces, they would not be those Erin and I found when we walked the beach together. They wouldn't carry the memories of those wonderful shared moments just as future walks along the Grayland beach won't be the same without Mom. I can still gather beach rocks and agates, sand dollars and shells, but they won't carry memories of the walks I shared on the coastal beach with my mother in the seven years and six days after Dad's death as the waters of the Pacific Ocean washed away her pain and carried away her memories.

∾   ∿

I drove the steep hill to Aberdeen Hospital, Mom at my side her arms wrapped tight around her middle as though holding herself together.

I'd arrived in Grayland the day before. That evening and the following morning, I watched Mom's repeated bathroom runs in silence. By late afternoon Friday, I couldn't keep quiet any longer. Something was wrong.

"What's up, Mom? Are you okay?" I asked.

"I'm having some trouble," she said. "Cramps. Bad cramps."

"Should we see a doctor?"

"Tomorrow. If I'm not better."

Tomorrow was Saturday and going to the doctor meant going to Aberdeen Hospital, the same hospital where Mom slipped Dad's jade ring from his finger, where I bent to kiss his forehead, where we said goodbye to his cold body.

We sat in the waiting room, Mom with her arms still clutching her belly against the spasms that kept her rushing to the hospital restroom. It was exactly one month to the day after Mom called 911 and paramedics failed to resuscitate my father.

When the receptionist called Mom's name, she stood and looked down at me. I remained seated paging through a tired magazine, wishing I'd thought to grab a book.

"Do you want me to go with you?" I asked her silence.

She nodded.

I didn't expect this. At twelve Erin had already insisted I allow her to see our family practitioner alone. I talked it over with the doctor, and we decided it was okay. It gave Erin the sense of independence she needed. Now my mother wanted me to go into the exam room with her.

I'd never seen more of my mother's body than bare arms and legs in the summertime. As I helped her out of her clothes and into the flimsy hospital gown, I wondered if she felt as uncomfortable as I did.

The doctor asked questions. Mom mentioned trouble sleeping and Dad's death. What about Maureen's murder? What about the Ridgway arrest? What about meeting your adult granddaughters for the first time at Dad's funeral? I wanted to scream. I wanted to complete the doctor's file on Mom's tragedies. But I remained silent. The respectful daughter, I was still acting the part of that child who had been taught to be seen but not heard. "It will take time," the doctor said. "We can give you something for the intestinal cramps and diarrhea, but the emotional stress on your body will take time to work through. Try to take a nice long walk or do something you enjoy each day. It will just take time."

But time was not kind to my mother.

ॐ ॐ

"How was your weekend?" asked the cashier at the campus cafeteria.

"Another Grayland visit," I said, more to myself than to her. Another long drive, another difficult goodbye.

"Grayland? Down by Westport, right? I love it down there," she said. "We camp at that state park every summer. Already got our reservations. I can't wait."

And that's it, I thought as I carried my soup and bagel up the stairs to my office. I went to Grayland every other weekend. A place most folks visited for vacation fun had become an obligation for me. Long quiet visits with Mom, struggling to find things to talk about. Grocery shopping and lawn maintenance, short walks on the beach and long evenings of crappy television. The beach walks were the best part of every visit. Odd I never thought of the place as a vacation destination. Or maybe not so odd at all.

Spring arrived in the Pacific Northwest. The early flowers – daffodils and tulips, lilacs and camellias – brought the fragrance and joy of new beginnings. In late April, I asked Erin what she wanted to do for her thirteenth birthday.

"Go to the beach," she said.

"To Grayland?" I asked. "You've got to be kidding. I thought you hated going there."

"I do," she said. "I want to go to Ocean Shores. Could we stay in a hotel? Could I invite two friends?"

"Five in one room?" I asked, failing to keep up with the spitfire speed of her planning process.

"No, Mom. We'd get two rooms. You and Dad could have your own."

"Ahhh, thanks."

"Come on, Mom."

"Let me talk it over with your dad." I used the standard delay tactic. The one I'd learned to employ whenever my daughter was thinking and talking circles around me.

A few weeks later, we were on the road for Ocean Shores, a coastal resort to the north of Mom's place. I remember the drive, three girls crammed into the backseat with pillows piled between them, the back of the station wagon loaded to the roof. I remember the stop in Aberdeen for rollerblading along the river. I remember the cool breeze of early spring and the pungent scent of fresh cut lumber from the mill on the opposite bank. I have a photograph on my bookcase at home, a photograph I do not need to remember the tight warmth and intense joy of my daughter's spontaneous hug.

We pulled into the hotel parking lot in Ocean Shores, and Tom tossed Erin the car keys. We grabbed our small overnight bags and headed to check-in leaving the girls to unload on their own. From a third floor window, we watched Erin and her girlfriends push an overloaded luggage cart across the parking lot.

"That's for one night?" Tom asked. "Looks like they're moving in."

I laughed. I had no idea what the girls had packed in their overflowing duffle bags, grocery bags and backpacks.

"Independence," I said. "They packed independence."

For a brief moment I thought about Mom. I wondered if she had found her own sense of self, her independence, when she left home after high school and moved into a dormitory room at Mounds-Midway School of Nursing in Minneapolis-St. Paul. I see my mother, a slender young woman, just over five feet with sparkling green eyes and long blond waves. I see her moving into a room for two, maybe four, young women like herself, all eager to become nurses by taking advantage of the new federal program of fast-tracked training designed to meet the growing demand. The country was at war. Nurses were needed.

I see these fresh-faced young women with their pressed white uniforms and starched nursing caps, and unwilling to set aside the vestiges of femininity, the bright red lipstick, the string of pearls. I wonder how much decorating went into that dorm room. Was Grandpa asked to paint the walls as Tom would later be when Erin moved into her first apartment? Were pictures hung and pillows fluffed?

Once Erin and her friends had settled into their hotel room, they headed across the dunes to the beach. "Check out the horses," I told them. "See if you want to do that Sunset Ride."

Tom and I sat on the balcony enjoying the afternoon sun sparkling over the Pacific. It wasn't long before we saw the girls climbing the dunes from the beach. Erin and one friend appeared. The other was missing. Crap, I thought. Why'd they separate? They weren't supposed to separate. I watched in relief a minute later as the third girl bounced over the dune, a boy on her heels.

"Crap," I said aloud.

"Don't worry," Tom said. "They weren't gone long enough to get into trouble."

"Teenagers. She's a teenager now. I don't think I can deal with this," I said.

"Do we have a choice?"

"I suppose not."

"Do you think they'll want to have dinner with us?" Tom asked.

"If we pay," I said.

It sounded harsh when I heard the words in my head, even harsher when I heard them aloud. But at thirteen being independent of us, the parental unit, was foremost. Yet without a source of money, without economic independence, Erin remained dependent. And she hated it. We continued to buy time with her, knowing, or at least hoping, that with a few years of maturity, she would once again enjoy spending time with her parents.

We had a late dinner that night when they returned from the sunset horseback ride on the beach. "They wouldn't let us gallop. It was so lame." Yet their complaints held little weight given the joy written across their faces.

After dinner, when they invited us down the hall to their room for birthday cake, we struggled to control our laughter. The small room was overflowing with pillows and piles, with magazines, photo albums, and clothing. The vanity counter was hidden under the perfumes, lotions, bubble bath, makeup, and costume jewelry of three young teenage girls. Pink, blue, and yellow streamers crossed the room from one corner to the other.

The piles held every kind of clothes imaginable – leggings, high heels, frilly blouses, T-shirts, jeans, shorts, bikinis, tennis shoes. I remembered the dress-up basket stuffed full of fancy old dresses, boas, and high heels now packed away in the attic at home. I saw these same three girls, a decade before, playing dress up together, each in as much grown-up clothes as they could layer on their small bodies, stumbling around in high heels many sizes too big for their little girl feet.

I remembered the ridiculous makeup kit my father – the man who often demanded to know why my sisters and I were wearing "war paint" on our faces – had given my daughter a few years earlier. It was a large, metallic silver box with multiple trays loaded with every eye shadow and rouge in the color wheel.

"I thought it was a tool kit," he smirked.

"It's for dress up," my mother said. But Erin was beyond little girl games.

These images of childhood flashed before me in that hotel room at the beach as the girls cleared off two chairs for Tom and me. We sang *Happy Birthday*, and Erin made a wish before blowing out her thirteen candles. We ate our cake, Erin opened a few gifts, and then there was a lull. A glance from one young face to the next made it clear we were no longer welcome.

We left them to their new game of dress up, or so I imagined. A game of putting together outfits, trying new makeup tips, taking each other's photograph. A game of fashion model photo shoot. A game of defining independence all night long, alone without adults, in a beachfront hotel room.

Tom wanted to plant himself in a sleeping bag on the floor outside their door for the night. "Fire code violation," I told him. Besides where would they go? Would they really want to go anywhere? I didn't think so. I suppose to this day I don't really know what they did all night, but they didn't get into trouble. We met for breakfast. They dragged themselves into the hotel restaurant half asleep, rumpled, unshowered, the telltale signs of exhaustion on their faces after a night of shared secrets.

The drive home was quiet with all three asleep in the back seat, cuddled together like so many puppies, a tangle of arms and legs. This is what the beach is all about, I thought. Only three months had passed since Dad's death and my heart was heavy, but those two days at the beach were a wonderful break, a reminder of why the cashier at the campus cafeteria looked forward to her family camping trip each summer in the wild beauty of the Pacific Coast.

My eldest sister's son was graduating from high school in California a month later. It seemed the perfect distraction for Mom and a chance to get her away from Grayland. We were still trying to convince her to stay with one of us – Marleen in California, Robert, Michael or Andrew in Hawaii, Charleen in Ellensburg just over the mountains in Central Washington, Doreen or me in Seattle. We figured she could spend some time with each of us. She was having none of it, insisting instead on staying alone in Grayland with Casey. Casey was the problem. She never wanted to leave the dog, and none of us wanted to keep him. He barked at everything and pulled like crazy on a leash. And he stunk. No matter how much you washed him, he stunk. It was as though he were rotting from the inside out.

To my complete surprise, she agreed to go to California.

"Will you go too?" she asked when I proposed the trip.

"Of course," I said.

"What about Casey?"

"We'll leave him with Tom and Erin and Mozart, okay? Casey and Mozart are great friends. They'll keep each other company."

"Okay," she said.

I bought plane tickets that afternoon.

At SeaTac airport, I ushered Mom through security to the gate and settled her into a hard plastic chair in the waiting area. She looked every bit a lost little girl with wrinkles and white curls, tiny and confused.

"I'll be right back," I said.

"Where are you going?"

"Just to the restroom. I'll be right back."

"I need to go, too," she said.

"Okay," I said. "Let's go together."

Like traveling with a two-year-old, I thought. I made excuses. She was out of her environment. She could function fine in Grayland where everything was familiar, but in new surroundings she got confused. I told myself this was normal. She was old. She was in mourning.

I linked my arm through hers and headed to the restroom. Later, as we sat waiting for our flight to be called, I saw my mother as a fearful shell of the woman she once was. This was the woman who once flew for United Airlines at the end of WWII when flight attendants were still called stewardesses and had to be registered nurses to qualify for the job. Now, we took a flight together, mother and daughter, with roles reversed.

My sister, Marleen, and her husband lived on a golf course. But Marleen was a walker, not a golfer. When Mom and I arrived to her hilltop home, the first thing we did was go for a long walk. The air was dry and warm, pungent with eucalyptus. But it was too much for Mom, or too hard for my sister to slow down so Mom could keep up over the rolling Moraga hills. The next day, Marleen showed us around by golf cart, the favored country club mode of transportation.

"Come on, Marleen, let me drive," I whined. Once the younger sister, always the younger sister.

She finally gave in, more because she could no longer stand being in the cart than because she was sick of my begging, I think. I'd never driven a golf cart before, but once we were back on the main road to her house, she pulled over and let me climb into the driver's seat. After a few brief instructions, she took off on foot, legs extended, arms swinging at her sides. Mom sat at my side laughing as I raced the golf cart up the hill challenging Marleen to keep up with us.

It was a warm spring, and the graduation was to be outdoors. Marleen insisted we all needed sun hats with broad brims. We took turns standing before the mirror in a local shop trying on straw hats – floppy and firm, fancy and plain – like little girls playing dress up, laughing and teasing until we each made a selection. We wore our hats to the graduation and throughout our weekend visit.

☙ ❧

From the day of her first ballet class at age two, Erin was a dancer. Later, she tapped and plié-ed her way through the confusion of adolescence. She danced through my mood swings and her own. She danced through tears and anger and pain. She danced through the arrest of the man who murdered the aunt she was robbed the chance of ever meeting, and then through her grandfather's death. On June 29, 2002 she danced across the stage of Seattle's 5th Avenue Theater for the first time in a school recital.

I remember the fear in my mother's eyes, the fear I'm sure was reflected in my own eyes, as Erin jumped from the car a few hours before the show.

"This is good, Dad," she said. She danced her way down the dirty alley, dodging trash bins as she made her way to the stage door carrying a large garment bag in one hand and a small dance satchel in the other.

"It's okay," Tom assured us both. "She's inside now. She'll be fine."

I'd gone to Grayland the day before and convinced Mom to come to Seattle for the show. After the trip to California, there was a bit of a shift, a willingness to venture out for brief visits, always with the promise of a ride home whenever she was ready. She never stayed for more than a night or two, which made for a very long weekend what with the drive both directions to get her and take her home, but still it was worth the effort. The change was good for her, I told myself. But the truth was I wanted her in Seattle to share my life and Erin's.

Later that Saturday, Mom walked down the sloping aisle of the 5th Avenue Theater, her hand in mine as we found our seats. We settled in for what I knew would be a very long show.

"Is it over now?" Mom asked when the lights came up.

"Only the first half," I said, worried she was ready to leave.

"That's good," she said.

I breathed a sigh of relief. I was certain Mom couldn't recognize Erin on the stage. The lights, the makeup, the costumes made it difficult for all of us. I was happy the music and color was enough of a thrill to keep her smiling.

∂∾ ∾ᖇ

I remember the day I became a writer. I still hadn't put pen to page
for anything more than journal ramblings, still didn't know what a
scene was, still hadn't heard of timed-writing practice, but as I look
back, I know that day was a turning point in my life. It was late
summer 2002. Dad had been gone for six months, the investigation
into Maureen's murder had reopened, and I was falling apart.

I don't remember why I was in my campus office or why Tom
was there with me. In over twenty years of teaching at the college, I
could count Tom's campus visits on one hand. I do remember the
bright sunlight flooding my small office through the second-floor
window. I remember the open door allowing a draft of fresh air to
flow through. I remember Tom standing over my left shoulder as I
sat at my computer.

"You have to do something," he said. "You've got to find a
release. A way out. You've always said you wanted to write, so
write. If counseling hasn't helped, maybe something creative will."

"But I don't want to do another master's, and I'd never get into a
doctoral program. Besides I'm sick of academia. I couldn't take the
pressure. Not now. Not ever."

"There's got to be other options," Tom said.

Since Dad's death, even before, I'd been in and out of
counseling. It kept my head above water, out of the oven. That
wasn't good enough anymore – not for Tom, not for Erin, not for me.
I had to find another solution. I had to find a way to understand and
release the pain inside of me before it destroyed the fragile joy Tom
and Erin had brought into my life.

Tom was an artist. He understood the power of creative
expression and pushed me toward a world I'd always been afraid to
embrace. I sat before my campus computer and began Googling.

As if by magic or perfect synchronicity, an aligning of forces or
just the tapping of the right combination of key words, up popped
the Writing Program offered through the University of Washington
Extension. My eyes scanned the screen. Memoir. Three-quarter
certificate program. A blurb about turning journals into memoir.

"Maybe I could do this," I said. "I've got stacks of journals."

"Sign up," Tom said.

Reading more, I learned of an orientation session. "Okay, I'll go to the orientation. I'll give it a try. But I don't promise anything. Not yet."

"Good enough."

A few weeks later as I found a seat in a UW classroom, I could feel a pit growing in my stomach, anxiety crawling my spine. I was back on the UW campus where I'd finished my Master's in Education a decade before, just after returning from years of self-imposed exile in Mexico. At that time I was still coping with re-entry culture shock, a failed first marriage, and the disappearance of my youngest sister. Just being back on campus was tough. I almost walked out.

But then we broke into small groups, and I found myself face to face with Jack Remick, one of the two professors who would be co-teaching the course. Gray ponytail. Black turtleneck and jeans. No nonsense. Abrupt. Serious. Dedicated. He reminded me of a political science professor I'd had many years earlier, also at the University of Washington where I was working on a Bachelor's degree while war raged in Southeast Asia. A professor who moved around the lecture hall plotting and prodding – the revolution within our grasp. But I was too messed up for revolution and belonging to anything was beyond me. Instead, I ran. Now three decades later Jack Remick challenged me again, but in an off-handed, not-giving-a-shit manner, to see if I could make sense of my life through words. Did I need a laptop? No, just pen and paper. Just show up. Just put in the seat time. I could handle that much, I decided. I registered for the program that night.

☙ ❧

Erin was pale with fear, her soft complexion blotchy and strained. She was sitting semi-upright in pre-op, wrapped in a skimpy surgical gown under piles of blankets, her teeth chattering. We waited and waited and waited. Thirty-five minutes was an eternity. The anesthesiologist arrived, and Erin clung to my hand.

"Will I wake up, Mom?"

"Of course you will, Sweetpea."

"Where will I go?"

"To sleep. Just like when you go to bed at night."

"But what if I don't wake up?"

The question cut like a knife. The same question had floated at the back of my mind since we agreed to this simple surgical procedure to remove Erin's tonsils and adenoids in hopes of reducing her sinus problems.

For an hour her question weighed on me as Tom and I waited, holding hands, trying to reassure each other all would be well. As we waited, I thought of other pain, other surgeries. I remembered the pain I saw in my mother's eyes when she was in a hospital many years before. I saw my own pain as I handed her my journal, the journal of my adventures in Mexico, because I couldn't find the words to talk to her. I didn't know how to build a bridge of words between us.

Mom once mentioned her work in a maternity ward in Merced, California. She commented on the Mexican women who "never uttered a peep" as they gave birth. Like those women, my mother did not complain.

Mom was a woman who gave birth to nine children. A woman who endured a hysterectomy and back surgery. A woman who worked as a registered nurse most of her adult life, working through the nights of my childhood so she was home when my siblings and I left for school in the morning and when we returned in the afternoon. And still, I cannot remember a whisper of complaint. Maybe I wasn't listening.

In the mid 1970s, I made my first solo trip to Mexico City, and then to Puerto Vallarta and Mazatlan on the Pacific Coast. I knew Mom was scheduled for back surgery and planned to be back in Seattle to help out as best I could. I traveled by bus and train. By the time I reached Los Angeles, I was sick with fever and diarrhea, unable to make it to Seattle before surgeons fused the vertebrae of my mother's lower back. I can still feel the desperation of those days as I vomited into a friend's toilet and worried about my mother. What were her odds? Would she make it? Would I see her again? We didn't talk of such things.

I was finally well enough to board a Greyhound, my backpack weighing on my shoulders. I don't remember reaching Seattle, where I stayed or even how I got there. My only clear memory is of that hospital room where my mother lay in traction. To my eyes, it looked like some kind of contraption Dad would put together to do a job that was too much for a single man, but still he'd do it, rigging up ropes and pulleys to distribute weight, to lift and move what one man alone could not. Now my mother was connected to ropes and pulleys, and I had no idea what to say to her. We never spoke much, never developed the easy rapport of mother and daughter. I didn't know how to tell her about the crowds and smog of Mexico City, the extreme contrasts of wealth and poverty. I didn't know how to share the thrill of climbing the Aztec pyramids of the sun and the moon in the dry arid air, or the weakness I felt at the high altitude of Mexico's central plateau. I couldn't find the words to describe the cobblestones and bougainvillea of Puerto Vallarta or the young man I fell in love with but didn't sleep with. I didn't know how to communicate with my mother, so I gave her my journal to read about my adventures as she lay stretched out in a sterile hospital bed. What teenage girl gives her mother her journal as hospital reading material?

My mother shooed me away, told me to get some rest, to see a doctor if I didn't feel one hundred percent soon. "You probably have worms," she said. "Did you boil the water?"

When I returned for another visit, my mother handed me my journal. "Your father and I are glad you got home safely." That's all she said, nothing more. We never talked about the places and people I described, not even about the boy in Puerto Vallarta. That evening when I opened my journal, I found Mom's words written in a weak hand at the end of my last entry: "P.S. And our prayers are answered, you are home safe and sound. Love, Mom."

Now, decades later, a nurse called our names, and Tom and I followed her into post-op. Again, Erin was cocooned in thin rumpled blankets, her pale face poking out from the pile. A short-lived smile spread across her face when she saw us.

"Is it over?"

"Sure is."

"It hurts."

"It'll get better," I said, knowing the orange icicle the nurse gave her would be the first of many.

On a clear Tuesday evening in late September, one of those crisp, cool days when you can smell autumn in the air, I climbed the worn steps of Denny Hall, the oldest building on the University of Washington campus. I made my way along the narrow corridors and into a classroom with a high ceiling, tall windows, and old wooden desks. I felt as though I'd stepped back in time, and I suppose in a way I had. I sank into a seat off to one side of the small room and found myself sinking lower and lower as introductions began, as the two professors, Robert Ray and Jack Remick, called roll and asked each of us what we were working on. When it was my turn, I wanted to disappear. I wanted a trap door to open in the old hardwood floor and swallow me, desk and all, into emptiness.

"Nothing," I said. "I haven't written anything. Just my journals."

We began with firsts and lasts. Five minute writes. Ten minute writes. The first time ... The last time ... By the end of that first class, my tears told me the story I needed to write. Maybe it was the lack of sentimentality in the room that allowed me to begin to explore my story, Maureen's story. Maybe it was my anonymity. I felt safe, even supported, among strangers. As the weeks folded into months, the strangers became classmates, the professors became mentors, but somehow I continued to feel safe. Maybe that person sitting at the hard wooden desk wasn't really me. Maybe the horrors she was facing weren't really mine. When each two-hour class ended, I packed that person away in my book bag with my writing materials and growing collection of work. I walked alone across the dark campus to the parking lot in a daze of memory and drove home leaving the stories, memories, and pain hidden in my book bag.

But just in the beginning. Soon the stories were flowing at home as well, and at coffee shops and libraries while I waited for Erin during swim team practices and dance classes. When Jack and Bob invited the class to join an open writing practice at a local coffee shop called Louisa's Café, I was ready. Nervous yes, but ready for the challenge. Within a month of that first day of class, as though I'd been prepping for the moment, my mother got a call from Detective Pavlovich of the Green River Task Force. He scheduled an appointment to drive to Grayland to take a DNA sample. The case against Gary Ridgway, the man charged with my sister's murder as well as that of forty-seven other young women, was open, and the Task Force was collecting evidence. Later in the month when I sat in my mother's living room, with Mom at my side and the detective in front of me, I put on the cloak of a writer. I separated the personal me, the sister, the daughter, from the writer me. A mental health specialist might say I was disassociating. I knew I was surviving. I was allowing myself the distance to listen and learn and to grow the confidence I needed to ask Detective Pavlovich for an appointment at the Task Force offices in Seattle.

In one short month, I'd become a writer, not a good writer, but still a writer. With my protective coating around my heart, I did the necessary research to face the truth of my sister's gruesome murder almost twenty years before. In the Task Force office, I paged through the heavy notebooks of evidence never used in court because a plea bargain rendered a trial unnecessary. I took copious notes.

Tuesday nights I returned to the classroom and dredged up childhood memories of my sister, myself, and the family that shaped us. By the end of that first quarter, by the date of Ridgway's confession, by the day my daughter and I sat side by side in court as Ridgway was sentenced to life in prison without parole on forty-eight counts of first-degree murder, I knew I was writing a memoir. I didn't know what would ever become of it, but I knew the story needed to be told, and I knew I needed to write it.

                                       * *

By fall 2002 I had a routine that involved a full-time job, the responsibilities of motherhood, a weekly evening class, writing practice twice a week, and one monthly weekend with Mom. Doreen and I alternated visits every two weeks having decided that going to Grayland every other week was more than either of us could handle. We decided weekly visits weren't essential. At least that's what we told ourselves. In truth, Mom still needed a weekly visit from one of us, hell, Mom needed daily visits, but we told ourselves we could skip a week, and she'd be okay. As long as the freezer and cupboards were well stocked and her car had a full tank, she'd manage.

I called from my office on Thursday to remind Mom I was coming for a visit.

"Really?" she said. "What a nice surprise."

"Are you in the kitchen, Mom?" I asked.

"Yes."

"Is the calendar there by the phone?"

"Yes."

"What day is it, Mom?"

"Oh, I don't know. I forgot to make the mark."

"Okay, well today is Thursday, October 17. Do you see that?"

"Yes."

"So cross out all the boxes that come before the 17."

"Okay."

"Do you have sixteen Xs?"

"Let me see, one, two, three, ..."

I waited in silence as my mother crossed off the first two weeks of the month and counted as she went along. When she was finished, I said, "Okay, now do you see Saturday, October 19? Does it say 'Arleen' on the 19?"

"Yes."

"So, that means I'll be there in two days, okay?"

"That'll be nice," she said.

I stopped at the public library on my way home from work to pick up a few audio books. It would be another month before I thought to get a Westport Library card and was able to check out listening materials at that end of the journey if I failed to stock up well enough before leaving the city. Without a good audio book for distraction, I'd find myself driving home with static-filled radio or lost in silence, haunted by the image of my mother waving from behind the heavy front gate.

I left home early Saturday morning. Within an hour I stopped at Top Foods in Black Lake, just past the capitol dome in Olympia. To stretch my legs and back, I told myself. With a double latte in hand, I drove another hour to Aberdeen, a depressed logging town with seemingly more boarded up buildings than open businesses. But just on the edge of town, a small shopping mall had opened with another Top Foods and Ross Dress for Less. I wandered the aisles of both stores, buying clothing I didn't need and food items I didn't know if Mom needed.

Back in my car, I phoned Mom. "I'm in Aberdeen, Mom. Do you want me to pick anything up for you?"

"Aberdeen?" she asked.

"Yeah, I'm driving down."

"Really? What a nice surprise."

I let it drop. I ignored the obvious. "So do you need anything, Mom?"

"Oh no," she said. "I go uptown when I need groceries."

"Okay. See you soon then."

A half hour later, I pulled into Mom's driveway and stopped in front of the closed gate. As I pushed it open, I wondered again how my mother managed to open and close the heavy thing. Yet she wouldn't think of leaving it open, convinced Casey would escape from his smaller fenced area into the larger yard, and from there leave and never return. No matter how often I tried to convince her that Casey wouldn't leave her, that he knew he had it good, she kept the front gate closed at all times.

As I pulled into the yard, Mom stuck her head out the front door. She watched as I parked the car and walked back to close the gate knowing I'd just have to reopen the thing a few hours later to take Mom for a drive before dinner.

"Oh, it's you," she said as I walked up to give her a hug.

"Who were you expecting?" I asked.

"Oh, nobody," she said.

"But I just called."

"You did not."

As I write these words so many years later, I feel foolish. How blind was I to not see, not acknowledge my mother's confusion? No, that's not right. I did acknowledge it, but I believed she could manage, and she did. Besides, she loved her little house, wouldn't hear of moving away from the beach, away from the home she had shared with my father.

"Have you eaten anything?" she asked.

"I had something on the drive down. We'll go out for dinner later, okay?"

"Okay," she said. "What's all that?

"Just my overnight bag and a few groceries."

"I don't need groceries."

"But I do," I said. "I like to eat a lot."

"But I have groceries."

"I know, Mom, but I feel bad if I don't bring anything."

"Okay," she said. "That's good."

We put away the groceries in silence. Mom rarely asked about my life or my work. Sometimes she asked about Tom, sometimes Erin. But mostly we stayed in the present. I turned to Casey lying at the sunroom door. "Ready for a beach walk? Come on, Mom, let's take a walk."

Again I worried Mom wasn't dressed warmly enough, and again I was right. Again, Casey led the way down the road and across the dunes to the beach, pulling on the leash, anxious to run free, but never allowed. It bothered me, this restraint, this limitation on the animal's natural instinct to run the beach. But Mom wouldn't allow it, convinced Casey wouldn't return, fearful, I suppose, of another loss. So we walked the beach with Casey dragging us along until he tired to a pace Mom was able to match.

After our walk it was time for a trip to the post office to get the mail, and then into the nearby town of Westport to watch for harbor seals. From there, it was on to the State Park to check on Dad's bench – a memorial bench we had installed along the three-mile path through the dunes from downtown Westport, past the State Park, to the Westport Lighthouse. The outing ended with chicken strips for Mom and a salad for me at the restaurant we always called the pizza place because neither of us ever bothered to learn its real name. After dinner, we went home for ice cream and Pepperidge Farm cookies with Hallmark Hall of Fame.

By midafternoon on Sunday, I had to head back to the city. Leaving was always the hardest part of every visit. This time was no exception. I gathered my bags at the door and pulled on my coat. Mom opened the closet looking for her own coat.

"I've got to leave now," I said.

"I'll get the gate," she said.

"Don't worry, Mom, I can get it."

"It's okay."

"But it's raining. You'll get wet."

"So will you."

"But I have to go out to the car anyway. Now give me a hug goodbye."

After a tight hug, I headed out to open the gate before backing around the rusting flagpole and stopping just beyond the open gate. There, I jumped out, pulled the gate closed and latched it. Mom stood, again her head poking from behind the screen door, waving goodbye. The loneliness cut so deep it was hard to leave. I felt torn between two worlds – my Seattle world with Tom and Erin, work and writing, and my Grayland world with Mom and Casey, slow walks and memories of Dad and Maureen permeating the air I breathed. I was torn between these worlds, pushed away by my teenage daughter in her struggle for independence and identity while clinging to my mother in a feeble attempt to get to know this woman I never understood, fearing, perhaps already knowing, that I'd waited too long. The relationship I wanted with my mother, a relationship of shared truths and passions, of deep conversations and daily nothings, I would never have. So I drove away in sadness, a smile plastered to my face, waving my fool arm out the open car window.

November 2002 was one of those months I'd rather forget. I was so distracted trying to understand the dynamics of my first family and how they contributed to Maureen's murder I ignored what was most precious to me – my daughter. Wrapped up in myself, in the ache of Maureen's death and Dad's death and all the unresolved questions surrounding both, I didn't see Erin's pain or realize the decisions and dilemmas she was facing.

To this date I'm not certain how the events unfolded. It's all a bit of a drug-induced blur. Early in the month I went in for jawbone implant surgery. After a decade of coping with a variety of dental bridges designed to compensate for the teeth and bone lost during a botched extraction a decade earlier in Mexico City that landed me in the hospital, I decided to follow my dentist's advice and get implants before progressive bone loss ruled out that option.

I was terrified. I suppose most of us are familiar with that fear of the dentist chair, but my fear was epic, my phobia of dentistry beyond measure. Memories of pre- and post-surgical suffering in Mexico haunted me. I remember one night sitting on the curb of a street in a rough area of northern Mexico City. I wasn't physically on my own, but still lost and alone in my overdose. I was alternating between three narcotic painkillers, trying to avoid an overdose of any one of the three, but I failed. I have lost most memories of those weeks, but I still remember the aching, spine clenching pain.

After I moved back to Seattle, it took about ten years of patient, gentle care to convince me not all dentists were sadistic butchers. Still I hesitated when it came to implants, and I knew cost wasn't the only thing stopping me.

My hesitation turned out to have some basis, but not because of poor dentistry. I was in excellent hands. Rather, it was my own body working against me in the way it chose to heal itself. Perhaps the same problem occurred in Mexico, but I'll never know for sure.

The surgery went well. I thought I'd sailed through it. I returned for post-op a week later and all was well. A week after that I was back in the surgeon's office with pain so intense the surgeon could do nothing. I wouldn't let him get close enough to get an injection in the right place and gas was having no effect. There was exposed bone. This was a Friday. The surgeon put me on Demerol for the weekend. Sunday night it was Demerol and Halcion. Monday morning he was able to make the bone bleed, stitch me up again, and send me on my way, pain free, but very drugged.

Two days before Thanksgiving, Tom drove to Grayland and brought Mom to Seattle for the holiday weekend. It was a quiet meal with just the three of us and Mom as well as Doreen and her husband. Nothing seemed out of the ordinary other than my limited eating ability and Erin's sullen unhappiness because we'd told her she couldn't take a bus downtown the next day with a friend. She had little bus or downtown experience, and we just didn't think the biggest shopping day of the year was a good day for gaining more.

The next day we let her go to her friend's house. After all her pleading and protesting the day before, she knew she wasn't supposed to go downtown. I thought they were going to wander around and do a bit of shopping in the local West Seattle Junction.

When Erin wasn't back by dusk, I began to worry. She knew she was supposed to be home before the streetlights came on and had always been good about sticking to the rules. I tried not to show my concern to my mother, but Erin wasn't home, and Tom was out with friends. I called the other mother and learned that our daughters' stories didn't match. They had, in fact, taken a bus downtown. As we were talking, the girls walked in her front door. Furious and humiliated, I asked her to put Erin on the phone.

"Get your stuff together. I'll be right there to pick you up," I said.

"But they invited me to dinner."

"Just like they, or rather she, invited you downtown? No, Erin, it's time for you to come home."

There was a brief silence. "I'm sorry, Mom."

"I'll be there in five minutes. Be ready. I don't want to keep your grandmother waiting," I said and snapped my phone shut.

"Is everything okay?" Mom asked.

"She went downtown," I said. "I can't believe she went downtown."

"But she's okay?" Mom asked.

"She's fine. But she lied. She's never lied before."

"She's a teenager now," my mother said, a hint of resignation in her voice.

I wanted to knock those words away, blow them up the chimney, clear the house of any trace. Instead, I said, "I've got to go pick her up. It's too dark for her to walk home now. Will you be okay for ten or fifteen minutes? We'll be right back."

That evening Mom and I shared dinner with a neighbor friend while Erin sulked in her room. We talked of the years we lived in

Issaquah and all our family adventures. The good memories of happy times.

"Someone should write the story before it's all forgotten," Mom said. "You could write it, Arleen. You could do it."

"I suppose the stories would be different depending on who was doing the writing," I said. "Do you really want our stories in a book?"

"Why not?" she said.

I wondered if she would understand or accept the memories I was writing every Tuesday night in that UW classroom. I wondered if those were the stories she wanted told. But I remained silent, unwilling to challenge her version of the past and unable to tell her my own. I doubted our versions were the same, but still a window had been opened, and I was ready to leap through it. As I curled in bed that night and scribbled in my journal, I knew writing was my lifeline to sanity.

The following day Tom took Erin with him to return Mom to Grayland, and I had a day to rest. My jawbone was healing, but the pain wasn't gone and neither were the painkillers. The dull bone ache was still there as though a warning of some sort, but it wasn't until Sunday that I learned the rest of the story.

The mother of one of Erin's friends called. She'd found an email. She wasn't prying, she said, it was a shared computer. The evidence was there in black and white. Tom had known Erin was at a sleepover, but he hadn't gotten the details. He hadn't checked with the other parent.

It must have been one of those weekends when I was strung out on painkillers, but I don't know. Erin had asked to spend the night with friends like she'd done so many other times. But this time, I didn't double check with the mom at the sleepover house. The friend told her mother she was staying with us, and the mother went out of town. The result: Erin spent the night at an unsupervised co-ed sleepover.

The truth unraveled through tears in front of a bright fire and a backdrop of holiday cheer.

"I know it was wrong," Erin said.

"Do you realize how much danger you put yourself in?" Tom asked, as he struggled to control himself.

"They're not like that," she said. "We just talked."

"But you're thirteen," I said. "You don't have co-ed sleepovers when you're thirteen. And you never have unsupervised co-ed sleepovers."

I was overwhelmed by a horrible sense of disaster. My daughter had not only lied to us, but she'd put herself in a potentially dangerous situation with boys we didn't even know. I wanted to believe her when she said they just talked all night. But two lies in one month were too much, and I was worn out. I wanted to scream and yell and shake her. I wanted to wring her neck and cuddle her at the same time.

The temptation to blame Tom for not checking on Erin, for letting the situation develop, for being too trusting was strong, but I knew the truth of the matter was that I'd never been able to build communication with my mother, and now I was failing with my daughter as well. I felt like a complete and utter failure as a mother. I was so consumed by my own grief and pain – both emotional and physical – that I was unaware of the emotional demons my daughter was battling. And the simple truth of the matter was she would not talk to me, would not share those demons with me. Her loyalty was to her friends, and I had become the outsider. The enemy.

"How will we know you're telling the truth now?" I said. "We'll have to figure out how to rebuild trust."

"I know," she said.

And we were silent.

Somehow we managed to tiptoe our way through Christmas. Erin was swamped with dance rehearsals leading up to the holiday recital, so we spent long commutes in the car struggling to bridge the chasm between us. Erin was desperate for independence while I was terrified of losing the final shreds of the loving daughter I once had, unable to come to terms with this sullen teenager sharing the car with me.

2003

IN LATE JANUARY a neighbor friend suggested a weekend ski trip to Whistler, the Canadian skiers' paradise just across the border to the north. I was complaining to her about our disastrous cross-country trip during Christmas break. When we'd made plans in late fall, Erin and a friend were excited. Then, at the last minute, the friend bailed. It was too late to invite someone else, so we made the trip just the three of us, despite Erin's protests. I hadn't told my neighbor about the unsupervised sleepover, but she knew enough, had probably heard enough – our houses being arm-reach close – to know Erin had become a handful.

"The best part of the whole trip was when we discovered this small ski bowl called Loup Loup in the community of Okanogan. It was like a miniature downhill run in the middle of cross-country paradise. Tom skied. Erin took a snowboarding lesson, and I had my first downhill lesson. I loved it," I said.

"So come with me and take another lesson at Whistler," she said.

The first half of the day at Whistler was fabulous. The sun was bright and the snow glistened. I was skiing on a real slope and loving it. At midday, the instructor told us to head in for lunch. It was on a run that changed difficulty level three times in a matter of a few narrow yards. I missed the final switch back. In quick succession, I heard a pop, fell, heard the instructor's "oh shit" and knew I was in trouble.

The ride off the mountain in a sled pulled by a little girl who looked Erin's age was total humiliation. I felt no pain. But I also had a leg that wouldn't hold me up. After hours at the emergency clinic, my friend and I spent the evening, my braced leg on a stool, sampling Scotch in a village bar. I was still ignorant of what lay before me.

The next month I had ACL transplant surgery followed by a night of such intensity it made my dental surgery seem like a minor discomfort. As the pain spiraled out of control, Tom found some narcotics left over from the implant surgery, and I was finally out cold. It was the weekend, and the surgeon had left on vacation before I was released from the hospital.

Within a few days my leg was swollen and purple. I struggled to get to the bathroom let alone start the physical therapy exercises I had been told to do. I saw the on-call surgeon. A blood clot and thirteen injections of blood thinners later I began to get around again. By then my blood was as thin as water, my poor husband was at the end of his endless patience, and Erin was fed up with her mother's problems. I couldn't blame either of them. Till death do us part should never include having to learn to give your spouse injections, especially since mine thought the whole ski trip was a mistake in the first place. He was right. I was still recovering from implant surgery and my back was still messed up from a ruptured disc a few years earlier. Why in the hell did I think it was a good time to take up a new sport?

I began to heal, to walk with a brace, to return to work, to begin winter term at the University of Washington, to continue work on the memoir that I'd put on hold. Through it all Doreen filled in for me with Mom, making extra visits to Grayland. At one point early on my mother was so worried she asked Doreen to bring her to Seattle to visit me. I don't remember who did the driving, where stinky Casey stayed or even where Mom stayed, but I do remember my mother sitting on the edge of my bed, her hand on my forehead, love and concern in her eyes. Despite her confusion and my pain, we connected through a mother's touch and the scent of miniature pink roses that filled the room where I lay. Doreen's and Mom's gifts. Two small plants that struggled to survive for several years in the garden – houseplants never intended for an outdoor environment any more than I was intended for a ski slope.

࿇   ࿇

The Easter floods of 2003 began on April Fool's Day, but unlike the later floods of 2007, these floods were indoors.

We live in a small West Seattle house built in 1943 – a war box of about 800 square feet on the main floor. Two bedrooms, a bath, kitchen, and dining room. The selling point for us was the dry, high-ceilinged basement. We moved in February 1991, just a few months before Erin's second birthday. We blocked the stairway to the basement with a baby gate, but there were four steps that led from the kitchen to the back door, steps that were higher than Erin's legs were long. I remember the look-at-me pride on her little face as she learned to crawl and then walk from the backyard into the kitchen.

By 2003, Tom had added a bathroom, laundry room, and two bedrooms to the unfinished basement, leaving a family room at the base of the stairs. He drywalled the basement and put up a ceiling. We were ready for carpet installation. Or so we thought.

On April Fool's Day we woke to a wet basement floor. The new toilet had backed up into the shower and overflowed. Like fools we didn't cancel the scheduled carpet installation. Instead Tom worked day and night replumbing the bathroom, and we plunged forward as planned.

Easter passed, and a second flood ruined our new carpet. At the same time my blood was thinner than the water soaking our new family room. I struggled with the stairs on a knee that still hadn't healed and spent each night trying to sleep in a contraption intended to straighten a knee frozen into a bent position.

At the end of April, the third and final quarter of my yearlong memoir course began. I skipped the first class, still unable to deal with the chaos of my life, still unsure how to move forward with the memoir I was now calling *The Thirty-Ninth Victim*. I was in a serious funk. When I received notice I'd been denied a sabbatical – the only sabbatical I'd ever requested in twenty years at the college – on the grounds that memoir writing was not of benefit to the institution, I was devastated. I hadn't realized the decision to grant professional leave was based on the design of a project that would directly benefit the college. Lifelong learning being touted as an institutional value, I was under the false assumption that a sabbatical was intended for personal professional development.

As I reread my journal of those months, I came across the pitiful words "what have I done to deserve all this shit in my life." I wondered all too often whether I should be writing a memoir about my family. Was it right, was it fair, was it honest? Was I being punished somehow? Then the rational me kicked in and told me I was being a self-pitying fool and to keep writing.

By mid-May life was feeling a bit brighter. I remember climbing the steep steps to a waterfront restaurant across from Alki Beach. Alki is one of those beaches dotted with volleyball nets and fire rings, great for afternoon games and evening bonfires, but the water is too cold for all but the hardiest.

Erin had decided that she wanted a beach party for her fourteenth birthday. Being hovering, at times overprotective parents and at other times neglectful as the experiences of previous months had shown us, we decided the beach party idea was great, but not without our supervision.

"But Mom, that's too embarrassing."

"What if nobody knows we're there?"

"That won't work. Everybody knows you and Dad."

"We'll hide," I said.

And we did. We hid at a second floor restaurant above the beach where we spent the evening over a long leisurely meal and a bottle of good Italian Chianti. It was Erin and a friend who came running across the street and up the stairs. She needed her dad to help set up the volleyball net we'd given her for the party because they couldn't manage to get it to stay upright in the wind.

I remember the beauty of the May sunset over Elliott Bay. I remember the flicker of fires, the whiff of driftwood smoke, and the sense of well-being the wind carried. And I remember a nagging fear it would all be very short-lived. I had to brace myself for whatever the next conflict or tragedy would be.

Until I became the mother of a school-aged child, I hadn't realized graduations as I knew them – ceremonies confined to the celebration of high school or university completion – had trickled downwards. Now we had preschool graduations, elementary school graduations, and middle school graduations as well.

I suppose by the time Erin graduated from middle school, the ceremony had already begun to lose its luster. Erin's focus was on high school, on leaving Madison Middle School far behind her. She always seemed in a hurry to grow up, but never was it more apparent than the spring of 2003. Middle school graduation was a non-event.

At the same time, I was distracted by my own graduation. The last time, the only time, I'd walked in a graduation ceremony was in 1972 when I wore a purple polyester gown and an unexpected parachute landing occurred in the middle of the football field – the graduating class of Issaquah High School being too large that year to hold an indoor event.

I didn't participate in my undergraduate ceremony having changed universities three times and moved to Mexico without finishing the research project required for University of California Santa Cruz graduation at that time. Years later I wrote a thesis, in Spanish, which was accepted. Eventually, UCSC sent my diploma to my parents' home, and I didn't see it for years. I don't know why I didn't walk in my Master's graduation from the University of Washington other than the simple fact that I didn't feel much like celebrating. My youngest sister was still missing, her remains yet undiscovered, my family was torn apart by grief, and my first marriage was in shambles.

But the graduation ceremony of June 2003 was different. I wasn't earning an academic degree, just a certificate in a continuing education program. There were no caps and gowns. Nobody in my extended family and none of my non-writer friends even knew it was happening. It was the most important, the most meaningful graduation of my life, but writing was still my secret, my near-solo journey into making sense of my world.

I sat in the dark auditorium on the UW campus with Erin on one side and Tom on the other. We watched as graduates of the various programs crossed the stage. When my program was called, I lined up with my classmates. I was fearful of the steep auditorium stairs, but when I walked across the stage and received my certificate with joy in my heart, I didn't feel my knee at all.

Despite the difficulties and challenges of the previous nine months, I'd completed the first draft of a memoir my professors believed was publishable. I still hadn't decided if publication was something I wanted, still wasn't sure if I was brave enough to share my secret manuscript with my siblings, but the simple fact I'd done it filled my heart with the pride of completion.

After the ceremony, my classmates and I gathered for a drink near campus. I've always been aware that Tom's shy discomfort often comes across as aloof arrogance, but there he was, quiet and solid at my side. Without him, I would not have been there at all.

Later that summer I visited a local frame shop in West Seattle and bought four bright wooden frames – yellow, red, blue, hot pink. I framed my diplomas and hung them on the wall of my campus office where they remain to this day.

అ ఌ

By August the inflammation in my knee was as warm as the summer sun, and Tom was ready to do more remodeling on the house before the autumn rains made outside work impossible. We'd already redone the kitchen, finished the basement, changed an upstairs bedroom into a dining room and added a sunroom. Now it was time to work on the exterior. During one of the earlier remodels, Tom had removed and replaced some of the siding when he put in new windows. In the process he discovered that the ugly asbestos siding covering our little house had been slapped on right over the original 1943 cedar siding. It was a bit like the earlier discoveries that the old carpet in the living room had preserved the hardwood floors underneath and the linoleum in the hallway could be removed with hot water to expose more hardwood.

Tom decided it was time to strip the house of asbestos siding. For several days he and a few workers dressed and masked like astronauts tore into the house, the screech of pulling nails worse than fingernails on a chalkboard – a cliché that dates me, but such was the sound. It was a sound that seemed to reverberate against the screw in the front of my knee holding the grafted ACL in place.

"That screw might need to be removed," the surgeon said when I complained of the inflammation and pain. "Sometimes the screw causes unnecessary discomfort." I wanted to know how much discomfort he felt was necessary, but I remained quiet. "Your body could be rejecting the screw," he concluded.

I agreed to go in for a second surgery with a surgeon I already held in very low esteem. Why I didn't go to someone else is still beyond me. I suppose I was just so totally burned out, I wasn't thinking. I knew this surgeon was covered by my medical insurance and had been referred by my primary care provider. Aren't doctors supposed to know what's best?

I did insist the surgery be performed on a day when the surgeon was not preparing to leave on vacation again. I got a guarantee he would be around for follow-up as needed. I'd gone off blood thinners some weeks before and was readied for surgery. "I want the screw," I said before I was put under.

Later I compared the screw the surgeon removed from my knee with the nails Tom was pulling from the outside of our home. Twice as big. Maybe more. I couldn't believe the size of that monster. Something that looked like any number of others in the bins at our local TrueValue Hardware had actually been screwed into my knee. I wasn't sure I'd ever be painfree, but I was happy to have it out of my body.

After weeks of puttying and sanding nail holes, the house was ready to paint. Tom and I pored over color wands from various Seattle paint distributors, unable to choose a color.

"I've got to start painting," Tom said. "What's it going to be?"

"White," I said, my leg on an ottoman to control the swelling. "If it's good enough for the president, it's good enough for me. It's a good base coat anyway. We can always change it later."

A decade later our house is still white. And my knee still talks to me.

        ❧ ❧

Erin was a shadow that summer. Around as little as possible. She spent her days with friends, coming home for dinner most evenings.

One afternoon I was invited along to see a movie with Erin and two of her friends. Or maybe I made the invitation – my presence was usually tolerated if I made my credit card available. Rather than sitting through the teen flick they wanted to see, I waited in the Barnes & Noble coffee shop at Pacific Place, a posh downtown shopping emporium. I wrote and waited as I often did when Erin was with her friends, in dance classes, or at swim practice. I didn't mind. It gave me the alone time I craved for writing. There was never enough time to write.

After the show ended, the three teens barreled into the coffee shop like a tornado. "Let's go get dessert," Erin said.

"How was the movie?" I asked.

"Fine. But let's go. We want to go to the Cheesecake Factory."

"Oh, I don't know about that."

"Come on, Mom. I really want to go there. It's just up the street. It'll be fun."

I didn't say no. I paused, and in that breath, the three turned on their heels and headed to the door. I thought about the close proximity of my car and the pain in my knee. I thought about the expense of four overpriced desserts in a downtown tourist trap hotspot. But still I gathered my notebook, pen, book, purse, sweater, and hobbled after them. They must have checked to confirm that I was coming, but if they did, I didn't notice. They, or maybe just Erin, seemed to assume I would follow and for a while I did. Up the block, three or four paces behind them, limping and pathetic.

"We're going ahead to see if there's a line," Erin called back to me. They picked up speed and disappeared into a crowd of shoppers crossing the street. The light had changed by the time I reached the intersection.

A few minutes later Erin was back. "Mom, can you stand in line and wait for a table? We want to run across to ..."

"No," I shouted. And then I cracked. "I don't want to do this anymore."

Maybe it was the word "stand." Maybe it was being treated as her servant. Maybe it was the argument a few days before when I'd accused her of the same thing – of suggesting an activity she wanted to do and including me because if I came along she knew I would pay. When I called her on it, when I told her I didn't want to just be her credit card, she exploded with a typical, rough-edged response of honest clarity. Clarity that went right over my head at the moment.

"We're not friends, you know. We're not the Gilmore Girls. I don't want a friend. I want a mother."

For a short while, I loved that silly television show. I wanted the open honest communication with my daughter that Lorelei enjoyed with Rory. I wanted the sharp, sassy humor and fun. And I was using a television role model to fill a void because I knew I didn't want to mother as I had been mothered. I feared the distance, the lack of communication, but that's exactly what I had created.

"Feels like you want a credit card."

"That would be great."

The exchange was harsh, cruel. And full of truth. Tom tried to comfort me, told me it was a phase, she was a teenager, it was normal. I didn't know what normal was, but I wasn't happy with the situation any more than I was willing to wait for a table at an overpriced restaurant for three teens who would have preferred I open a tab for them and disappear.

"I don't want to do this, Erin," I said. "I'm going home." With that I turned around and started limping back to the parking garage.

"But why? What's wrong? What did I do? I didn't do anything wrong. You're so mean." The protests continued, loud, long, embarrassing. And maybe I was being mean. My mistake was not having been decisive enough from the beginning, and now I was reduced to black-red fury. I wanted to run away, but even walking was painful. I wanted to cause pain. I wanted to slap her. Right there in the middle of a crowded downtown sidewalk. I was so full of rage I wanted to slap my daughter.

I hit Erin only once, and the memory still fills me with shame. She was three or four, and a terror. Always determined to get her way, always bright enough to out-smart and out-debate me, always articulate enough to talk her way out of just about any situation.

I no longer remember the circumstances surrounding the slap, what we were fighting about – me fighting with a four-year-old. Pathetic. I only remember I gave her a light slap on her fanny. To this day, I feel horrible. I never wanted to be a do-this-because-I-told-you-so mother. I wanted something different. I wanted something more democratic or even consensus-based where all conflicts could be resolved through rational conversation. What I failed to realize when my daughter was a child was that I also had the emotional maturity of a child.

Now my daughter was a fourteen-year-old who felt she could boss me around. What might have been cute, or at least bearable, when she was a child was no longer cute as a teenager, especially a teenager who had the mature look of a young woman in her early twenties. As I limped back to the car in a rage, fighting the urge to strike her, another memory surfaced, a memory of the one time, the only time that my own mother slapped me.

Mom had just returned from grocery shopping. The back of the large International Harvester was full of bags from the Prairie Market, the first discount, mark-it-yourself, overstock grocery store in the Issaquah Valley. She pulled into the carport and struggled up the back steps into the kitchen, her arms loaded. I was upstairs in the girls' dormitory bedroom watching from the back window. I wasn't alone. "Shhh …" somebody whispered. "Maybe she won't know we're here." The lazy not-so-innocent innocence of an early adolescent.

"Arleen, come down here and give me a hand with these groceries. I know you're up there. I stumbled over your dirty boots on the steps."

My cover blown, I made my slow slide down the stairs.

"Give me a hand with these bags," Mom said as I poked my head into the kitchen.

I don't remember what I said. I don't know if it was my words or attitude that caused my mother to crack. All I know is she slapped me across the face – hard, fast, and unexpected.

As I look back from the perspective of a good four decades or more, I'm not sure who was more shocked, her or me. We disappeared in opposite directions, losing ourselves in space. I don't think there was ever an apology from either of us, or a hug of reconciliation. It just happened, and it was over. Then it was ignored. In my parents' world, what was ignored could be forgotten, or at least set aside, as though it had never happened at all. But for me it remains an indelible imprint on my brain. Just as I remember the one and only time I slapped my own daughter. But when I slapped Erin on her bottom for a reason I can't recall, there were hugs and tears and endless apologies. As I begged Erin for forgiveness in a manner disproportionate to the offense, I was begging my mother for forgiveness for the many, many troubles I caused her.

I can only now imagine how overwrought Mom was the day she lost control and slapped me across my face to quiet the sassy, nasty words I'd had the nerve to spew in her direction. I had no comprehension of her suffering, the suffering of a woman with six or seven kids already and another on the way. I simply didn't care, didn't have the capacity for empathy in my early teens to look beyond my own myopia.

In that brief moment of realization, my rage toward Erin dissipated like a popped balloon. She neither understood nor cared about my physical and emotional pain. She was busy with her own teenage burdens of trying to make sense of the world and the people in it. At fourteen she was light years ahead of me. She just needed to learn to be a bit more respectful.

Respect. Now there's a word that has challenged my ability to parent. Like my father, I always wanted Erin to question all authority and to understand why she was doing what she was doing, why a rule or law existed and the fairness or equity of that law. As a mother, I couldn't say, do, or ask anything without a challenge. Why should I do this or that? Why do I have to? Why is it important? Why don't you trust me? Why? Why? Why? The questions didn't stop in front of friends – hers or mine. At times I could find logical answers. At other times, most times, I floundered into muteness as I had when Erin insisted on going to the Cheesecake Factory.

There was silence in the car as I drove the girls back to West Seattle. Finally I heard, "I'm sorry, Mom." Then, "Could we stop at Safeway to get some dessert?" The apology and the request, one on the heels of the other, the second diminishing the value of the first. Still it was something.

"I'm not getting out of the car," I said. "And I don't have any cash."

I waited in the parking lot while the girls argued in the store – something Erin told me the next day when she was complaining about the failure of the sleepover. Apparently, the girls just hadn't gotten along well. Like most friendships, too much of a good thing had its ups and downs. At that point, I was no longer Public Enemy Number One, and she was no longer showing off in front of her friends. I was just Mom with a shoulder to cry on.

❧ ❧

We were sitting in the living room amid tears of frustration and anger – both Erin's and mine. I have no doubt that Tom shed his own in private.

"You've been telling us for the past year that you wanted to go to West Seattle High School. Why the change now?" I asked.

"I don't know. Just because."

"Because your friends didn't get into West Seattle."

"No, that's not the only reason."

"It's not a good school, Erin. You're going to West Seattle as planned."

"It's getting better."

"True, but not fast enough."

"I won't go."

"Then you'll have to deal with the consequences."

The argument repeated itself throughout late August. That summer of breaking way, of becoming a teenager, was ending. Erin wanted it to continue with a palpable passion, and she no longer wanted to attend the high school she'd dreamed of throughout her childhood. She'd watched the remodel of West Seattle High School with anticipation. The beautiful brick building was where her grandfather had once been a football star decades before. Now she was fighting to go to what was often referred to as one of Seattle's worst schools, a school with the lowest test scores and graduation rates in the city at the time.

"I want to run away," she told me a few days later through a veil of tears. "But where would I go? I have nowhere to go."

"Is it so horrible here?" I asked.

"I feel trapped."

"I know. We all feel trapped sometimes," I told her.

"But you never let me do what I want."

"Sometimes your dad and I have to make the decisions we think are best for you."

"You can't make me go there."

"You can go anywhere else. Any good school, public or private, but we're not going to allow you to throw your education away."

For a day or two, she researched private boarding schools in Hawaii. Could she find something more remote, appealing, or expensive? We took boarding schools off the list of options. Public or private within driving distance, we told her.

But that wasn't really the issue. The issue had to do with one group of middle school friends going to one high school and a different group going to the other high school, and Erin feeling like she was in the wrong group. Tom and I held our ground.

When the first day of school arrived, Erin refused to go. The second day and the third came and went. Both Tom and I went to work and ignored her for those first few days. Then we reminded her that by state law, she had to attend school, and if she didn't show up pretty soon, they'd come looking for her. At the time, she had a neighbor friend in juvenile detention who I'd taken her to visit. She knew she didn't want to end up there. Begrudgingly she got up and went to school before the first week ended. Tom and I breathed a shared sigh of relief.

✿ ✿

After twenty years of ineptitude, the Green River Task Force had finally arrested the worst serial killer in American history at that time, a man who had preyed on young women, a man who they had suspected and questioned while my sister was still alive. Had they done their job, Maureen might be reading these words. Or other words, for these words, these exact words, would never have been written. I would never have begun writing to comprehend the tragedy of my sister's murder.

On November 5, 2003 I sat with my mother in her tiny living room watching the television. Together, we heard the words:

"How do you plea?"

"Guilty."

After the telecast, we drove to Seattle. We kept Mom with us for a week, fearful the press might find her alone, confused, and mourning on the Pacific Coast. I felt torn between my daughter and my mother, incapable of giving either the attention or support she needed. At the same time, I wasn't sleeping at night. I struggled to fall asleep only to awaken a few hours later wet and clammy in a pool of perspiration. As if the realities of my daily life weren't tough enough, my body decided it was time to change and my hormonal levels were free-flying.

In mid-November my insurance coverage ran out on the device I was required to wear each night in an attempt to straighten my knee to full extension. I'd been using the awful thing since shortly after the surgery in March, after the blood clot had dissolved, after I'd begun physical therapy. For over six months I struggled to sleep in this incredibly uncomfortable splint which I learned years later had over-stretched the ACL transplant tissue – a bit like an old rubber band – to the point of lost elasticity, thus making the whole damn surgery a failure. It was nice to sleep again, between night sweats anyway, with the luxury of a brace-free leg.

Two weeks after Mom insisted she wanted to go home, my mother-in-law arrived for a visit. At the time, Lucy was spending winters in Florida and the rest of the year floating between the homes of her children and sister. Her visits are always a pleasure. She's one of those women who seems able to find something positive in every person or situation. I remember sitting on the front steps of the house in freezing weather trying to cool from a hot flash and her gentle laughter and touch on my shoulder told me it was okay, told me she understood, told me I wasn't alone.

Thanksgiving dinner 2003 was one of those rare occasions when my daughter sat at the table flanked by both of her grandmothers – one divorced, the other widowed. Tom was the odd man out, the lone male surrounded by women. The older women gave me comfort despite the limited direction or parenting advice I was able to glean from either of them. Despite the difference in their ages – one so young she could have been the daughter of the other – what the two grandmothers shared was their reticence to voice opinions or advice.

My mother's faltering memory and confusion were more apparent with each passing week. With the stress of the Ridgway confession and the resurgence of the painful losses of both Maureen and Dad, she seemed to shut down. She sat in mute confusion at our Thanksgiving table despite our gentle attempts to include her in the conversation. Still, I treasure the image of my tall, slender daughter towering over her grandmothers, arms draped over their shoulders, laughter in her eyes.

The week before Thanksgiving dinner, just about the time Lucy arrived in Seattle, I received a phone call from the King County Prosecutors office informing me that the sentencing of the man who had confessed to my sister's murder would be on December 18th. Families would be welcome to address the court either in writing or in person. A week later I mailed a letter to Judge Jones sharing my feelings about the case. In the meantime, Erin told me she wanted to go to the sentencing with me. It had been a tough autumn. I knew some of Erin's friends were either troubled or getting into trouble, and I knew Erin was torn between her sense of right and wrong and her desire, her visceral need, to be part of that group of friends, some of whom she'd known since elementary school.

Her desire to go to the sentencing, her insistence, caught me a bit off guard, but Tom and I decided nothing negative would come of it.

And, because the sentencing was not being televised, I was not quite so worried about being with Mom. Two weeks after Thanksgiving, fall quarter ended and plans were in place for the Erin and me to go to the sentencing. At the same time, I had a bulky pile of manuscript pages needing my undivided attention and a soul needing some respite.

A friend offered her weekend home in Cannon Beach, a small coastal resort town in Oregon. With manuscript, laptop, and overnight bag packed, I left home planning to return on the eve of the sentencing, pulled back to Seattle by my determination to be in the courtroom to see my sister's killer and by the promise I'd made to Erin to take her with me.

For five days I wrote, walked, ate, and read in silence. I had piles of manuscript pages spread over every flat surface. Because I hadn't thought to bring a printer, I resorted to old-school techniques. As I moved scenes and chapters to restructure the story, I cut and taped the pages into a new patchwork of scenes. Once satisfied with the revised structure of each chapter, I typed in the changes. A slow process, but far from tedious. I'm a very tactile person. I needed to see the words, feel the paper between my fingers, smell the ink.

As we move into a world of digital books, I fill our small house with bookcases and scour bookstores for those copies I can't live without. I continue to write, pen scratching words on the pale green lines of an old world steno pad. The shape and size is perfect, line length limited to a half dozen scrawled words. The spiral at the top doesn't impede the glide of my hand across each page. The words, the ideas, the memories, flow from brain to heart to hand in a steady stream. A compact size that fits into every handbag I own. I buy bags based on whether they will hold my notebook and a book. I don't know what I'll do if Staples ever decides to stop producing these steno pads I buy in bulk every six months. Maybe I should stock up. Would a dozen a year for the next twenty-five years do the trick?

I went to Cannon Beach with steno pads, both full and empty, a manuscript, both hard copy and electronic, and the determination to restructure the story and pull together a final draft worthy of submission. I left Cannon Beach both refreshed and exhausted with a manuscript ready to print. It wasn't finished, but I had a structure I knew would work.

The morning after I returned from Cannon Beach, my daughter and I sat in a downtown courtroom only a few rows behind the man who deprived Erin of ever knowing her auntie. We sat, we listened, and we walked away knowing evil wore a very normal face, and nothing at all would ever change the tragedy of our family. The bitter tears that ran our make-up could do nothing to wash away the pain.

Later as we sat in a bookstore coffee shop and ate lunch, Erin insisted there was some good in this man, that all humans have some good in them. I knew she was still battling her own demons, with friends she loved who she knew were making lousy decisions, and perhaps, with some of her own decisions and mistakes.

The following morning I was drinking coffee alone at the kitchen table when Erin walked in and sat down beside me. She was silent.

"Good morning," I said. "What's up? Are you okay?" I wondered if she was struggling with the events of the day before.

"Will you promise not to tell the other moms?" she asked.

"No, I can't do that." The words were out of my mouth before I could stop them. I immediately rephrased. "You can tell me anything. As long as it's not a matter of personal safety, I won't say a word."

But it was too late. I led with the negative, and Erin clammed up. I still wonder what she wanted to tell me and how desperately she needed a mom she felt she could talk to about anything and everything she wanted to share. I failed her at that moment, and I knew it, just as I knew there was no way to rectify my blunder.

The next day Erin danced in the final dress rehearsal for her winter show while I headed to Grayland to bring Mom to Seattle. As I drove, I thought about that brief conversation and wondered what she might have been trying to tell me. I kicked myself again for speaking without thinking and worried over how I could learn to listen to my daughter in a way that would help her open up to me. I was glad Erin had dance – her physical, emotional, and creative outlet. She danced away her troubles as a teenager just as swimming had eased her soul when she was younger. The girls she danced with were not her high school friends, not the friends she'd known since elementary school, so with them she could be herself, even recreate herself with greater ease and fewer expectations.

She danced throughout middle school and the first few years of high school – jazz, ballet, tap, flamenco – the rhythms and steps and beats washing her heart free of Boppa's death, Nana's confusion, the sentencing of Auntie Maureen's killer, my physical and emotional roller coaster ride as well as her own teen struggles. I was grateful for dance, for her passion that granted her some release.

2004

THE GUEST BEDROOM in my mother's house was cramped, dusty and filled to the walls with a double bed. A blue comforter covered the bed set on blue carpet. Heavy blue curtains covered the high, narrow window. The curtains allowed no draft of cold air in the winter, no breeze in the summer. Late at night the silence was heavy and comforting with the crash of waves just at the edge of awareness like elevator music in a downtown skyscraper. I lay wide awake in the too-soft bed. My mother slept just beyond the wall separating the bedrooms.

Earlier that day I had arrived for another overnight stay. As always when I visited, I poked around the house looking for changes, for signs of my mother's activities or needs. Signs she could no longer care for herself. I saw a large gift box in the bay window seat.

"What's this, Mom?"

"Oh, just an old album. Doreen got it out when she was here."

"Really?" I asked. "I wonder why."

"She was looking at it."

I knew my sister hadn't visited in several weeks and nothing stayed in the same place for that long in Mom's house, but I said nothing. Instead, I opened the box and found the album of photographs and memories from my parents' fortieth wedding anniversary party.

December 1986. My sisters and I had planned a large celebration, asking friends and relatives to send memories, stories, anecdotes to commemorate my parents' forty years of marriage. The party was held only four months after the heart attack and triple by-pass surgery that almost took Dad's life.

I sat on the sofa with Mom at my side, opened the album, and turned the heavy pages. I read positive, powerful memories of my parents' goodness, laughter, and joy. And yet as I read, I noticed everyone had written about the early years of their marriage, the Seattle years, the first decade or so, before they bought ten acres of undeveloped land and moved their growing family out to the Issaquah Valley. There were also a few memories of the early Issaquah years, but nothing more. No one had mentioned the later years, the second half of my parents' life together. Those were the dark years, the years when my parents' dream of an idyllic country life fell apart, when my older siblings became teenagers, and my father lost control because he could not relinquish it with grace and respect. As the youngest of nine children, most of my sister Maureen's short life had been in the second half of my parents' marriage.

My mother and I kissed goodnight and closed our bedroom doors. As I struggled to find sleep, I was flooded with memories of my father. I tried to understand this man who, like Maureen, was now gone. Who was this man, this source of so much joy for some and so much pain and confusion for others? My father was a strong, controlling man, a man who insisted we live by his rules, or we were no longer part of his life. He refused to speak to or even hear mention of the three eldest of his nine children for varying lengths of time. I was the middle child. When it was my turn to be a teenager, I was also disowned for a while. With time all but one of us were reinstated into the family circle by changing our ways, by accepting the conditions of my father's love.

Unable to sleep, I tried to name the gifts my father gave me, the teachings, the values, but I came up empty. I tried to remember the happy, singing, joking man others remembered, but I couldn't. Instead I remembered the silence. What did my father teach me? I learned hard work, but little pleasure. I learned to be focused and organized, but also controlling and fearful. I learned the judgment silence held, but not the acceptance. I learned the power and beauty of boundless creative energy and the destructive nature of conditional love.

Up early the following morning, long before my mother would awaken, I headed for the stretch of Pacific beach in front of her home. I walked the sands, breathing the misty salt air, and talking to Maureen. Unlike my father's ashes still held in a sealed urn in Mom's living room, my sister's ashes were not contained. Years before my parents released her to the winds over the Pacific Ocean from the stern of my father's fishing boat. They did it alone without the knowledge or involvement of their other eight children. Still, I'm glad they did it, for it is at this beach that I feel my sister's presence, in the power of the waves crashing on the sand. Those waves contain my sister, her ashes, and it is there I am at peace.

If my father taught me the silence of conditional love, Maureen's gift was voice – voice to speak, to scream, and finally to break the family code of silence enforced by our father. Since that day a year and a half earlier when I sat searching for direction in my campus office, my window overlooking a large grassy area with a clock tower and student center in the distance, I have written daily. I signed up for a writing program with no clear idea why, only that I needed an outlet, a creative release, a safety valve. Within a few weeks I was writing Maureen's story. Through my pen I became her voice, and with time, I began to find my own.

By late afternoon another short visit with my mother was over, and it was time to face the long drive back to Seattle, back to my husband and daughter, back to the circle of love we have created together. I packed my small overnight bag, set it by the front door, and folded my mother into my arms.

"Goodbye, Mom. I'll see you again soon. I love you."

"Drive safely," she said. "I love you, too."

Then, as always, I looked up at the ceramic urn on the top of Mom's bookshelf, red and green swirls over a black enamel finish, and I whispered a quiet goodbye to my father. I climbed into my car, promising my mother that I'd call when I got home. As I drove out of the fenced yard and headed toward the highway, I scanned the beach, gave Maureen a nod of gratitude, and felt my spirit soar.

❧   ❧

I wasn't snooping. She never accused me of snooping. It was a rare afternoon when I was at home. The door was open, and I went into her bedroom with an armful of folded laundry to set on her bed. As I was leaving, I noticed a pile of jewelry on the corner of her dresser. All silver. All with tags still attached. I knew my daughter didn't have the resources to buy that jewelry. It was odd the way it was there on the dresser in plain sight. A memory intruded. "If I tell you, will you promise not to tell the other moms?" I felt she was telling me something with that pile of jewelry. In my gut, I felt she wanted me to see it, to confront her, to set the limits she was already fighting.

Or maybe I just convinced myself of this to give me the courage to do what I knew I had to do. I didn't call Tom right away. I wanted to talk to Erin first. Later that day we were in the car together – that enclosed capsule, perfect for important conversations. I'd just picked her up from track practice. She was attempting track, not because it was something she enjoyed, but because the practices were held on a field shared by the high school we had not allowed her to attend. Track offered an opportunity to hang out with her friends at the other school.

"Erin, I was putting some laundry on your bed today," I said.

"Yeah?" she said, distracted.

"There's a bunch of brand new silver jewelry on your dresser. Where did it come from?"

She began to cry.

"Erin?"

"I knew it was wrong when I did it. I didn't want to do it."

"You stole it."

"It wasn't really like stealing. I mean, it was so easy."

"Did you pay for it?"

"No."

"Then you stole it."

"Yes."

"Were you alone?"

"No."

I pulled the car to a stop at the side of the road to look at her, tears streaming down her cheeks, still rosy from her workout. I saw her as a little girl in an adult body making adolescent mistakes because of peer pressure and an intense desire to belong.

"I didn't know what to do."

"Did they dare you?"

"Yes."

"You weren't able to wander off to another department this time?"

We'd had a conversation before, months before, when a few of her friends were caught shoplifting. I'd asked her if she'd ever been with them when they were doing it.

"Yes," she'd said.

"What do you do when that happens?"

"I just go someplace else."

Tom and I had worried, the worry of any concerned parents about the friends their child was keeping, but we knew trying to ban her friends, trying to tell her who she could or couldn't be friends with would only backfire. Instead, we decided we needed to be vigilant, to watch, to talk, to hope she made wise decisions that kept her out of trouble and safe. But she was teetering. She was more than teetering. She'd fallen off the ledge, and I was terrified for her.

"What if you'd been caught?"

"I know."

"Now what should we do?"

"I don't know."

"You need to return it."

I saw the flash of terror in her eyes. Intense and real. "But they'll arrest me," she said.

"Do you deserve to be arrested?" I asked.

"Yes." It was more a whimper than a word.

"Well, I don't want you to be arrested. I also don't want you to be shoplifting or hanging out with friends who are shoplifting or doing other stupid things. So what are we going to do?"

"I could mail it back."

"With an apology."

"Do I have to sign the letter?"

"No. And no return address, okay?"

"Okay."

"What about the friends?"

Again she started to cry. I could see the fissures in her heart. These were girls she'd known since primary school. "They're my friends," she said. "I can't tell them what to do."

"I suppose not," I said. "But you can tell them what you're going to do. And what you're not going to do. Can you handle that?"

"Okay. Are you going to tell the other moms?"

"Should I?"

"I don't want you to."

"Can I trust you'll never ever, ever do this again?" There was that word again: trust.

"Yes," she said.

Her eyes told me she would never shoplift again. I knew there would be other challenges she'd have to face, it was never going to be easy sailing for her, but at least we'd managed to talk our way through this one.

"Do we have to tell Dad?" she asked.

"Yes," I told her. "Your dad has the right to know. I don't keep secrets from him. Or from you."

Again, she began to cry knowing her father would be disappointed in her, knowing she'd let him down.

"It'll be okay." I unfastened my seatbelt and reached over to wrap her in my arms. I felt her body relax into my embrace and for a brief moment my teenage daughter was again a toddler relieved of the weight of pending adulthood, her tears soaking my shoulders.

∂≈ ≈∂

When Mom fell on the Grayland Beach, it was Casey's fault. Her beloved old golden retriever was getting fatter in seemingly equal proportion to Mom's weight loss. He was heavy, he was untrained, and he pulled hard on his leash no matter where they were headed. Both Mom and Casey loved their daily beach walk, but Casey pulled so hard Mom struggled to keep up. Still, she refused to allow him off leash despite the endless stretch of beach for him to run and explore. Casey tugged and pulled in frustration. At the rise of the last dune on the narrow trail to the beach, the Pacific Ocean lay ahead in all its endless majesty. Between the top of that last dune and the hard-packed beach, the sand was loose and soft and scattered with driftwood.

There in the deceptively soft sand Mom fell. She landed hard, her tailbone hitting something other than soft sand. A neighbor found her lying on the ground with Casey at her side and helped her limp home. She insisted she was okay and refused to see a doctor. The neighbor called Doreen. Doreen called me, and I left campus by midafternoon on St. Patrick's Day, a day loaded with Irish tradition when Dad was still with us. Was Mom thinking about Dad when she fell? Was she not being vigilant, not holding Casey with a firm hand?

When I arrived, Mom was on the loveseat with her legs propped up. Always the polite hostess, she didn't stand to greet me when I walked through the front door, so it was odd to see her sitting there.

"How you doing, Mom?" I asked.

"Oh, I'm okay."

"I hear you took a fall."

"I did?"

"That's what Doreen told me. You're a bit sore, aren't you?"

"Oh, I'm okay."

"Well, you have an appointment tomorrow morning with the doctor to make sure nothing's broken, okay?"

"I don't need a doctor."

"But I need you to go. Just so I don't worry so much about you. We can go out to lunch at Duffy's afterwards. Does that sound good?"

"We'll see," she said, still not moving from her place on the small sofa.

Later, we ate dinner at home instead of going out to our regular restaurant. The following morning, Mom still refused to admit she was in pain, but she didn't fight me about going to the doctor.

After hours of waiting and x-rays and more waiting, we were assured Mom had no broken bones, just a badly bruised tailbone. For the next six months her living room and kitchen had a scattering of various shapes and sizes of donut pillows Doreen bought on-line and had shipped to Grayland. Mom must have loved opening all those packages. I was never as good as I could have been about sending cards and packages to her. I remembered the big things – holidays and birthdays – but I wasn't good at just sending notes, cards, little gifts. Anything at all to fill her Grayland mailbox, anything that would make her daily trip to the post office worthwhile, anything that would break up the monotony of her daily life. I imagine Doreen's donut pillows were a fun distraction for a few months.

ও   ৎ

"Can I drive, Dad? Please?"

"We're twenty feet long, pulling a fifteen hundred pound boat, Erin. Not this time. Not yet."

"I can do it," she said.

"I'm sure you can. But not this time," Tom said.

In early summer, Erin had completed driver's education and was eager to drive every time anyone got in a vehicle, even if it was Tom's huge GMC van, fondly referred to as the Big Green Jelly Bean. The truth was, Erin was an excellent driver. Sure, she drove fast and didn't always leave sufficient car lengths between her and the car in front of her, but she had excellent perception and response. She was quick and seemed to be able to sense what other drivers were about to do. That summer and into the fall she had dance classes once or twice weekly in Burien, a half hour drive to the south. That was her driving time.

I remember the first time I allowed her behind the wheel. Tom had already taken her to an open, empty parking lot a few times to get the basics. It was time for road practice. I took her to a quiet residential area with wide streets, wide parking strips, and no sidewalks. It was midafternoon, so few cars were parked in front of the homes and fewer people were present to witness the lesson.

"Okay," I said. "Are you ready?"

"Sure," she said with the confidence of a seasoned driver. That first day she drove the neighborhood with the skill of someone who'd been driving for months. She made the turns, the stops, the yields without a hitch. Driving made Erin happy. Driving gave her that sense of adulthood she craved. It would still be a long time before she could drive alone – sixteen in Washington State – and even longer before she could drive with friends in the car without an adult present – sixteen and a half. But she was determined to learn, to be ready when the time came.

We were headed to Ike Kinswa State Park on Mayfield Lake in southern Washington for a few days – the three of us and one of Erin's friends. We always let her take a friend whenever possible. Without siblings, we wanted Erin to have someone to play with when she was younger, to commiserate and just hang out with as a teenager. They had their own tent. They had a sense of independence. And they had Tom to drive the ski boat.

It would've been a wonderful trip, but I freaked out. I was so buried in Maureen's death, I was terrified for Erin. She was a fifteen-year-old who looked at least five years older. I wanted her to be twenty, but she wasn't. I wanted her to survive past nineteen, Maureen's age when she was killed. In the depths of my illogical terror, I somehow felt that if she made it past nineteen, she'd be okay. She'd be safe.

The second day at the lake, while Tom was docking the boat for the evening, I went back to camp alone thinking I'd meet up with Erin and her friend. Instead, I found a note saying they'd gone for a walk. I panicked. Night falls late but fast in the wilderness, and dusk was already upon us. It was a large park divided by a small country road, but a road nonetheless, a road leading away from the park. Where was my daughter? I ran back through the park to the dock to find Tom and insisted we search for the girls.

"They're fine," Tom said. "They just lost track of time."

"No," I screamed. "We have to find them. I'll do it alone if you won't help."

Begrudgingly Tom joined me, and we began a search of the large campground.

"Have you seen two pretty blond teenagers?" I asked each stranger I passed.

"Yeah, I saw two girls with a young man," another camper said. "They were headed down toward the beach."

We headed in that direction. There was a grassy knoll with a concessions stand and bath house above the swimming area. The restrooms were closed, the area empty, dark and, to my eyes, frightening. Then I saw them. Two girls deep in happy conversation walking down the park road toward us. I collapsed into tears of relief.

"We left you a note," Erin said. "I'm sorry. Is it really such a big deal?"

At fifteen Erin was fed up with her emotional wreck of a mother. When she was younger, it had been easier to hide my terrors. I was loving and gentle. I wasn't great at games and make-believe, but I loved her deeply, intensely, and she felt it without feeling smothered. Now as a teenager, the hours of reading aloud together, of coffee shop journal writing, of beach walking were gone. Now, as she approached the age when Maureen was murdered, my fears were out of control, and in my fear, I was clinging so tightly I was suffocating her.

"Where's the boy?" I demanded.

"What boy?" the girls asked in unison.

"Another camper said he saw you with a boy," I said.

"Wasn't us," they said.

"Come on," Tom said. "Let's go make dinner."

But it wasn't so easy. I was having a two-year-old temper tantrum, and Erin was angry I'd made such a big deal out of nothing. Angry because I'd embarrassed her in front of a friend. I knew I was pushing her away, but I was lost in a black blur and couldn't seem to stop myself. We headed back to the campsite in silence.

ã¿ â

In September 2002, Mom's seventy-eighth birthday had been a quiet affair. Only seven months after Dad's death, she was in no mood to celebrate. None of us were. But by September 2004, two years, seven months and nineteen days after Dad's death, Doreen and I knew it was time for the family to come together again and celebrate Mom's eighty years of life. We had navigated our way through over two and a half years of foggy, blurry confusion and pain together. Dad was gone. Maureen's killer had been sentenced to life in prison without parole. Mom was alive. Alive with early signs of dementia, but still remembering Dad's eightieth birthday, remembering the celebration we had in his honor, and reminding both Doreen and me she would soon be eighty years old.

Just as I was waiting for Erin to turn twenty so she would be safe because some twisted logic told me if she got past nineteen she'd never be hurt, I now had a whole new set of fears around Mom turning eighty. Would eighty be enough for her? Would she then let go, give up, follow Dad? So in addition to my desire for my daughter to reach an age of safety, I feared my mother reaching an age of letting go. For those first few years after Dad's death, my fear about Mom's physical longevity overshadowed my concerns about her mental health. Only later did I realize I was worrying about the wrong infirmity.

Early summer, Doreen and I got busy planning a party. We contacted each of the siblings, including Laureen in Turkey and our three brothers in Hawaii. The message was the same to all eight siblings and grandchildren: there would be a party and all were invited.

The cold Pacific winds pounded the old clapboard two-story building, a remnant of the 1800s, a reminder of times past. Majestic and beautiful, once a resort destination for travelers up and down the west coast, the Tokeland Hotel is a national historic landmark on the tip of the Willapa Peninsula, just past Washaway Beach, and through the tiny Shoalwater Indian Reservation with its small casino and a trail of fireworks stands, boarded up ten months of the year. Drafty and smelling of a hundred years of musty decay, the Tokeland Hotel still stands, a graceful, aging beauty. A bit worse for the wear. Still majestic. Still proud. Traveling from various points worldwide, eight siblings, spouses, and children, as well as some of our cousins, converged on this tiny point of windswept Washington coastland to celebrate. Most hadn't seen our mother since Dad's funeral.

Mom, confused and overwhelmed by excitement, stood in the middle of the lobby surrounded by family. A cold rush of September wind blew through the room as the front door opened. From a far corner, where I was discussing the table arrangements with the restaurant staff, I saw my middle brother, Michael, hobble through the door on crutches, his leg braced from ankle to thigh. Andrew, my youngest brother, held the door.

I saw Mom's face freeze in surprise. Her hands flew to her cheeks as though on wing.

"Sorry we're late, Mom," Michael said, a tease in his voice.

"You're here," she said, unconvinced.

As I stood back and watched Mom's gesture of surprise, I saw her mother, Grandma Huber, on the front steps of her two-story, white clapboard home in Herried, South Dakota when we drove into the yard after traveling cross-country from Seattle for a summer visit.

I watched as Michael made his way toward Mom, as her hands sailed from her own cheeks upwards to those of her middle son, as she held his face in her hands in disbelief. Michael passed his crutches to one hand, doubled over and embraced our tiny, frail mother. She disappeared in his arms. Then it was Andrew's turn. A bit more reserved, never as free with his emotions, Andrew too wrapped Mom in a bear hug.

We found seats around a long table. It wasn't so much what was said, or even what was not said, that mattered. Rather it was that we were together – all of the living family members, all of the living siblings, together in one room to honor Mom's eightieth birthday. The food was mediocre at best, the restaurant drafty, but the bittersweet joy of being together sufficed. In a way I'm not sure any of us really knew what to say to each other. It was awkward. Dad had died, Laureen was reunited with Mom after a lifetime of banishment, and Maureen's death still hung in the air since the announcement of the arrest of her killer in the local papers the day of Dad's eightieth birthday almost four years before. A birthday we had celebrated in the same fashion, in the same room, in the same beach hotel, with almost the same cast of characters. I felt awkward. I didn't know what to say in that noisy room with the clatter of utensils and talk of nothing at all.

It was binding love that brought us together on September 21, 2004 to the tip of the Willapa Peninsula to surprise Mom on the day of her birth, the day marking her eightieth year on earth. There was deep love, but little understanding among my siblings. We lived very separate lives. Distance, both physical and emotional, came between us. We were bound by shared blood, genetics, DNA. We were bound by familial love born of a shared or somewhat shared childhood, but how shared can a span of fifteen years from eldest to youngest really be? Still we were and continue to be bound by family love and separated by profound ignorance of each other's lives, interests, values, or passions. We don't know each other. We simply think we know each other because we're siblings, because we're supposed to know each other, because we are bound by blood.

The following morning was clear and blue at the beach. The family gathered at the house and walked – a long line of siblings, spouses and grandchildren – along the trail, over the dunes and out onto the wide Pacific beach, Casey leading the way. It was my niece's husband who thought to bring a camera. He found a large piece of driftwood and slowly, meticulously wrote our shared family name and the date in huge block letters into the hard gray sand. All caps. Proud and strong. I could have kissed him. He lined us all up along the shore and started snapping pictures, the Pacific waves crashing behind us, a strong cold ocean wind whipping our hair across our faces, the sun unusually bright overhead. Proof we were still family: eight siblings with Mom. Maureen in the waves, in the air, in the sunshine that warmed us. Then the next generation, the cousins, frozen in gray tones on white paper.

But Maureen was not mentioned at all. As we walked the beach, as we stood and laughed and had our photograph taken, I was overwhelmed with a sense of guilt and dishonesty. My siblings had gathered. We joked, reminisced, talked. Dad was remembered, the good memories, the early memories. But not our sister. And deep inside of me, I carried a secret none but Mom knew about, and she wasn't telling anyone. She couldn't. She'd already forgotten.

I didn't tell my siblings I was writing, I'd taken a course at the University of Washington, I'd finished a memoir. I suppose I feared there would be serious trouble once they knew, and I didn't want that trouble to overshadow the celebration, Mom's celebration. But still I felt like I was lying to them.

෯ ෯

The month after my mother's eightieth, I turned fifty. When Tom asked me what I wanted, I said, "A party. I've never had a birthday party."

"Never?"

"No, not really. I mean we always had family parties with a cake and candles, but I've never had a party with lots people of my own choosing."

"Okay, so who do you want to invite?" With that, Tom planned a wonderful party for me at a local wine shop.

As though part of his arrangements, only days before the party, I received a contract offer to publish *The Thirty-Ninth Victim*. Just after the party, I signed the contract.

As high as I was flying that month, I crashed to the opposite extreme only a few weeks later. I'd written in secrecy because I feared my family's judgement and condemnation. When I made the decision to seek publication, I'd told Tom that as soon as I signed a contract, as soon as I was certain *The Thirty-Ninth Victim* would be published, I'd have to give copies to my siblings. That seemed a fair to me.

"I always figured I wouldn't tell them unless it was going to be published," I said. "Now that I've signed the contract, I need to do it."

"Why tell them at all?" Tom asked. "They'll never know unless it becomes a bestseller."

"And what are the chances of that?" I said with a laugh knowing my little independent publisher wasn't going to carry the book to any bestsellers list. "Still," I said. "I need to tell them."

"I wouldn't do it if I were you," he said. "All hell's going to break loose."

As was often the case, Tom could read the inevitable with far greater clarity than I ever could. Maybe this was due to the lack of emotional baggage he carried and his lack of concern about my siblings' reactions. His concern was about me and about how struggles with my siblings might affect my well-being and that of our small family. He was the compass I used to guide my way. But this time I ignored my compass and faced the consequences.

I made a couple of errors: I failed to mark the manuscript as a draft, and I had the copies bound for easy reading. I suppose I was proud of my work, and I wanted it to look good when I finally shared my secret with my siblings. But by giving it a finished appearance, I left no room for compromise.

Our family code of silence was stone solid. Only Dad's death freed me to write anything more than a private journal. I knew if I shared my writing too soon, I risked allowing my siblings to silence me just as I had allowed my father to do so. I gave him and them an illogical power over me. I knew this. I recognized my weakness and kept my writing a secret until the manuscript was complete and the publishing contract signed and mailed. Then, I sent a copy of the manuscript to each sibling with a brief letter telling them of my plans to publish. The letter was upbeat. I was sharing my good news.

The response was fast. Emails claimed I was destroying the family name, dishonoring our father's memory, and shaming our sister.

At first I tried to respond to every email, every accusation.

"Remember what that child development expert told us?" Tom said one day in the midst of my tears of exhaustion. "Disengage. Don't make it worse. They're acting like children so just disengage."

This time I listened to him. I stopped responding. I read and printed everything, but responded to nothing. That was when I got the phone call from my eldest sister. "Will you meet us to talk?" she asked.

2005

I WALKED INTO Alki Bakery checking my watch. 9:23 a.m. I was seven minutes early. I figured I'd have a few minutes to collect my thoughts before they arrived, but I was wrong. There they were, three of my four sisters, settled at a window table in the back of the room, deep in conversation. It looked like they'd been there a while. I imagined them plotting how best to deal with their renegade sister. The outsider, I approached the table with as much confidence as I could muster. But it was all an act. I hated confrontation, and I'd spent the weeks leading up to this meeting an emotional wreck. I'd been dealing with written confrontation for two months since I mailed the manuscript in November. The holiday season passed without extended family. Now, mid-January, it was going to be face to face, three against one, and I dreaded it.

"Hi," I said.

"Hello, Arleen. You look great," Marleen said.

"Thanks. I feel great. Better than I've felt in years," I said as the butterflies fluttered and flapped.

"Really?"

"Yup." Confidence oozed, false confidence, a tough façade ready to take whatever they chose to dish out.

"Let's all get some coffee and sit down and talk."

"Sounds good." I was still on my feet. I set down my coat and headed to the counter to order. I'd already put in my order and paid by the time my sisters were out of their chairs and looking over the selection of breakfast scones and muffins.

"Wait, let me get that," Marleen said.

"I got it."

"Don't you want something to eat?"

"No, thanks. Just finished breakfast with Tom and Erin."

That was Marleen's big sister thing. She always paid. Always generous. But for me it tilted the playing field. We never took turns like friends. Like the friends I'd always wanted us to be. Not this time, I told myself. This time I was standing strong on my own two feet and her generosity was not going to soften my resolve.

I headed to our table in the corner. The table outside the bathroom doors. My least favorite table in the place, but I knew why they chose it. In the back corner away from most of the other tables and people who crowded this popular beach spot, this table offered a bit of privacy. I sat and sipped my decaf, inhaling the rich aroma, trying to relax as my sisters made their selections, waited for their orders, and doctored their drinks. I thought about my eldest sister, the sister who was not only my "big" sister, but also, at times, my surrogate mother. The sister who took me in and supported me when I returned from years living abroad, when I suffered a loneliness so intense I would spend nights in her spare bedroom rather than go home to my empty apartment. The sister I thought I could depend on for support.

Marleen was always positive and upbeat regardless the situation. She always had something nice to say, even when it felt fake to me. As I sat waiting, I remembered a conversation with Tom a few days before when we were walking Mozart along Alki Beach.

"If you always see the glass half empty, at least you started with a full glass. That's why you're always disappointed, Arleen, because you have such high expectations. You want to keep the glass full, even when it's not possible. But people like Marleen, who always see the glass half full, started out with an empty glass. The way you see life is a net gain."

I wasn't sure if Tom's logic made sense to me, but as I sat waiting for my sisters, it somehow made me feel stronger.

A few minutes later, they sat down. I avoided starting the conversation by looking out the large window next to our table. A covered bus shelter blocked the view of Elliott Bay. Buses came and went on a regular schedule. People waited even on this cold Saturday morning in mid-January. Doreen and Marleen sat on one side of the table, Charleen and I on the other. Doreen sat in front of me, but both Marleen and I angled our chairs, our bodies, to look toward each other. That angle also allowed me a better view beyond, where I found solace in the gulls as they dove for food in the garbage can next to the bus stop and soared over the water in the distance. I wanted to be with the gulls.

"So, I guess we're here to try to resolve this situation," Marleen said.

"I'm here because you asked me to be here," I said.

"Why, Arleen? Why did you do this?"

"Why did I do what?"

"Write this thing," Marleen said.

"Both my kids read it," Charleen said. "It's not just us, Arleen. They even said it was pure sensationalism. You can't publish *our* stories."

"I've been writing for as long as I can remember. I started journaling as a kid. Remember, Charleen? You gave me my first journal. But I could never put anything together, could never finish it. This I could finish. This is what I needed to say."

"But you can't do this. It's wrong. You can't tell our stories."

I continued, ignoring Charleen's choice of words. "It's a book about communication. Family communication and what can happen when there's a serious lack of communication. It's *my* story."

"Then names don't matter," Marleen said. "Change the names. All the names. First and last."

I could tell by the nods of approval from Charleen and Doreen that this was not a new idea. This was a bargaining chip they'd agreed on before I walked into the room. But I wasn't willing to give in so easily.

"I can't change Maureen's name. Like it or not, she's a public figure."

"Yes, you can," Marleen said. "It doesn't matter."

"I can't, and I won't, and I'm not changing my name either."

"How can you do this to Mom, to Dad's memory?"

"What about Maureen's memory?" I asked. "Can you all just forget she ever existed? Forget what happened to her?"

"You're trashing that, too," Marleen said. "You're not honoring her. You're destroying her memory. Don't fool yourself."

Again, nods of agreement from the other two sisters.

"I'm sorry you feel that way," I said.

"The point is, you didn't know her," Charleen said.

"You're right. I left home when she was still a kid. But it's my memoir. It's not a biography about Maureen. It's about my life and my relationship, and lack of relationship, with Maureen."

"You can't publish this thing," Marleen said. "I respect the work you put into it. I really do. I know how hard it is to write, and it's even harder to edit and rewrite. I've done two books, and they're not this kind of book. It's well-written. It's a good piece. But you can't publish it."

"I can, and I will," I said.

"You have to change it then. The bottom line is I don't want to be in it."

"What are you so afraid of?" I asked.

"I'm not afraid of anything." Marleen glared at me.

"Like it or not, you, all of you, are a part of my life, of my adolescence. Your actions, Dad's and Mom's actions, affected who I was then, and who I am today. We are intertwined, our histories, our lives are intertwined. And I have the right to tell my story."

"You don't have the right to tell ours," Marleen shot back.

"Where it touches mine, I do. I sent you the manuscript as a courtesy. And as an opportunity to point out inaccuracies as you see them, though I may or may not agree with your point of view. With nine kids over a fifteen-year span, Mom and Dad changed, their life circumstances and their parenting were different. As the middle kid, I had a bird's eye view."

"Look, Arleen, the Feeney name is important to us," Marleen said. "I can't believe it isn't important to you. The men in the family all use the name. The siblings, nephews, and nieces, too. We draw strength from the name. It's on my book jackets. How can you trash our name?"

"It's my name, too," Charleen said. "My legal name is hyphenated."

"It's just a name," I said. "Google it. There's a ton of them out there. But that's not the point. The point is the name was trashed, if you want to call it that, long before I wrote this manuscript. Do you really think there were secrets in the Issaquah Valley or within our extended family?"

"If you publish this thing …"

"Marleen, it's called a manuscript," I said.

"If you publish this manuscript you need to make sure it's clear this is only your version of what happened. You need to add a postscript that says something like 'My family doesn't agree with my depiction of our family or the events in our shared childhood. All family names have been changed'."

"No," Charleen said. "It's a simple matter of right and wrong, black and white. You can't publish it. It's is just plain wrong."

Dad's words, I thought. Dad's words flowing from Charleen's mouth. I bit my tongue and said nothing.

"Wait a minute, Charleen," Marleen said, interrupting her, slowing her down. "So, Arleen, I can see how you might need to write in order to understand and find some sort of closure, but why publish?"

"Because that's what writers do."

"But if you did it for catharsis, you reached your goal. You worked through it. You've done what you felt you needed to do, though frankly I can't understand why you needed to do it," Charleen said. "Now why can't you just put it in a drawer and forget about it? Or at least wait until after Mom is gone."

"Charleen's right. You can't do this to Mom," Marleen said. "You've trashed her husband of fifty years. You've trashed everything that's important to her. And you're just plain wrong if you think she won't find out about it because she will. None of us will tell her, but sooner or later somebody will. You can't do this to her."

"I resent the suggestion that I'm not aware of or concerned about Mom. I see her once or twice a month. How often do you two visit? But that's a whole different conversation. Just don't tell me I'm being insensitive to Mom. I don't believe I trashed her or Dad in the manuscript. I was as honest as I could possibly be, and I showed all sides of a very complex man."

"All sides? You didn't show anything but the negative. What about the happy, singing, whistling man? The man who loved life?"

"That man was the father you remember, Marleen. That man was long gone before I reached my early teens. And what about the man who disowned his third child? Didn't speak to her for over thirty years. What about that man?"

"Laureen was never completely disowned," Doreen said, finally breaking her silence. "She's in their will."

"A will is just a legal document. He didn't speak to her in over thirty years. In my opinion that means a whole lot more than any piece of paper," I said.

"He was changing," Marleen said.

"He came to my house when Laureen and her daughters were visiting," I said. "He refused to speak to her and made a beeline to the car with Mom running behind to catch up. He was so angry he wouldn't talk to me for months. That was only a few years ago. How many opportunities did he need?"

"Okay, he made some bad decisions he just didn't live long enough to retract," Marleen said. "You have to give a more balanced view of him. You have to think of Mom, of all of us. He wasn't the culprit you claim he was."

Later I looked up the culprit reference that Marleen mentioned. It was on page four of the manuscript. I wasn't even referring to Dad in the sentence. Still, I changed it.

"Look, Arleen, everybody has a tough time in their teen years," Charleen said. "They grow up and move on. They get over it."

"This just sounds so whiny. So poor me. Even Michael said you should get off your pity piss pot."

"Yeah, Marleen. I heard that one, too."

"I keep a journal," Charleen said. "But I'd never show it to anyone. It's personal. There are parts of me nobody knows, and I like it that way."

"I write, too," Marleen said. "When I'm upset or angry, I scribble like crazy. Pages and pages of bile. Then I burn them, and I feel better. I'd never dream of sharing them with anyone."

"Nobody?" I asked.

"No, nobody. Why?"

"Because our feelings are a large part of who we are. In any case, journal and memoir are two very different things. Memoir is a reconstruction of the past from the writer's perspective."

"Don't lecture me on memoir." I could hear an edge of anger creeping into Marleen's carefully controlled speech. She was the university professor. She held the only doctorate in the family. "I've done my research," she continued. "I've spoken to the head of the English department. You're going by one narrow definition of memoir. There are many others, but you've chosen to be with the minority who think they can say or do whatever they want, that truth doesn't matter."

"Whose truth? I wrote my truth. I'm sorry you don't want to hear it."

Again, Marleen shifted the conversation. Tried another approach. "Why, Arleen? Are you doing this for work?"

"Work? Oh, you mean as in 'publish or perish?' No, nothing like that."

"I thought they paid for classes or something. There's something in the acknowledgements, I think."

"Yeah, they did. But that was just professional development grant money I applied for. No, I don't need to publish to keep my tenure. I'm at a community college, not a university. Look, I wrote this because I wanted, I needed, to write it. Is that so hard to understand? I'm publishing it because I can. Because that's what writers strive to do."

"A writer? You want to be a writer?"

"Always have."

"You mean you'd quit your teaching job to write?"

"In a flash. No, wait. I love teaching, too. I love the students, but I hate the politics. Besides the benefits are good. I'm not sure what I'd do if I had the choice. Maybe teach part time. I really don't know. It's a moot point anyway."

There was a pause in the conversation. I wanted to think my sisters were beginning to realize how little we knew or understood about each other's lives and passions, but I think I was wrong.

"Lucy Williams," Marleen said.

"Yeah, what about her?"

Marleen only stared at me, her blue eyes pinning me to my chair. Dad's eyes.

"What about her?" I repeated. "She's my mother-in-law."

"I know," she said. "I've met her. Dare2Dream publishing, right?"

"Yes."

"There's a Lucy Williams with Dare2Dream."

"What? You've got to be kidding. My publisher is not Tom's mother." I was too stunned to explode. Not only had she been researching my publishing company, but she was insinuating that the only reason I was getting published, able to get published, was because my mother-in-law was behind it. I should've stood up and walked out, but I didn't. I let it roll over me like the winter waves crashing on Alki Beach, and somehow I remained afloat.

I remembered years before when I'd just returned to Seattle after almost a decade away. I wrote a short story and asked Marleen to read it and give me her opinion. I never heard a word back from her and was too timid to ask. Our parents taught us that if we didn't have anything good to say we shouldn't say anything at all. So I simply assumed my story was a piece of crap. Marleen's insinuation that my mother-in-law was my connection to a publishing contract reminded me of how little faith my sister had in my writing. But this time I realized it was not the weakness of my writing that put my sister off, but the power of my words.

Two and a half hours into the conversation, I'd had enough. It felt a bit like childbirth. I'd been terrified going into it. I'd braced myself, but to my surprise, it wasn't as bad as I'd feared, and I came out stronger in the end.

We said goodbye and parted ways. I went one direction, and the three of them went in the opposite direction. I assumed they came in one car and left together, but I didn't know and didn't ask. I assumed they went back to Doreen's house to rehash the meeting. I knew I was right when I received their email later in the day. Subject line: "Meeting and manuscript recap."

☙ ❧

My mother was never one for annual checkups, for herself or for anyone else in our large family. I'm not sure if that was a bi-product of necessity. How could you manage medical and dental checkups for nine kids and two adults? It wasn't just a matter of having good health insurance. There was a time factor involved as well. Or was it that she just didn't think they were necessary? Even when the kids were grown and gone, she and Dad rarely went to the doctor, limiting visits to address an absolute and apparent need. Unless they were sick, hurt, or in extreme pain, they saw no need to visit a medical or dental clinic. So as Mom aged, getting her in for a physical exam was a challenge.

Several years earlier, when Dad was still alive, Mom fell and hit her head on a bedside dresser in the middle of the night. Dad found her on the floor beside the bed. I never knew if a CT scan was done at the time, but the story we were told was that the doctor thought she'd had a minor stroke. She was on blood thinners and other medications for years even though she always insisted she was fine.

By spring 2005 Doreen and I were concerned about Mom's inability to remember to take her medications on a regular basis, medications we were unconvinced she really needed. We worried that by taking too many pills one day and skipping the next day, she was putting her health at risk, and that perhaps her inconsistent dosages could be contributing to her lack of mental clarity. We wanted her off all medications unless they were absolutely essential. We wanted to know what she really needed to be taking, how much and how often. I wanted to bring her to Seattle to doctors I knew and trusted, but she'd never agree to that, so Doreen and I started a slow campaign to get her to see a doctor closer to home.

"When was the last time you had an annual physical?" I asked her one day when I was visiting.

"Oh, I don't know," she said.

"Well, they're supposed to be every year. That's why they're called *annual* physicals."

"Oh, I'm fine," she said with a laugh.

"Yeah, you're stronger and healthier than I am, but wouldn't it be great not to have to take these pills every day?"

We were sitting in the kitchen. I picked up one of her pill bottles from the placemat in the center of the table and shook it for emphasis. "Sounds like this one's almost empty. Before we refill it, let's find out if you really have to keep taking them, okay?"

"That would be nice."

"So, if I make an appointment, will you go?"

"To the doctor?"

"Yes."

"Will you go with me?"

"Yes. We'll go see that young woman doctor, okay? We met her when you fell and hurt your tailbone. You liked her because she was funny and nice." I didn't remind her that she thought the young doctor was a nurse. In Mom's world women were nurses. Doctors were men.

"Okay," she said.

With that slim agreement, I made an appointment. I mentioned we were concerned about memory loss and asked if a CT scan could be arranged the same day as I'd be coming from Seattle to drive Mom to the appointment. I also said Mom was a bit reticent. The doctor's office was very accommodating. I'm sure I wasn't the only out-of-town adult child bringing in an aging parent. That demographic was a reality of this coastal community.

"There's no evidence of a stroke here. What we do see is a series of tiny black dots in the lower back lobe of her brain. These dots indicate what's called multi-infarct syndrome. It's a common form of dementia," the doctor told us a few weeks later.

"Can it be stopped or controlled with medication?" I asked.

"No. There's really nothing that's been found effective. This is a normal part of the aging process, but it's more pronounced and occurs with greater frequency in some than others."

"Is it like Alzheimer's?"

"There are many, many forms of dementia, but this is not Alzheimer's."

"Can we take Mom off the other medications she's been on?"

"Yes. But gradually."

I didn't think to ask about progression or prognosis. I didn't go home and do an internet search. I heard "normal" and focused on the fact that the doctor found no evidence in the scan of an earlier stroke, that for over a half dozen years my mother had been taking drugs she might never have needed at all.

Throughout the year leading up to Erin's sixteenth birthday, she had a goal she rarely lost sight of. She wanted a car. As with many things she wanted through her young life, when she started talking about a car, Tom and I told her we'd go halves. She did babysitting and odd jobs and saved almost every dollar that passed through her hands. On her sixteenth birthday the dream of having her own car became a reality.

Erin's first two years of high school weren't great academic successes, but she maintained a decent, if not stellar, GPA. By her second year, she wanted out of the high school scene all together. She was frustrated by the attitudes and behaviors of students and teachers alike. She complained of being treated with more respect, more like an adult, in elementary school than in high school. She was looking into new options.

Washington State's Running Start program allows high school students to attend community college and earn both a high school diploma and an associate degree at the same time. Students can do all college classes or they can have a mixed schedule, taking some classes at their high school and others at a local college. The program is only available to those high school juniors or seniors who are able to test into college level English or Math classes. I suggested she talk to her high school counselor about the program.

Two years after those tears and struggles in our living room over which school she would attend, I sat outside the Assessment Office at the college where I taught in West Seattle. Erin walked out of the office glowing. "I did it, Mom," she said. Her arms wrapped me in an exuberant hug. "I'm in."

"Congratulations! What's next?"

"Well, I have to see my high school advisor to find out what classes I need, and then I have to see the college advisor to register for classes at the college that will fulfill those requirements and my AA requirements."

"I'm so very proud of you," I said. My heart danced. I knew Erin needed a challenge – both intellectual and social – to keep her engaged. I hoped that attending college would be that challenge.

By midsummer Erin was registered for college classes, working as a Starbucks barista, and driving her own car to dance classes. In July she danced across the stage of the 5th Avenue Theater in her fourth and final recital. The girl was flying.

As I sat in the audience in that beautiful ornate theater, I remembered a very little girl, a girl at her first ballet recital when she was just barely three years old. Tom and I were the excited parents. We held a tiny wrist bracelet of baby's breath and miniature pink roses. The music began for her number. Her classmates trailed onto the stage – little pink legs and fluffy white tutus. We watched each girl, straining to see our own. But Erin didn't appear.

"Is that all?" I whispered to Tom. He nodded. "But where is she?"

"There, do you see her to the right?" he said.

I looked in the direction he was pointing and caught a brief glimpse of Erin's face peeking out from the wing, terrified and refusing to move onstage. A few minutes into the number, we silently made our way to the exit. We headed backstage but found our way blocked by the assistant director of the dance studio.

"We want to see Erin," I said.

"She's okay."

"She's terrified."

"She'll be okay. She's with the other dancers. We've done this before."

"But we want to see her now."

"Really, it's best if you just leave her for now. Nobody's allowed backstage during the show. We'll bring her to you when it's over."

I looked at Tom, unwilling to leave my daughter to cry in some stranger's arms, uncertain how to make the right decision, unsure whether the studio policy was what was best for Erin or simply what worked best for the school. We went back to our seats, but I couldn't sit still any more than Tom could, so we returned to the lobby where we paced until the show ended.

Finally, the house lights came up, and the wait was over. The lobby was flooded in a sea of pink and white tulle, face makeup smeared and costumes askew. And there was little Erin, her pudgy face streaked with tears, clinging to the hand of one of the older dancers, now a teaching assistant. Her face lit up when she saw us in the crowd, and then, just as fast, her eyes dropped in embarrassment and shame. My heart dropped with them. She made her way to us through the crowd and into my arms.

"Mommy, it was so long," she said.

"It's okay, honey," I said as I held her tight in my arms, reluctant to loosen my grip even for Tom's embrace. I can still feel her warm little body in my arms, a bundle of disappointment.

"This is for you, sweetie," Tom said as he handed her the tiny bouquet.

"Do I still get it?" she asked. A timid, tiny voice fighting back tears.

"Of course you do," he said. "You practiced hard for a long time."

"Thank you," she said.

"Here, let me help you put it on," he said. He gently fitted the floral bracelet on her wrist. "There, you look very pretty."

To this day I don't know if leaving her backstage with the teachers and other dancers was the right thing to have done. I know I wanted to storm past the director's assistant blocking the stage door and rush back to hold my crying baby in my arms. Instead, I listened to the voice of dance authority and waited. At the time, Tom and I thought it would be the traumatic end to her interest in dance. But she overcame her stage fright and danced until that final recital when she was sixteen in the summer of 2005.

 ஒ   ல

Almost six months had passed since the discussion with my sisters at Alki Bakery. Doreen and I continued alternating visits to Mom, but our communication was limited to short, precise emails about our mother. When are you going? What does she need? What did the doctor say? For months, the subject line read: Mom.

I finally got fed up with the emails and picked up the phone. She didn't refuse to answer despite caller ID. A good sign, I figured. "Can I talk to you?" I said.

"Is something wrong?" she asked.

"No, I'm just tired of all these emails. It's getting a bit silly. We haven't talked in what, six months?"

There was a silence for a moment. Then she said, "Okay, what's up?"

We talked about Mom and finalized a schedule of visits for the next month. Before I ended the call, I decided to push a bit more. "Can I call again?" I asked.

"Okay," she said. "To talk about Mom."

"Can't we just agree to disagree about my writing?" I asked.

"Alright. But I don't want to hear about it."

"Agreed," I said.

I was pleased when I hung up. Pleased I'd made the call. Pleased it was a small step in the right direction, in the direction of restoring communication with my sisters at a time when everything else was clouded by uncertainty.

A few weeks later, it was Doreen who called me. Surprised, I thought something had happened to Mom.

"Is she okay?" I asked.

"Yeah, I just wanted to let you know Michael and Andrew are in town, so you don't need to go to Grayland this weekend."

"Really?"

"Yeah, they're headed there now. I guess they rented a van and are doing some sort of road trip with all their kids."

"Wow, that's a first," I said.

"They'll be in Seattle early next week. I don't know where they're all going to stay. I've got to work."

"Well, let them know they can stay here if they want. It's summer break now, so I'm not working. They can set up tents in the yard for all I care."

To my surprise, I got a phone call a few days later from Michael. "Hi, Arnie." His special nickname for me.

"Hi, Michael," I said. "I hear you're coming to town."

"Yeah, we're at Mom's now. We went surfing today."

"Lord, I bet you froze your butts off."

"Yeah. Wet suits and all that shit. It's tough, but the boys caught some good waves."

"Fun," I said.

There was a pause.

"We're coming up there tomorrow," he said.

"You want to do a barbecue?" I asked. "The weather's beautiful. You're all welcome to stay. There aren't enough beds, of course, but there's plenty of floor space."

"We've got sleeping bags and camping shit."

"Okay, then, we'll see you tomorrow."

I clicked the phone shut and turned to Tom who'd been listening to my end of the conversation. "They're coming?" he asked.

"Yeah, weird, huh? What am I going to do? What if they confront me like the sisters?"

"They won't," he said.

"How can you be so sure?"

"Because they're guys. They're your dad through and through. They don't want to talk about it. They want to forget it, pretend you never wrote it."

"I suppose you're right," I said. But still I couldn't sleep that night. I tossed and turned, running imagined conversations through my nervous brain.

Our narrow, neighborhood street rarely experienced the noise and craziness of that sunny Saturday afternoon. Between the two of them, my younger brothers have five sons and two daughters. At the time, the kids ranged from single digits to early twenties. All well-mannered, free-spirited island kids, they arrived early afternoon in a large van. I watched as the side door slid open and kids, long boards, and duffle bags piled out.

"Here we go," I said to Tom, who stood at my side.

"Come on, Mom," Erin said as she walked behind us. "It's going to be fun."

Tom just gave me an encouraging back pat. We opened the front door as Andrew and Michael lumbered toward us. No wives or girlfriends. Just my brothers and their kids.

"Hey, Arnie," Michael boomed over the noisy chaos. "We're here."

I hadn't seen my brothers, nieces, or nephews for several years. Hadn't talked to either brother since I mailed the manuscript six months before. I'd heard comments attributed to each, but had spoken with neither by phone or email. There was little new about that. We weren't a close family. Not close in that way some siblings are with regular phone or email conversations. A year could pass without an exchange between us. That had been our pattern since I left home at seventeen when they were still in elementary school. Still, despite the distance and silence, love tied us together – an awkward love, a love of blood, but not of understanding and acceptance.

I rubbed my sweaty palms on the seat of my jeans and walked forward to receive my brothers' embraces.

Most of my nephews were surfers, and even those who weren't, excelled on long boards. Only moments after their arrival and brief greetings, the boys had set up a ramp over the steps between our yard and the sidewalk. For hours they skateboarded, making impossible jumps and putting on a show unlike anything our quiet street had ever witnessed.

Later, with the aroma of barbecued salmon in the backyard, kids running through the house and up and down the street, Andrew and Michael settled at the picnic table with beers in hand, I passed Tom in the kitchen. "Don't leave me alone with them," I whispered.

"Okay," he said. "But stop worrying. They're not going to say anything. They just want a nice visit before they get on that plane tomorrow and head back to work."

I knew I was being ridiculous. But I clung to Tom all afternoon and evening, determined never to be caught alone in a room with either of my brothers. With both together I felt a bit safer, certain that unlike my sisters, neither brother would say a word about the manuscript in front of the other.

We ate and drank and talked for hours, reminiscing about our childhood in Issaquah, worrying about Mom, avoiding the personal present. Later, the sofas and floors were covered with sleeping bags, and the brothers tossed a coin for the guest bed. By the time I was up the next morning, all trace of chaos was gone. The kids had rolled their sleeping bags and repacked their backpacks. Like a well-oiled road crew, the van was repacked and the gang was ready to head to the airport. Coffee, orange juice, milk, breakfast muffins for all, and they were gone. It happened so fast, it almost felt like a dream. And, of course, Tom was right. Not a word was muttered of the manuscript.

ॐ ॐ

Earlier that summer of 2005, I had learned Blue Feather Books, Ltd. had taken ownership of my first publisher. I contacted them, and it wasn't long before I got a response. I was told it would take some time for them to get fully up and running. They asked if I could send another copy of my manuscript and if by chance I also had a copy of my contract. I sent both and felt as though I were starting all over again. Unsure whether the contract would be honored or whether the trouble with my siblings had been worth it.

I began second guessing myself. Maybe I should never have sent the manuscript. Maybe I should have listened when Tom advised against sending it. Maybe I should have felt the weight of the published book in my hands before telling them about it.

A few weeks later, an attorney for Blue Feather Books, Ltd. called me. She said she'd found an email addressed to my original publisher dated February 9, 2005. It was a threat to file a lawsuit if *The Thirty-Ninth Victim* were released. It was from Feeneys7@aol.com. She told me the message was followed by a list of names, and she wanted to know if I recognized them. I listened to her read the list and then told her the names were indeed those of my siblings. She wanted to know if I was aware of this threat of legal action. I assured her I knew nothing of the email or the threat and that my siblings had told me nothing about it. I tried to calm the trembling in my hands, the spasm in my lower back, the knots in my stomach.

It wasn't until that moment I realized the depth of my siblings' condemnation. I had been disowned just as my father had disowned Laureen decades before. The cycle continued. Not Feeneys8, but Feeneys7. I was no longer one of the family.

Before she ended the call, I thought to ask the attorney if she could send me a copy of the email. A few days later I received copies of both the email my siblings sent as well as the attorney's response negating their legal rights to stop publication. But it wasn't the body of the email that took my breath away, that landed like a punch to the gut. It was seeing that address: Feeneys7@aol.com typed out in black ink on white paper. They did not write, sign, and mail a letter or provide any physical address. Instead, they created an electronic address, choosing a name that intimated I was no longer one of the eight living siblings. They closed their message with a list of names, in chronological order from eldest to youngest, and sent it only three weeks after our meeting at Alki Bakery.

By late summer I still didn't know the fate of my manuscript, but I remained silent, refusing to give my siblings the pleasure of learning, of hoping, the book wouldn't be published. As difficult as it was that email address and the secret threat to my publisher on the tail of our conversation fortified my desire to publish the book and try to break the family cycle of silence.

❧　❧

The turkey was in the oven, the house fragrant with holiday goodness, when I walked Mom up the front steps and in the door, leaving Casey to sniff the yard. I'd driven to Grayland the previous afternoon and spent the night at Mom's, unwilling to drive the five hours down and back, probably more with holiday traffic, in a single day. Tom was cooking Thanksgiving dinner – his holiday feast of family specialties and southern tradition.

We'd planned a long weekend for Mom, a visit we hoped we might be able to prolong for the full four days, better yet a full week and two days until the following weekend. As we saw it, there was really no reason for Mom to return to Grayland. Tom and I had discussed the possibilities of remodeling again, of adding a mother-in-law apartment to our house, of convincing her to live with us. At least we wouldn't worry about her being alone two and a half hours away. We thought she'd be happier surrounded by family. Alone during the workday, but together for breakfast each morning and dinner every evening. Wouldn't that be better than weeks alone in

Grayland with only Casey for company? We thought we could start with long visits, trial runs, to see if she, if we, could make it work. I suppose what we didn't think about was that it would always be our home, not hers. And Mom was a very independent woman.

Again, we'd invited a few friends as well as Doreen and her husband for Thanksgiving dinner. We looked forward to a full house, great food, drink, and conversation. It was a bit odd socializing with Doreen with the shadow of the lawsuit hanging over me, but going into the holidays, I just wanted to pretend we were a big happy family again, and I was excited Mom had agreed to come, so I said nothing. Only my willingness to cart stinky Casey to Seattle with her and the promise to take them both home, whenever she was ready, sealed the deal. That promise was a bit of a stretch, given I worked full-time, but I figured, worst-case scenario, I'd take a personal day to keep my promise.

It was about noon when we walked in the front door. I settled Mom into the only bedroom on the main floor of our small house – my writing room. I'd cleared off my desk for her small suitcase. My writing routine was put on hold for the duration of her visit. This too, my husband and I had discussed. If Mom lived with us, I would never be able to work or write at home. I'd have to resort to coffee shops or my campus office. When I was at home, I would be with Mom, just as I had been when Erin was a young child – on call at all times unless she was napping. Being with Mom was the same. She was unable to allow personal space. When awake, she needed full attention and interaction. Still, we could make it work we decided, if only she'd agree. At the very least, a few weeks with us every so often, particularly in the winter months during the holiday season would be nice.

"Where's Casey?" Mom asked.

"Just outside, Mom"

"I don't see him." She was standing in the living room searching the front yard through the large front window.

"He's in the backyard with Mozart."

"Can he get out?" she asked for what seemed like the hundredth time in the first hour of her visit.

"No, Mom. The yard's fenced all the way around. There's a gate on both sides of the house. They're locked tight. He can't get out. Look there's one gate." I pointed out the southern-facing living room window. "See the gate's right there, and it's locked shut. Now come here. I'll show you the other gate." I led her into her bedroom and pulled up the blind covering the window on the north side of the room. "See, Mom, there's the other gate closed tight. Casey can't escape. Besides, he likes to play with Mozart. He won't go anywhere."

"But where is he?"

"Well, you can look out this window." I pulled the blind on the west window with a view of the backyard. "Or, you can look out the kitchen window. He's right there, see him? And he can come into the sunroom whenever he wants through the doggy door."

"Really?"

"Yeah, he can just come right into the sunroom."

"Let's keep him inside," she said.

"Later, we'll keep him inside, but right now Tom needs to go in and out a lot through the sunroom. See, he's cooking the turkey outside in that big barbecue."

"Okay," she said.

Throughout the afternoon Mom moved from window to window, back and forth, from the kitchen to my writing room in search of Casey. Tom was busy trying to cook dinner, dodging my mother to work on his favorite traditional side dishes: Southern corn pudding, Bourbon sweet potatoes, and baked dressing balls. When my mother couldn't see Casey in the backyard, she wandered into the living room. Back and forth from living room window to dining room window, both with full views of the front yard.

"Mom," I said. "Casey can't go to the front yard. He's only in the back yard. See there's a gate here. He can't get through. And see, there's a gate on this side too." I took her hand, like a small child, and again led her from the south window in the living room to the north window in my writing room, pointing out the gates.

"Is the front gate locked?" she asked five minutes later.

"Yes, Mom." I gave up trying to explain that Casey was in the backyard with our dog. That it was impossible for the dogs to even get into the front yard, let alone out the front gate.

A few minutes later Tom pulled me aside. "She's trying to put out the candles," he said. Sure enough, she was in the living room worrying over the candles on the mantle, each enclosed in its own little glass. Safe candles. The only kind I've used in my home since Erin was a child.

"The fire's big," Mom said.

"It's okay, Mom," I said.

"The fire," she repeated, and I realized she was talking about the flames of the gas fire in the fireplace.

"It's okay, Mom. See we can just switch it off."

"Really?"

"Yeah. Look." I hit the switch, and the fire was gone.

"Where's Casey?" she asked.

By midafternoon, our dinner guests began to arrive. The table was set, and the turkey was ready. We began carrying food to the dining room. Everyone gathered around the table and found places to sit. I took a moment in the kitchen. Do we have everything? I asked myself and took a deep calming breath.

"Who are all these people, and when will they go away?" my mother asked.

"Oh, Mom," I said, a bit startled that she'd followed me into the kitchen. "I thought you were at the table."

"When will they go?" she repeated. "I want to go home."

"It's okay, Mom. They're just family and friends. They'll leave after dinner. Come on. Let's go eat. Are you hungry?"

"Hungry?" she asked.

The living room and connected dining area were again ablaze in candlelight and flames from the fireplace. I led Mom back to the table and sat beside her. "Sensory overload," I whispered to Tom in response to the question in his eyes – the same words we had used to describe our daughter when she was a toddler and dissolved in unexpected tears.

Dinner was fabulous. Tom's annual treat, with special dishes added by friends. We ate, drank, and talked. Mom seemed to relax, join in. Our friends graciously pulled her into the conversation, reducing it to a level she could follow. *How's Casey? Was it a nice drive from the beach? How long will you stay in Seattle?* With each question, she looked in my direction, seeking the words, and I would provide those words just as I had done many years before when Erin was a very young child, still too timid to respond to an adult's question, an adult who was not a parent.

I cleared the dishes and prepared dessert. I was at the kitchen counter when again Mom came up behind me. "I want to go home now," she said.

"Are you tired, Mom?"

"Too many people."

"I know. It's a bit crazy, isn't it? Do you want to go to your room for a while? You don't have to stay up, you know. It's okay. You can go to bed."

"Really?" she said.

"Of course. Come on. I'll help you." I led her to my writing room and again showed her the adjacent bathroom. Opening the slats in the back blind, I said, "Look Mom, you can see Casey sleeping right there through the windows. The doggy door is closed, so Casey and Mozart will stay in the sunroom. Say good night."

"Good night, Casey," she said. Then I gave her a kiss, and she climbed into bed.

I returned to my guests. A temporary weight lifted from my shoulders as Mom slept.

2006

IT WAS A clear, winter day in Grayland. A rarity. We'd already walked the beach. A long walk for Mom. Not nearly long enough for me. Now the long afternoon lay before us. Empty.

The boredom of the Grayland visits was the boredom of endless television. Because my siblings and I rarely watched television growing up, it was odd to be in Mom's house with a television turned on every waking hour. I knew it was her company, the noise in the house that warded off loneliness. The summers were easier with longer beach walks and puttering in the garden. The long, dark, wet winter months were a challenge.

I searched for ideas, trying to come up with activities to fill the hours and to get Mom out of the house when I was visiting. We took long drives, watched the seals in the Westport harbor, and poked around the library. Mom did not check out books. She was no longer reading more than short articles in the local newspaper, but I got my own library card and always insisted on going to get another audio book for the long drive home, even when I already had several in the car.

I also began collecting antique dinner plates. The last thing I needed was more dinner plates – new or antique. But if I was going to collect something, plates were easy to stack, and besides, they conjured summer garden parties with white linen table coverings and flowers and candles aglow. Alluring romantic images of a life of leisure and beauty.

Despite the limited options for shopping in the Westport-Grayland coastal communities, two types of businesses seemed to flourish like mushrooms in the rain-soaked foothills. The first was the touristy knickknack shops with the inevitable ice cream or taffy dispensary in the corner and the bins of shellacked shells and starfish imported from overseas. The other type of business was the antique shops. Both were intended to fill the lonely hours of the wives of the weekend fishermen out for the day on the deep-sea charter boats. I had no interest whatsoever in the knickknacks, but I could easily spend an hour or more wandering an antique shop with Mom. Collecting dinner plates just gave those wanderings a hint of purpose.

After our morning walk, we drove to the post office to pick up the mail, to Westport to check for seals in the harbor, and to the state park to visit Dad's memorial bench.

"Now what, Mom?" I asked.

"I don't know."

"Library?"

"I don't need to go."

For a second I wasn't sure if she meant that she didn't need to go to the library or to the restroom, but I let it drop. "Well, how about the big red antique store?"

"Why?"

"Because it's full of cool antiques."

"Old stuff?"

"Yeah, old stuff," I said.

"Why?"

"To see if we can find another dinner plate, okay?"

"Why? I have plates."

"I'm collecting antique dinner plates. Pretty old ones," I added for clarification. "I only have six. I need eight, maybe ten. Will you help me find another?"

"Okay," she said.

I drove back toward Grayland and stopped in front of a large antique store. It was a big red barnlike structure along the coastal road, just across from the turn-off to the Grayland Post Office and the cranberry bogs, ANTIQUES in large white letters above the front door.

"Come on, Mom," I said. "Let's see what we can brush the dust off of in there."

"Oh no," she said.

"Okay then. Let's just look around."

"But not touch."

"Okay, we won't touch anything," I said. I helped her from the car and walked behind her up the rickety wooden steps to the large barn door.

"Why are we here?" Mom asked.

"To find another dinner plate."

"Why?"

"Because I only have six, and I need at least eight. Will you help me find another one?"

"Okay," she said.

The shop was large, but cramped. Like many antique malls, it was divided into a myriad of small spaces, each space holding the merchandise of a separate vendor. The result was a crazy crowded maze of small cubbies and narrow passages, of frilly cloth doilies and hanging gilded birdcages, of floral dinnerware, porcelain tea sets, and silver serving platters. The air was musty, with hints of the fading fragrance of artificial Christmas. Fake garland, tinsel, glass balls, Santas, and angels in every size and shape, candy canes so old the white had turned to pale beige, and innumerable nativity scenes added to the chaos and confusion of the place.

I began to wander as is my habit whether at art museums with Tom or department stores with Erin. It was just our way. We always seemed to know when to check back in and how to find each other if we were too far separated. I forgot for a moment I was with my mother.

I glanced around and realized I could not see her. I began to retrace my steps, trying to remember which way I'd walked through the complicated maze, cursing myself for letting Mom out of my sight. I was at the front door and still no Mom. I ran out to the parking lot to check the car, the street. No Mom. I returned to the store and again retraced my steps to the center of the building. There I heard her voice.

"My sister … no daughter," she said. "Where … "

I didn't wait for a response from the bewildered cashier. "I'm here, Mom," I said.

"Oh, okay," she said.

"I thought I'd lost you," I said.

"Oh no. I'm not lost."

"Good. Did you find any plates for me?"

"Oh no," she said. "They're too old here."

ล่   ดง

On Monday, August 29, 2005, the city of New Orleans was devastated. Hurricane Katrina struck a chord in the hearts of people around the world. The city of jazz destroyed. Still a child, already an adult, Erin had turned sixteen just three months before Hurricane Katrina slammed into the coast of Louisiana. As a Running Start student attending classes at a politically active urban community college, her eyes were open to the world around her. Now, as her seventeenth birthday approached, she knew what she wanted long before she shared her plans with us: a plane ticket. A ticket to New Orleans and our permission to allow her to spend her winter break doing hurricane relief work. The catch? She wanted to go with her boyfriend.

They'd done their homework, found a reputable organization that provided room and board in exchange for work, an organization that didn't require more than the two-week commitment they were able to give. She laid out the plan, showed us detailed information about the organization they had selected. In this age of paying to volunteer, this organization, like so many others offered teens and adults alike free room and board, but the volunteer needed to cover travel costs. Erin didn't want the normal teenage birthday gifts – new phone, computer, clothes, music – she wanted a plane ticket to New Orleans and our signature on the permission form that would allow a minor to participate in the program.

Tom and I weren't so naïve as to ignore the multiple layers of the situation. The desire to do volunteer work, to have a sense of participation in a national tragedy was laudable. Doing so as a seventeen-year-old with her twenty-one-year-old boyfriend was what caused us many sleepless nights of endless discussion and long mental lists of pros and cons. In the end, we let her go knowing she could not go without her boyfriend. As a minor she could only volunteer in the custody of an adult. In the end, we signed over custody to her boyfriend for the duration of the trip.

Age is a relative thing. A four-year age difference can seem huge in the teen years. Ten years later it's nothing at all. With Erin and her first boyfriend the ages often seemed reversed. Somehow from thirteen to seventeen Erin had gained the emotional maturity of a woman far beyond her years. We were certain the experiences and understanding she would gain in New Orleans far outweighed our concern about their age differences.

So in mid-May, as we ate birthday cake and celebrated, we told them they could go. We gave Erin the plane ticket, and once again we crossed our fingers that we'd made the right choice. Choices – the constant challenge of parenting. How many times had we struggled to figure out the best path? How many times would Erin decide she wanted something, do extensive research, lay out the options in such a way as to show us whatever it was she was lobbying for made perfect, logical sense? How many times would I go back re-research and find no flaw in her arguments? I learned the more loudly she argued for what she wanted, the weaker her argument. I think she learned that lesson as well, and with time, she stopped pushing for those things she knew weren't in her best interest. When she asked for a plane ticket to New Orleans, she simply sent us the website for the organization and the travel costs.

ॐ ॐ

My parents' closet ran the length of their bedroom. Two sets of louvered doors. His side and hers, divided in the middle by a stack of floor-to-ceiling shelves. The closet, lined with cedar, filled the small bedroom with the rich fragrance of a cedar grove each time the doors were opened. I wasn't aware of my father's love of clothes or my mother's inability to throw anything out until I began emptying that closet.

After Dad's death I made it my personal mission to empty Dad's half of the closet. I'm not sure if my need to find something to keep us busy or my envy of that long cedar-lined closet and my desire for my mother to use the space propelled me into action. Perhaps I was pressuring her to have what I would like to have: closet space. I was also convinced that half a closet and a dresser full of Dad's clothing served as excessive reminders that he was gone. Clearing the closet offered a certain kind of distraction and a sense of accomplishment. Each visit I'd show up with a few large black plastic bags. I remember the concern in Mom's eyes when I led her into the bedroom the first time and pulled out an empty black garbage bag.

"Oh no," she said.

"Don't worry, Mom. Nothing's going into the garbage. Remember, we talked about giving some of Dad's heavy clothes to the poor people? It's going to get cold out this winter and lots of people could really use some of this stuff."

She knew I meant business. I'd mentioned it weeks before, days before, even on the call I always made before leaving Seattle and on the second call from Aberdeen. She needed to know I was coming. She needed enough reminders so she wouldn't be able to forget. So I called and told her we were going to sort the closet. I even stretched the truth a bit and said it was her idea, an idea she'd mentioned to Doreen, a great idea I was glad she'd come up with. When I laid it on thick, I never knew where the breaking point was, that point when she realized I was full of bullshit. I wondered sometimes about how easy it could be to convince her that she'd said, done or decided innumerable things.

She tried to delay the inevitable. "Do you want a cup of tea, Arleen?"

"No thanks, Mom. Let's just get started. I know you really want to get this done today."

"You're not going to throw everything in the garbage, are you? It's good clothes. Maybe the boys will want it."

Again I reminded her "the boys" – my three brothers all decades beyond boyhood – had already told her they couldn't use Dad's clothes. And no, I wasn't going to throw it all in the garbage. There were many, many cold homeless men living under Interstate 5 who would love Dad's clothes.

"Will you give it to them?" she asked.

I assured her I would and barged into her bedroom.

"But what about the boys?" she asked again a few minutes later.

"Michael, Andrew, and Robert already took what they wanted when they were here for your birthday party. Robert's too small, and

Andrew and Michael are too tall for most of Dad's stuff. Besides they don't need any heavy clothes in Hawaii," I repeated, holding tight the fragile thread of patience.

"Okay," she said. "Give it to the poor people."

"Let's start with the dresser, okay?"

I pulled open drawers I would never have dreamed of touching when Dad was still alive. It was easy dumping dozens of old work socks, underwear, T-shirts into bags. I didn't even look at them. Didn't want to think or sort. I just wanted to get it out of Mom's way and help her find a new lease on life.

I pulled open the double doors to Dad's side of the closet with flourish, a two-handed sweep. Together Mom and I began pulling out shirts and pants, folding, stacking, making growing piles. My father had been a union steamfitter, a man who wore work clothes every day of his life. Even after he retired, he was always working on a project of some sort and always in heavy work pants or jeans. We got rid of the work clothes first. I expected the work clothes. What I didn't expect were over two dozen pairs of slacks – wool, khaki, gabardine. What did a retired man of eighty need with two dozen almost new pairs of slacks? Who was this stranger with two dozen pairs of slacks? Some still with tags on them.

My father was not one to use a fitting room. And he'd never even consider returning an item. If you bought it, you kept it. You made a commitment, you stood by it.

Reusable work clothes went into one bag. Dress slacks, shirts and jackets, tags and all, went into another bag. Work clothes worn to a state of disrepair even the homeless would reject went into the garbage bag. The bag I lied about to my mother.

After several weekends of sorting, my father's side of the closet stood vacant, stripped of life, of the history of a man. Maybe they did more than just walk the mall on those long Grayland winters. They apparently filled more empty hours with shopping than I realized.

My mother's side of the closet was packed tight. Mom never threw out anything, convinced sooner or later somebody would be able to use it, sooner or later it would be back in style. But my mother was also totally unaware of current style and lived her entire working career in nursing whites. There was a shelf above the copper rod in her closet stacked to the ceiling with boxes: cardboard gift boxes from various department stores, some long out of business and clear plastic storage boxes, perhaps a one-time attempt to keep track of what was hidden inside so many boxes. The rod itself was crammed with hangers each loaded with multiple clothing items. The hangers were a mismatched collection – plastic, metal, wooden. Under the heavily laden rod rested my mother's cedar chest, a chest she owned since she left home, a young nursing student in the early 1940s. On top of the chest were more stacks: shoeboxes, piles of clothing Mom could no longer find a home for, piles of unfiled papers. Her mantra, "A place for everything and everything in its place" had slipped away with the passing of years. The piles in her closet attested to her inability to live by her own rules. The white Mexican blouse I'd brought home for her thirty years before, a Hawaiian muumuu from a long-ago vacation, white nursing shoes unworn since retirement piled together with old bank statements, holiday cards, and photographs. Piles of chaos.

"Come on, Mom," I said on another gray afternoon as I took her by the hand and led her into the bedroom. "Let's make this closet of yours a little more user-friendly. How much of this stuff do you actually use?"

"Oh, I don't know," she said looking down at the sweater she was wearing, both hands pulling it from her body for a better view of the Arizona motif across her chest and belly. It was the same sweater she'd been wearing every time I'd visited for the past several months. "I like this one," she said.

I pulled open the doors on what was once Dad's side of the wall length closet. "Wow, Mom. Look at all this great space. I wish I had half this much closet space."

"Really?"

"Yeah," I said as I moved toward her side of the closet. "And look at this. All jammed in so tight, I don't know how you ever figure out what to wear."

Another little lie. I knew perfectly well how my mother decided what to wear. She simply wore the same thing she'd worn the day before. The week and month before. She rarely changed unless there were obvious food or garden stains on her clothes, and given her failing eyesight without the glasses she rarely wore, the stains had to be big. Then, she'd throw her clothes in the washer and put on whatever was still in the dryer from the last time she'd done the laundry.

Was it the chaos of her closet that made choices difficult, I wondered? Or the chaos of her mind? Had she reverted to her early teachings as a young mother, perhaps the early learnings of her own childhood? When I was a child, we had farm clothes and school clothes. The farm clothes were worn until they were too dirty to be allowed in the house. The school clothes were worn for a week. One dress for five days. Eventually, it became two dresses a week, and finally, probably when we hit those teen years, the rules were dropped.

I started pushing through her packed closet, finding blouses and skirts I recognized from my childhood. "So, let's go through this stuff and decide what you want to keep, okay Mom? We could even put a few outfits together. I'd never be able to decide what to wear each morning with this much stuff to choose from."

She looked at me, flustered, confused, a bit unwilling. Her hands on the hangers, pushing tiny gaps, breathing space between the garments.

"Tell you what, Mom. Let's do this like a fashion show. I'll hold something up, and you decide if you want to keep it or give it to charity. You should keep anything you think you'll wear, okay? Why don't you just sit there on the edge of the bed?"

"Okay," she said, a look of relief in her eyes. "But we're not putting it in the garbage," she said as she fingered the pile of large, heavy-duty garbage bags on the bed beside her.

"Oh no," I said. "We'll give everything you don't want to the poor people who need it." My second little lie of the day. I knew darn well many of the items in my mother's closet were long past their day, even on the charity circuit.

And so we began. I'd hold something up – an old wool skirt, a stained T-shirt, a pair of worn white nursing shoes – she'd shrug her shoulders and I'd decide between the empty side of the closet, the charity bag, or the denied, but very real, garbage bag.

As we inched deep into the back corner of the closet, my hands landed on a light brown corduroy jacket hanging over a maroon corduroy skirt. "Look at this, Mom," I said. "This was mine. I remember when you and Laureen, or maybe it was Marleen, gave it to me on my first birthday home after I moved back from Mexico City."

"Try it on. Take it," she said.

"I was skinny then, Mom. It'll never fit me now. That's probably why you have it. I'm too fat."

"You're not fat," she said with such conviction I wanted to believe her. I pulled the outfit from the closet, unable to resist the urge to try on the jacket. I knew the skirt was out of the question, but just maybe the jacket would fit. I figured it'd look great with a pair of jeans. As I pulled the jacket off the hanger, I discovered a tan leather purse hidden underneath, between the jacket and the skirt. The long strap of the purse was looped over the hook of the hanger, completely hidden by the collar of the jacket.

"Oh my god, look at this, Mom."

"What's that?"

"Your purse. The tan leather purse you and Doreen were searching for a few weeks ago. The lost purse."

"I didn't lose my purse," she said.

I sat down on the edge of the bed beside her and opened the purse. A small leather bag, the last handbag Dad had given her. A prized possession we'd thought was permanently lost. Over the past few weeks my sister had gone through the stressful, time-consuming process of cancelling Mom's credit card and putting holds on her bank accounts. Just the weekend before she'd taken Mom to get a new driver's license, half hoping she'd be denied a license and at the same time worried about how Mom would cope without a car. Not a week later I opened the purse with Mom to find her old driver's license, her Visa card, her AARP identification, and her medical insurance information. All there, all intact, all perfectly worthless. And all I could think of was homemade cookies.

Throughout both our pre-teen and teen years, my sisters and I took turns baking cookies. It was one of the few chores I didn't mind. I ate as much dough and as many fresh cookies as I wanted as long as Mom and Dad weren't home when I was cooking. I could double the recipe and still get a full batch. But once the cookies were cooled and put into a cookie canister, they disappeared. With nine kids and a husband with an uncontrollable sweet tooth, the only way Mom could be sure to have enough cookies for school lunches and, more important, for Dad's box lunch each day was to hide them. It was a serious matter to Mom, but a game to us kids. Whenever we were at home without Mom or Dad, we'd search the house to find the cookie stash. We usually failed, but then I don't ever remember searching their bedroom. That was their special place. I never entered without permission. Undoubtedly that's where the cookies were hidden.

Now Mom was hiding her purse, and we were still failing to find her hiding places, places she could no longer remember at all.

☙ ❧

October arrived and with it another birthday. Nothing I was looking forward to, no special plans. I was beginning to feel old. My body was fighting against me, and it wasn't my doing. It wasn't a ruptured disc or an ACL transplant. It wasn't because of some fun activity, a sports-related injury. No, age was against me, and my body was changing. I'd always been moody, swinging from rage to joy, from tears to smiles in a matter of minutes, even seconds. Now the roller coaster of emotions was threatening to veer off track. That's when the night sweats and hot flashes took over in earnest. I had friends who complained of having to change their pajamas, their sheets in the middle of the night. I never had it that bad, but I couldn't remember the last full night of sleep I'd enjoyed. I went to the doctor and was assured all was well. All was normal. "What about all this fat?" I whined. "This isn't normal for me." By then I was a good twenty pounds heavier than I'd ever been except during pregnancy. I knew I was a wreck despite what any doctor told me. If this was normal, I didn't want to be normal.

On the day of my fifty-second birthday, I came home from work to find a beautiful autumn bouquet – dahlia and zinnia, hydrangea and eucalyptus – in the middle of the dining room table. I leaned in and took a deep breath of the heady aroma, then headed into my writing room and clicked on my computer. Early on in the agent/publisher query process I'd become a lovesick teenager checking all forms of communication throughout the day. I checked and rechecked my email in hopes of a nibble of interest in my writing.

As I stepped out of my work clothes, I clicked on Outlook. Distracted. I wondered if Tom had made dinner plans for my

birthday. I didn't want to cook. I glanced at the screen and saw Blue
Feather Books, Ltd. I took a deep breath and scanned the message. I
clicked on the attachment and then the print key with screams of
delight. I grabbed at the pages as fast as the printer could spit them
out and danced around the house hollering my fool head off. When
Tom walked in the front door only moments later, the startled look
on his face made me laugh with pleasure.

"I've got it," I said. "I've got it. I've got it."

"The new contract?" he asked.

"Yup. I never thought I'd really get it."

"I never doubted it for a minute," he said. "It's a good book.
Happy Birthday."

"The best birthday present in the whole world," I said. "How'd
you arrange it?"

He laughed. "You can thank me for the flowers, but the
contract's all your doing."

"Thank you for the beautiful flowers." I stood on my tiptoes to
kiss him.

"So, are you going to sign that thing and let me take you out to
dinner?" he asked.

We sat at the kitchen table and compared the new contract to the
old one. Satisfied, I signed, folded, and sealed my new contract. My
birthday contract. Apparently, my siblings had not replied to my
publisher's response to their threat of a lawsuit, and I decided to
ignore it. I was hopeful that the trouble with my siblings had been
for nothing, the publication delays were over, and my memoir
would be published before I was so old I'd need bifocals to read it.
And it was. But just barely.

☙ ❧

With new contract in hand, I was feeling strong and flying high.
Doreen and I were talking; my brothers had visited. By late 2006 I
decided it was time to try Marleen. As the eldest, she was the sister
who had been an odd mix of sister, friend, and surrogate mother for
much of my life.

It was a Friday evening. November 18th. I was alone, both Tom and Erin out with friends. I knew I couldn't just write an email and send it. I knew some careful thought, some deep writing, had to go into this message. So, I took out my pen and notebook and began to write. I told her how much she meant to me, how much she'd always meant to me. I acknowledged it had been two long years of stressful silence. I told her people changed, and perhaps I was no longer the sister she once knew and loved, but I hoped she was willing to give this new me a chance because I liked the new me a whole lot more than the old me.

I wrote and wrote and finally worked my message into a four-paragraph letter. Then I set it aside. I went to bed knowing it was best to give these things time. The following morning I sat down to reread my letter. Satisfied I'd said all I wanted to say as clearly as I could say it, I typed it into my laptop, my fingers sticky on the keys. I pushed the send button and began waiting. A week passed. Then another. I was convinced that I'd screwed up again, that my sister's love was indeed as conditional as my father's had been.

On December 4th I began my day as I did almost every other day. I poured some coffee and clicked on my computer. There it was. My sister's name in my inbox. I hesitated. I set down my cup and settled into the desk chair. I clicked on her name and got one of those "you've received an e-card" messages. I clicked again, and my eyes filled with tears of relief. I played and replayed the silly image of a tiny goldfish circling in its tank. I read and reread her words: I got over being angry. I got over being angry. I got over being angry.

Those words told me Marleen was not my father. She could get angry, really horribly angry, and then let it go. I knew it was just the beginning, there were bridges that needed serious construction work, but still I was thrilled. I'd taken the first step, and it had paid off.

The following spring she was in Seattle visiting her son who had just moved up from California. She called and invited me to meet for lunch. When she asked about including her son, I suggested bringing Erin as well. We had our buffer zone, a focal point for the conversation. It began strained and loosened as the minutes ticked away, as we settled in and talked of college plans and new jobs, as we worked our way slowly back to a peaceful balance between sisters. The bridge was not completed in that one day, but at least the supports were in place.

❧ ❧

For over a year, Mom had been pointing out the slow construction progress on the new Westport Library, a library built entirely on private donations in one of the most economically depressed areas in Washington State in the early years of the new millennium. A sweet little building when finished, with blue shingles, a high roofline, and white trim, it reminded me a bit of something I'd expect to see in Cape Cod.

Finally opening day arrived. December 5, 2006. A community ribbon-cutting, cake-eating celebration. Always looking for something to do while visiting, I saw the announcement in the local paper.

"Hey, Mom, the new library's opening today. Let's go check it out!" I watched her pull away. Pull inward without a word. "Come on, Mom, you've been showing me the outside of your new library forever. Let's go see what it looks like on the inside."

"Well, okay," she said.

We finished breakfast and headed to town.

"Let's go to the library first, Mom. Then we can go shopping, okay?"

"I don't need anything."

So predictable, I could've said it for her, and yet the refrigerator was empty but for the bread we'd scrounged for breakfast toast. "Well, we still need ice cream to eat with Hallmark Hall of Fame tonight," I said with a laugh. "Would you look at this parking lot? I don't think I've ever seen this many cars in one place in Westport except maybe on the beach during open clamming."

Searching for a parking spot, I should've known the whole idea was a big mistake, but I was determined to get Mom, to get us, out of the damn house. In the first few years after Dad's death, I'd bugged her about getting involved in the community, doing some volunteer work, reading to kids at the library. I knew she loved little ones and figured a weekly reading circle might be great for her as well as for the kids of the Westport/Grayland area. But she pulled inward with force that matched my own. I found the swimsuit, goggles, and cap – testimony of my attempt to get her to join a senior swim class – unused in the bottom drawer of her dresser when we were sorting her clothes.

I stopped, got out of the car, and opened Mom's door. Was she really struggling with the seatbelt or just procrastinating like a three-year-old fearful of new places, new people? I took her hand, helped her out of the car, and led her into the library.

The parking lot overflowed into the large, vacant lot next to the library, and the small library was the inside of a sardine can. We arrived just as speeches began. I shoved our way around the perimeter of the room and between the open stacks searching for a chair for Mom. Finally someone offered her a seat where she sat through several long-winded speeches thanking a litany of people we'd never heard of. There was generous applause followed by an invitation to cake and other refreshments.

"Can we go now?" Mom asked.

"Of course, Mom," I said. "Do you want some cake first?" I watched her scan the crowd and shake her head. "I'm sorry. I didn't expect such a crowd."

"It's okay," she said, always gracious, always a smile on her wrinkled face. "Let's go now."

"We'll come again," I said in response to the questions at the door as we squeezed our way out into the cold salt air. A relief, not so much from the tight confines of the small library – for me it was a little glimpse of Norman Rockwell, small town America, and I loved it. Rather, it was a relief to see the strain leave Mom's face, to watch her body relax as she hurried across the parking lot and climbed into the safety of my car.

❧ ❦

I leaned against the doorframe of the large opening between the kitchen and the dining room, an opening Tom created in one of many remodels that transformed the little house into our home.

Remodels that shaped ourselves and our relationship as much as they shaped the physical structure of the house itself.

I scanned the living room. The Christmas tree lights twinkled in multiple reflections on the front corner windows; Erin and Mom sat next to each other on the sofa in front of the crackling fireplace.

"I've got them all over me, Nana. See they're on my arms and legs," Erin pulled up the legs of her baggy flannel pants. "Here on my tummy, too."

"Don't scratch them," Mom said.

"I've got bug juice all over me, but they still itch. I've never seen so many mosquitoes. They were huge. It was damp and moldy and warm and dirty. It's good to be home."

"Where?" Mom asked.

"Louisiana. I just got back."

"Why?"

"I went there to do volunteer work. There was a bad hurricane in New Orleans. Did you see it on the news?"

"I've been there," Mom said.

"Really?" Erin asked. "When?"

"Oh, a long time ago."

As I stood shamelessly eavesdropping, I remembered snippets of stories of Mom's early years. I remembered a mention of her flying into New Orleans during her brief stint as a United Airlines stewardess before marrying Dad. I realized that Mom was remembering a time when she was only a few years older than Erin was now, when she too was in the city now devastated by natural disaster. Only later did I realize the rarity of this moment of connection between my daughter and my mother, as Erin tried to speak in a simple way her grandmother would understand, and Mom tried to find the words to share her thoughts and ask questions. Or maybe I did realize it then, as I stood and watched my mother smooth Erin's silky blond hair still damp from the shower and hold her hand to still the temptation to scratch the bug bites that plagued her.

When Erin arrived home earlier that day from the gulf shore of Louisiana, I'd never seen her so dirty, bug bitten, exhausted, or content. She dropped her bags and collapsed on her bed. "It feels great," she said. The bed? Being home? Being away from the misery of Katrina? For two weeks she'd helped prepare and serve meals to the homeless in the collapsing remains of a gutted school. She organized activities for the children in the largest and most dangerous FEMA trailer camp in the area. In doing so, she saw life as she had never imagined it, and she returned home more grateful than ever for the life she enjoyed and with greater determination to do something with that life.

Later, she explained how the gymnasium floor, still damp from the flooding and continued rains, was covered with wood pallets. Tents of the volunteers – they had to bring their own – covered those pallets. Rodents made homes underneath them. There were outhouses, but no showers. All water was trucked in. She spoke of intermittent electricity and lights that flickered when the generators were low. She spoke of the stench.

The stories came out in bits and pieces over the week between Christmas and New Year's. She told of the daily visits to the FEMA trailer parks where attempts to organize activities for the young kids fell flat, the children too traumatized to partake of the activities the endless stream of young, predominately middle class, white volunteers came to offer. Even the youngest kids seem to know the volunteers were only temporary; they would leave without a trace. Allowing attachment would only lead to more suffering.

Erin spoke of long conversations into the night with homeless, shattered men, men who had lost everything, men who had little before Katrina hit, men who had nothing after. Not even hope. Men who told her not to fool herself, that the work she was doing was more for her and the other volunteers than for them because their reality would never change.

As I stood and watched and listened to my beautiful daughter explain to my once beautiful mother her experiences in New Orleans and the help she was trying to give, I felt a surge of love so intense tears blurred my vision. And as I listened to my mother trying so hard to keep up her end of the conversation, when I heard the repeated questions and the struggle to find words, my heart broke.

The moment passed, as these moments do. The Christmas tree lights flickered. Erin yawned and stretched her arms over her head, her back the arch of a ballerina.

"I've got to go to bed, Nana," I heard her say.

"Me too," Mom said.

A hug, a kiss and each went to her own bedroom.

2007

THE NEW YEAR blew in with several inches of heavy snow. Like a kid, I woke up and danced around the house. Snow day. It was only the beginning of winter quarter, and already I was behind schedule and would have to adjust my syllabus, but the pleasure of an unexpected day off was pure ecstasy. I was again a child.

The world outside the front windows was sparkling white. Icicles hung from the bare tree branches. It was January 11th and the Christmas tree still stood in the front corner. We rarely kept the tree after winter quarter began, but Erin, just was home from Louisiana, hadn't had enough holiday beauty. She begged me to keep the tree a bit longer than normal. I used the first snow day to take it down. After removing the woven straw figures and brightly painted tiny gourds from Mexico; Erin's seventeen ornaments from Tom's mother, one marking each Christmas in Erin's young life; the dozen hand-painted balls, I took off the string of lights and hoisted the tree out to the backyard still in the tree stand.

I'd already packed away the collection of children's holiday picture books. For years Marleen had sent Erin a book each Christmas. While boxing the books, I'd reread one about not wanting Christmas to end. I moved the barren, drooping tree outside where it stood in clear view of the kitchen window, and then I hiked through the snow to the hardware store to pick up a few birdfeeders. The idea was quickly abandoned later that afternoon when both Erin and Tom pointed out that we could hang the feeders from any one of the living trees in the yard and that the poor, old Christmas tree just looked pathetic.

I spent the rest of the day cleaning and putting the house back together. Another year. A new year. A month of off-and-on snowfall and late starts. A month of helping Erin with university applications. Months and months of editing *The Thirty-Ninth Victim* in its slow crawl toward publication. Months of trying to find my way into my first novel. I remember complaining to my mentor, Jack Remick, about not knowing how to write fiction, not having time to write anything, not being able to juggle editing one manuscript while writing another. I got an email from him: "Writers write. One-book-wonders ponder. Which are you?"

I wanted to be a writer, but I struggled with so much going on in my life. I was terrified of the impending publication of the memoir. I was preparing my first book for publication and writing a new novel. Getting my only daughter ready for university and bracing for an empty house without her. Navigating through all the impending changes in my mother's life, and by necessity, my own. All these preparations resulted in a lot of worry. It was no wonder, I suppose, that Tom and I were also going through one of the stormiest periods our marriage had experienced. My weekends in Grayland and long hours spent writing were taking a toll, and we simply hadn't put the time or energy into keeping our marriage strong. I held my breath and hoped against all odds that we'd make it, that we'd find our way through the storm.

I was seeing a mental health therapist at the time who suggested Julia Cameron's *The Artist's Way,* and I began doing morning pages, working my way through her book with a vengeance, determined to find balance in a life that seemed to be spinning.

"Are you willing to face the consequences?" the therapist asked.

"I've already done that," I said. "I've already given it to my siblings."

"And the general public?"

"I think I can deal with that."

But still I was nervous. My siblings' reaction had shaken me. I was no longer certain what I'd written was even worthy of publication. As I continued to work through my emotions, I saw patterns of synchronicity everywhere. It was as though I could step outside of the daily stress and chaos to view my life as an outsider. The perspective was good, but the fear of going public with my first memoir was still daunting.

A friend from the University of Washington memoir program continued to encourage me. One evening she invited me to an open mic event at a local bookstore and pushed me to read. Trembling, I stood before my first audience and read a short scene from *The Thirty-Ninth Victim*. The room became silent, and I knew they were listening to my words, that my words had the power to captivate. I was thrilled.

Throughout the year, as I worked with Blue Feather Books editing the manuscript and designing the cover, I was terrified about the future – the book release, Erin's graduation and departure, Mom's failing mental health, my rocky marriage.

Tom and I tiptoed through winter, looking toward spring, toward graduation, publication, resolution, in hopes that our marriage would gain strength instead of falling in pieces around us. Then, shortly after Erin's eighteenth birthday, Tom's divorced parents began making plans to come for Erin's high school graduation. His father planned to take advantage of the trip to the west coast by scheduling a cruise to Alaska. His mother just wanted to be with Erin and not cause any complications. But avoiding complications in a tiny house with divorced in-laws would be nothing short of miraculous.

Benaroya Hall, Seattle's premier symphony and literary venue, was crowded and raucous. Balloons, flowers, and cheers competed for air space. The West Seattle High School graduation ceremony followed that of another city school, and families crowded to get the best seats while others exited. We greeted Erin in line with the other graduates waiting to file in, and then we found seats in the crowded hall. We were a small group. We sat quietly, surrounded by large noisy extended families. There was little pomp and circumstance at this graduation. Speeches were made, speeches that were at times difficult to hear. Then the graduates were called. As each name was announced and the graduate crossed the stage, the screams, whistles, and applause roared from different corners of the large hall.

I smiled as I looked around the large room and took in the faces that testified to the wide range of racial, ethnic, and religious diversity rarely seen in most parts of the world, the country, or even this state. I loved it. I loved the chaos and noise and fun. I realized graduation day wasn't a time for solemn pomp and circumstance for all. For some it was a time to scream and holler and create more of a sports event atmosphere than a traditional graduation ceremony.

I was filled with intense pride as I watched my daughter cross the stage knowing she had decided to study summer and fall quarters in order to complete her Associate of Arts degree by Christmas and transfer to a university midyear. As a college student, Erin had already learned that being treated as an adult was far superior to the alternative, especially after attempting to take one last course at the high school during her senior year.

At the end of the first day of school, she came home, dropped her backpack on the kitchen floor, and said, "I'm not going back there. I'm dropping that class."

"What happened?" I asked.

"You won't believe this," she said. "I actually had to ask permission to go to the bathroom."

That was the last day Erin attended high school. She went back for some of the social events, but she was finished with high school classes. Still, she wanted to graduate with her friends, and I was thrilled to be part of her celebration.

Somehow we made that family visit work. I relinquished my writing room to my mother-in-law, feeling very Stephen King when Tom set up a writing table for me in the laundry room. He also set up a bed in his studio for his father. It an odd sort of way, it all worked out. I'd hoped to be able to have Mom join us as well, but there just wasn't any space left in our house. After talking it over with Erin and Tom, we decided the crowds at graduation and at Erin's party might be just too overwhelming for her anyway. We'd go to Grayland together for a visit instead.

The day after graduation, we had a party. Erin wanted a big barbecue. Nothing fancy. Just hamburgers and hotdogs and lots of people. She invited everyone on both sides of the family, all her friends and neighbors she'd known her entire life. The weather cooperated, and the yard was full of laughter and energy, music and conversation. Erin and I crossed paths in the kitchen at one point in the afternoon.

"How's it going?" I asked. "Is this what you wanted?"

"It's perfect, Mom," Erin said. "Thank you so much. It's just perfect."

જ ન્

Summer flew by and Erin's work schedule as a Starbuck's barista kept her busy most weekends. It wasn't until September that she was finally free to join me on a trip to visit her grandmother.

Friday afternoon traffic was horrible. Erin and I didn't get to Grayland until late afternoon. Mom greeted us at the door with that look of surprise painted on her face. She'd completely forgotten my phone call only an hour earlier.

"I didn't know you were coming. What a nice surprise!"

"Hi, Mom. Yes, I brought Erin for a visit. For your birthday."

"My birthday? It's not my birthday."

"Sure it is, Mom. September 21st. You're eighty-three today."

I wrapped Mom in a tender embrace. She was tiny. She seemed smaller with each visit.

When we entered the house, I saw the remains of a loaf of bread and an almost empty peanut butter jar on the table. No dirty plates in sight.

"Were you making lunch, Mom? Have you eaten today?" I looked at her again. She'd lost weight since my last visit only two weeks prior. She looked good, but her slender frame was verging on too thin. I looked in the refrigerator. Nothing.

"Oh, I'm done with that. Let's put it away," she said.

My daughter looked over my shoulder into the empty refrigerator. We caught each other's eye. There was nothing in the refrigerator. Nothing. We checked the freezer. Frozen peanut butter cookie dough. Nothing more. We checked the cabinets. No cereal, no crackers, no cans of soup.

"Mom, you don't have any food in this place," I said. "We're going shopping."

"I have … a problem," she said. "I don't have money."

"But you have your credit card, Mom. Remember?"

"I can't find it."

"Let's see, Mom. It's usually right here in the side pocket of your purse." With a glance to check for her approval, I opened her small handbag and pulled out her plastic. "See, Mom. Here's your VISA card. You can use this any time you run out of cash."

"Oh," she said, sounding totally unconvinced.

"Have you used all your cash? You used to have a stash in your top drawer." Again I saw the confusion on her wrinkled face, her eyes as wide as a child's. "Come on, Mom, let's check your dresser drawers."

As we headed to her bedroom at the back of her small house, I tried to make light, to joke and keep her laughing. I played the clown, the entertainer, unwilling to upset her, to ruin her birthday, or whatever shard of it she held in the recesses of her fading memory. We searched her drawers. Nothing.

"Well, Mom," I said. "The bank is only right down the street."

"I know," she said, an edge of irritation creeping into her voice. "I was going, but it's closed on the weekend."

"It's only Friday."

"Well, you came too soon. I didn't get to go."

"Okay, let's make a shopping list. We'll go to the bank and the store, okay? We'll have an outing." I figured there was no point in arguing logic. What mattered was to refill her food supply and take her out for a nice birthday dinner.

"Okay, let me go to the bathroom," Mom said as she headed back into the bedroom.

Erin and I shifted into high gear, making a list of everything we thought she might eat and that required minimal preparation. She didn't even have any tea left, her comfort staple. As we poked through her kitchen we found two grocery receipts, each for one loaf of bread. An 89-cent total on one, $1.09 on the other. I held back my tears and looked again in Mom's purse. It held pennies, a nickel, a dime. Nothing more. She'd been living on bread and peanut butter. For how long? I failed to read the dates on those two receipts. I thought I'd stocked the kitchen with sufficient food when I was there two weeks prior, but I was wrong. I'd also forgotten to check her cash supply. It was clear Mom could no longer use credit and hadn't written a check in several years. Now it seemed she was uncomfortable or unable to go to the bank alone for a simple cash withdrawal.

After banking and shopping, when I felt confident there was food for a month and enough cash for little outings for cookies and ice cream, it was time to take Mom out for her birthday dinner.

"Where do you want to go, Nana?" Erin asked.

"Oh, no" Mom said. With a sweep of her arms she opened the refrigerator. "Lots of food here."

"But that's for you. Let's go out to some place special tonight to celebrate your birthday."

"Birthday?"

"You're eighty-three today, Nana. Happy Birthday!" Erin said.

"Really?" Mom asked.

I was tired of the same pizza place we always went to, the same salad for me, the same chicken strips for Mom. I knew Erin would rather go somewhere different as well. So I said, "They've redone the restaurant in that old hotel at the harbor. Let's go there, okay?"

"Okay," Mom said.

But it wasn't okay. It was young and creative with fast-talking waitresses. The music was loud, the light was low, the room was on the chilly side of comfortable. And there were no chicken strips on the menu.

"It'll be alright," Erin whispered as she tried her best to keep Mom engaged and comfortable.

"I have to go," Mom said.

"Me too," Erin said. "Can I go with you?"

"Okay."

I gave Erin a smile of appreciation and watched them walk across the room. Erin stood tall and slender, with the graceful posture of a dancer, her long blond hair pulled into a loose ponytail. At her side Mom, tiny and thin, her gray-white hair in need of a good shampoo and cut, wearing the same clothes, the same sweater with the Arizona motif she'd worn on my last visit.

I sat alone and struggled to hold my emotions in check, unwilling to confuse Mom with my tears. I knew the time had come. I knew my mother was no longer able to care for herself. A decision had to be made. I reminded myself that Doreen was looking into home health care services and soon we'd have someone checking on Mom at least once, maybe twice, a week. That would help, but still it was only a matter of time.

On the drive home the following day, both Erin and I were subdued. It was Erin who broke the silence. "It's so sad, Mom. It's hard to leave her there all alone."

"I know, honey. I know."

"But it's where she wants to be," Erin said, more to herself than to me. "We can't force her to move. That wouldn't be right."

"The day will come when we may have to," I said.

"That's not fair."

"Maybe not, but it's not right to leave her there if she can't take care of herself, is it?"

"No," she said. "But she's okay now, isn't she? I mean as long as she has food and she has Casey."

"I think so," I said. "And she'll have someone checking on her soon, so that will help too."

"Good," Erin said.

Good, I thought. She'll be okay, I told myself. But what's okay about an eighty-three-year old woman losing herself to dementia?

ॐ ॐ

When we got the news Erin was accepted to the University of Washington, we danced around the living room. After considering various universities, Erin had set her heart on the UW, ruling out all others. Because she submitted only the one university application, leaving herself with no back-up plan, the acceptance brought a huge sigh of relief.

I'm not sure what combination of concerns or interests solidified Erin's determination to get into the UW. Friends? Fear? Nostalgia? I remember one conversation we'd had early in the decision-making process. We'd been going out to dinner together on Friday nights while Tom was out with friends, a little routine we'd established that gave us time to connect. We were talking about a university in Oregon that looked interesting.

"But if I go there, you'll come and visit me whenever I'm homesick, won't you?" she asked.

"Of course," I said.

"Every weekend?"

"Every single weekend until you're absolutely sick of me," I said.

I realized she was feeling the same kind of separation anxiety I was feeling. She didn't want to leave the only home she'd known, her safety net of family, dog, and friends. It was so different from my own desperation to get away from home as soon as possible when I was her age I had been unable to recognize how she was feeling.

In mid-November we were moving her into her first apartment. She didn't want to live in the dorms, and she didn't want roommates. A single child, she'd always had her own space, and she wanted to try living alone. We supported the idea. There are challenges and rewards to living alone, especially at eighteen, not the least of which is the process of learning your own strengths and limitations. Tom and I were happy to give her the opportunity while she was still close enough to come home whenever she wanted family support.

We walked the UW campus, only blocks from her new apartment. We bought her textbooks and found her classrooms. There were several long days of drop cloths, purple paint, and pizza as we helped her make her apartment feel homey despite being in a converted hotel with long, cold hallways that would never be anything but lonely.

Still, it wasn't really the apartment itself that made her decide to move back to West Seattle six months later. It was the walk to and from the university past the panhandlers harassing her for spare change each day. It was the difficulty of building new friendships among other commuter students who rushed to and from classes and then off to jobs, just as Erin was doing. She completed the school year in that first apartment before moving home for the summer, her first real break from school since she'd entered Running Start.

ご゛ くゔ

The year had started with a snowstorm and was now ending with flood waters. Severe winds took out power line, and rains raised rivers to unprecedented flood levels. It was early December.

"Do you have food, Mom?" I asked when I phoned to check on my mother.

"Food?"

"Yes, food that's not in the refrigerator? Do you have bread and peanut butter?"

"Why?"

"Because you don't have power. Are you warm enough?"

"It's a little cold."

I heard her walking down the hall. I could see her flicking the light switch off and on, off and on. Then pushing up the thermostat, confused by the chill in the house and the hall light that wouldn't turn on.

"It doesn't work," she said.

"No, you don't have power. You need to put on more clothes, Mom. You need to put on another sweater, and then you need to eat a peanut butter sandwich."

"Why?"

"Because the storm blew down the power lines."

Doreen and I both called several times that day and the next. Every time the same conversation. Doreen called Larry and asked him to check on Mom. By the second day of the outage, I started making plans.

"I'll leave work early and take a personal day," I told Tom.

"It won't work."

"Why?"

"The roads are flooded. You can't get through. The stretch between Olympia and Aberdeen is closed in a couple of different places," he said.

I checked the Department of Transportation website by the hour throughout the following morning waiting for the road to reopen. I made phone calls and finally got a tentative okay from a DOT representative. They were opening and closing the road as needed dependent on water level. For the time being, the road was open. The car packed with emergency food and water, blankets and clothes, I headed south determined to reach Mom by early afternoon and, if possible, turn around and bring her to Seattle before nightfall. I knew it was a gamble, but so was leaving Mom alone in a cold house with no food for a third day.

Most of the route was clear, all but one section, a low area near the tiny town of McCleary. The ditches were wide and deep, full to overflowing. With the road itself covered by at least an inch of water, it was impossible to see where the road edge ended and the ditch began. Traffic crept along. At one point a flooded underpass forced a detour through the small town and back onto the road a mile or two farther along.

I reached Grayland relieved and still confident I could get Mom back to Seattle safely the same day. The front gate was open when I drove up. And the garage door. Odd. The garage door was electric. Larry must have come over and opened it so Mom could get to the grocery store. Relieved, I knocked. No answer. I knocked again, louder. Still nothing. I was headed for the hidden key, a tinge of fear climbing my spine, when a truck pulled into the driveway.

Larry hopped out with a big grin on his face and helped Mom out behind him. Another neighbor was driving. "We were just up with the Indians," he said. "The casino is the only place for miles with a generator. They're serving one hot meal a day. Thought your mom might want to come eat with us."

"It was good," Mom said.

"Thank you," I said. "Thank you so very, very much for watching out for her."

"Oh, we've been okay," he said. "You going to take her to Seattle with you?"

"Yeah, as soon as I can pack up a few things. Will you keep an eye on the place for us? Maybe check everything when the power comes back on."

"Sure thing," he said. "Bye, Sally. Have fun in Seattle."

"Oh, I will," she said.

"Okay, Mom, let's get you packed," I said as Larry climbed into the truck.

"Packed?"

"Yeah, you're coming to Seattle with me."

"Seattle?"

"That's right. You're going on a little vacation to a place with electricity, heat, and warm cooking."

"Oh good," she said.

The drive back to Seattle seemed easier somehow. Maybe the shoulders were wider. Maybe the ditches weren't quite so close to the edge of the pavement. There were no detours and less traffic. The biggest distraction was my mother's repetitious stream of commentary.

"It's a long way."

"Yes, it is a long way," I said. "That's why I want you to move closer to Seattle. It would be easier, and I could visit you more often."

"Oh, no," she said. "Are we almost there?"

"No, we're only about half way, Mom."

Five minutes later. "It's a long way."

"Yes, Mom. That's why I want you to move closer to Seattle. Wouldn't it be nice if we could visit every week instead of just once a month?"

"That would be nice," she said.

"Will you move closer to my house? Will you come live with me and Tom and Erin?"

"Oh no," she said. "I have a house."

I remember that week of fear and frustration as the reality check Doreen and I needed to push us into action. That's when we came to the heart-wrenching realization Mom could no longer take care of herself. She needed home health care. The decision to get help, that Mom could no longer be left entirely on her own between our bi-weekly visits, was made. We knew we could not depend solely on the goodness of neighbors to make certain Mom was safe and her basic needs were being met on a daily basis. The flooding made it stark clear to us that another winter alone in Grayland was not an option for Mom. If she refused to move, at least we could get someone to help her, to shop and cook for her once or twice a week.

Doreen made the phone calls, worked with a local agency, set the schedule, and sent in the payment. She handled all the arrangements, interviewed the providers, and had someone sent to the house. As with all matters financial, Doreen was in charge, which was totally fine by me. More than fine. I preferred to be as uninvolved as possible. Since Dad's death, our roles had become increasingly defined. Doreen took care of all the serious concerns while I tried to make Mom laugh and have some fun.

When the first caregiver arrived, Mom wouldn't let her in the house. The second time the woman made it in the door, but Mom told her to leave and never come back. Both Doreen and I struggled to get the story from Mom, but it only came in bits and pieces over time. She said the woman was fat and smoked and smelled bad. She said she didn't need or want anyone to help her. Other times, she denied anyone came to the house at all. After several weeks of admitted failure and pressure from my sister, the agency sent someone new. Somehow Eleanor was able to wheedle her way into Mom's house and heart and in the process give her the much needed care neither Doreen nor I were able to provide. At least for a while. At least until it became obvious to all of us that home health care wasn't enough. That Mom would have to move.

In late December Doreen and I began what would be a yearlong search to find a new home for our mother. The first challenge was figuring out what we were searching for – assisted living or dementia care. The second challenge was to find a place where we believed Mom could adjust and be happy. Over time we defined our parameters. We wanted single level, garden areas Mom could dig in if she wanted to, interesting walking paths, a casual atmosphere with a friendly loving staff, and a culture supportive to the residents and communicative with the families. And finally the third challenge was finding weekends when we were both free, when neither of us was in Grayland, when we could visit facilities together.

2008

THERE WERE TWO Caseys in my parents' retirement years. They were both pure-bred Golden Retrievers. Both un-neutered males. But there the similarity ended. Casey #1 was a well-behaved, healthy, happy dog. Casey #2 was the complete opposite, an overweight, neurotic, stinky beast.

But the difference did not lie with the dogs, with genetics, with "good seeds" and "bad seeds" as Dad might have claimed. The behavior of the dogs was a mirror of the life and care they were given. Casey #1 was the lucky Casey. Dad and Mom were in their early years of retirement enjoying long walks on the Pacific beach and even longer road trips between Seattle and Arizona. When Dad walked the beach, Casey #1 ran free, jumping the waves and chasing the tight flocks of Sand Pipers that rose in synchronized formations. Anyone who happened to be on the beach would stop to watch the flocks of tiny birds rise in unison from the shore just inches above the joyous barking of the beautiful Golden Retriever.

Casey #1 raced the beach in full extension, flying across the sand. Dad told the story of an Iditarod racer who trained his dog sled team on the hard sands at water's edge one year, about how this man once stopped him on the beach to ask if he might be interested in selling Casey #1.

"I could use a dog with that kind of speed," the man said. But Dad only laughed and repeated the laughter with each retelling of the story.

Casey #1 lived to a healthy old age at Dad's side.

Casey #2 was a dog with a different life story. He joined Dad's life at a time when arthritic knee pain limited his owner's ability to walk. He was never allowed to run the beach, to chase the birds, to race the waves. Mom often claimed that once, still a puppy, he escaped from the yard and was hit by a car on the beach, the Westport-Grayland beach being one of few strips of west coast waterfront still bearing a state highway designation.

Years later, on a vet visit, in a feeble attempt to understand why Casey stunk so badly and limped so painfully, I asked about possible damage from this earlier accident. The vet found no evidence the dog had ever suffered the type of impact Mom described. There was no scar tissue that would evidence the type of impact Mom described nor cause the discomfort Casey suffered. The only obvious problem the animal had was that he was overfed and not getting enough exercise. But Dad was gone, and Mom believed her own stories. No amount of veterinarian science could deny the history her mind had created.

Casey lived for six years, one month and five days after Dad's death. In the years when Mom still drove, they would go for drives each day – her and Casey – to nearby Westport. Mom would park at the harbor, and she and Casey would watch for seals or for the feral cats living in the rocks of the bulkhead protecting the harbor. Casey loved the cats. Or maybe he hated them. Many a visit, I'd be in the car with them.

"Look at the kitty, Casey," Mom would say, pointing to a cat on a rock. "Kitty, kitty, kitty," she'd call out her opened window. Casey's eyes would follow the line of her pointing finger until he saw the cat. Then he'd start barking like crazy, and Mom would laugh in delight.

Their other favorite haunt was the state park and the huge area of adjacent land – the land that was supposed to be turned into a golf course, the dream of economic salvation for the depressed area. But for the seven years and six days Mom lived alone, the land remained blessedly undeveloped and home to a small herd of deer. When they were visible, grazing in the field along the road, Mom would pull to a stop and watch in silence. Casey recognized the change of mood, and he remained silent watching Mom watch the deer. Mom loved the deer and hated the cats. Casey mirrored her emotions. Once Dad's dog, he was now her dog, her meaning and purpose in life. Day in and day out Casey was her sole companion. Unlike Doreen and me, who came and went at intervals she struggled to keep track of regardless of how carefully we maintained the large calendar next to her telephone on the kitchen counter, Casey was a constant in her life, always there to greet her in the morning, to walk the beach or the neighborhood midday, to watch Hallmark Hall of Fame with her each evening. Mom couldn't find the motivation to cook for or feed herself, but she fed Casey to obesity, and the dog suffered the expected consequences.

By spring 2008, it was clear Casey was on his way out. He may have lasted a few more years but for the way Mom fed him. It wasn't just the table scraps that took their toll, but rather the simple fact that Mom couldn't remember she'd fed him five minutes after filling his bowl. Casey was one of those dogs who ate anything and everything put before him and still whined for more. So each time Mom filled the bowl, Casey emptied it and begged for more. Mom, convinced that "Poor Casey" was starving, refilled his bowl. This pattern repeated itself throughout the day, every day. With no husband or kids to feed and care for, Casey garnered all Mom's attention. Sadly, it probably cost him a few years of life.

The phone call, when it came, was really not much of a surprise. "I got a call from Eleanor," Doreen said.

"What's the problem?" I asked.

"It's Casey. He couldn't get up. I'm not sure it was just today or longer. But Eleanor said Mom was pretty upset when she got there today. They tried to help him get up a few times, but they couldn't, so I guess Eleanor just lifted him up and put him in her car, and they went to the vet."

"Good thing Eleanor's so strong," I said in a feeble attempt to find some positive in what I already feared was coming.

"That's for sure. Anyway, I guess the vet said Casey's body has shut down and he recommended putting him to sleep."

"Lord," I said. "How'd Mom take that?"

"Eleanor said she doesn't think Mom really understands," Doreen said.

"So, what happened?"

"Eleanor told the vet she didn't feel she had the authority to make that decision. So the vet's going to call me, or I should call him. But I don't know what to do."

I understood my sister's concern: she wouldn't want to be blamed for ending Casey's life. It was a tough spot to be in. "Where's Casey now?" I asked.

"Eleanor left him at the vet's and told Mom they needed to leave him there because he was too sick to go home."

"Bless that woman's heart. I don't think we pay her enough," I said.

"That's for sure. She said she could just tell Mom that Casey died in the doggy hospital. But it's still going to be so hard on her."

"Yeah, she won't have anybody to talk to or take care of at all."

"I don't know what to do," Doreen said again.

"Do whatever the vet recommends, I guess. He's the expert. He knows what Casey's condition is and what his chances of survival are. Ask him and then follow his advice. That's what I'd do, Doreen. I know we waited too long when Mozart died. Because of that, it was a harder death than it needed to be for the poor boy. What if it happened in Mom's house, and she was alone, and Casey was left suffering? Anyway, I'd follow the vet's advice."

"Okay," Doreen said. "I think I'll just call him now and get it over with."

"Sounds good. Let me know what happens. And thank you, Doreen. I'm really sorry you have to handle all this stuff."

That's how Mom lost her last connection to Dad. I'm not sure how well she understood what happened. I know Casey was euthanized as soon as Doreen spoke with the vet. The poor dog was resting comfortably, and the vet recommended we allow him to slip away in peace. I know Eleanor told Mom that Casey died, and she made extra, uncompensated visits to make sure Mom was doing okay. I know, when I called Mom, she told me Casey was gone just as she had told me almost seven years before that my father was gone.

એ ન

Erin was no longer living at home, so the holidays and the possibility of sharing them with her held greater importance for Tom and me. But Erin had a life of her own, and she decided Easter was a kid's holiday – a time for egg hunts, too much candy, and ham dinner. She wasn't interested in any of it, so like St. Patrick's Day only a month before, she chose to ignore Easter. Instead of the ritual family dinner, she went on a road trip with friends to spend the holiday with someone else's family. Hurt? A bit. Understanding? I tried. An only child, Erin was always seeking large family gatherings, the more people the better. Family holidays at our house often meant just the three of us, especially of late.

Midweek before Easter, Erin called. "It's over," she said.

"You're finished?"

"Yup. I'm walking home right now."

"When do you leave for Idaho?" I asked.

"Day after tomorrow."

"Can you come to dinner before you leave?" I asked, aiming for casual, trying hard not to sound too needy. I was so proud of her. She'd just finished her first week of final exams as an eighteen-year-old junior at the University of Washington. I wanted to celebrate.

"Sure," she said. "Tomorrow okay?"

"Perfect," I said.

A few days later, on Good Friday, I drove to Grayland and brought Mom to Seattle. It was with a sense of relief that I locked her front door and settled her into the front passenger seat. Relief to know that at least for a few days, she wouldn't be alone and that maybe, just maybe, she'd decide she liked being with us in Seattle now with Casey gone.

I was wrong. Saturday morning Mom walked upstairs carrying her little green floral suitcase. She crossed the living room and set the bag by the front door.

"All packed?" I asked

"Yes," she said.

"But Easter Sunday is tomorrow," I said. "Aren't you going to wait for the Easter Bunny?"

"Really?" she said.

"I'll just put this back in your bedroom and then we'll have breakfast, okay? Tom can help you make a cup of tea."

"Come on, Sally," Tom said from the kitchen. "Let's get you a cup. We can put some tea bags right here so you can make more tea whenever you want."

"Okay," she said.

Relieved, I carried her small suitcase back down to the bedroom. The bed was made. The room looked unused. I checked the space heater. She'd turned it up to the highest setting. Was she cold last night or was she trying to turn it off this morning, I wondered. I reset it and returned to the kitchen.

Easter morning was pouring rain, dark gray, and cold. Again the suitcase found its way to the front door. Again we went through the routine, but this time she was a bit more obstinate.

"I want to go home,"' she said, loud and clear.

"It's Easter Sunday, Mom. I want to stay here and make a nice Easter ham for dinner with you and Tom. I don't want to drive all the way to Grayland on Easter Sunday. It's such a long drive. Remember how long the drive was?"

There it was again, that awful word: *remember*. I saw the confusion in her eyes. I saw a flash of struggle, of pain. Or perhaps it was my pain. I knew she didn't remember. I knew when I drove her home the next day she'd spend the two-hour drive commenting on how long it was and asking if we were there yet. And I knew that unlike the questions of a young child, my mother would never grow out of her endless repetitive questioning. What I didn't know at the time was those annoying repetitions were preferable to the muteness and humming that would come with her growing loss of words. What happens in the brain when one loses language, loses words? Are all thoughts lost as well? Is there silence in the brain? Is there nothing at all?

We had a simple, quiet Easter dinner, just Tom, Mom, and me. We watched something on television and went to bed early. The following morning, the third in a row, Mom's suitcase again made it to the front door, and this time I agreed to take her home.

Later I drove back from Grayland with questions doing somersaults in my brain. I realized I knew nothing about dementia, about what my mother was experiencing, about what to expect. Sure, the doctor had explained there were many causes of memory loss and that Mom had something called multi-infarct dementia, but I still knew nothing at all. The following morning when I poured myself a cup of coffee and turned on my computer, I began a long-overdue search.

I learned multi-infarct dementia is the second most common form of dementia after Alzheimer's. I learned it is caused by vascular disease and strokes, tiny microscopic strokes that cause damage to the cortex of the brain when blood clots block the small blood vessels and destroy the brain tissue necessary to store and retrieve language and memories. I learned dementia is not a "normal" part of the aging process despite what the Aberdeen doctor had told me. I learned it is neither curable nor reversible and that while the causes are unknown, depression, nutritional deficiencies, and thyroid disease are among the contributing factors.

My mother's depression and current nutritional deficiencies were obvious even to me. I was unsure whether or not she'd ever been diagnosed with thyroid problems, but I knew several of my siblings were dealing with hypoactive thyroids and even thyroid cancer. After speaking with a few doctors, I resigned myself to the reality that there was little I could do to help my mother apart from improved nutrition. I also knew I needed to get my own thyroid checked.

 via ໑

I spent much of early 2008 learning what I could about book marketing, a world as foreign to me as quantum physics. Or neuroscience. It was only the beginning of a very exciting adventure, an adventure my siblings knew nothing about. When I learned *The Thirty-Ninth Victim* would be released in April, I began planning a launch party, but finding a date was more complicated than I anticipated. It couldn't be too soon – I had to be able to order and receive copies of the book – but I didn't want to wait too long either. In an odd sort of synchronicity, the most logical date for the launch was also the date of Erin's nineteenth birthday. Even though I thought there was something very right about celebrating my two most important accomplishments on the same day, I wasn't at all certain my teenage daughter would agree.

"So, what do you think?" I asked. "Could we do the release party on May 17th?"

"On my birthday? Why?" Erin asked. "It's my birthday."

"I know," I said, "but it's the best day for the launch. I can get copies of the book. Louisa's Café is available. And Dad will be gone the rest of the month."

"Why can't you wait 'til June?"

"It's too long. The book comes out on Amazon in early April. The sooner, the better."

She understood the logic but still wasn't convinced. "It won't be all night, will it?" she asked.

"No, of course not. Just a few hours in the afternoon."

"Oh, that's okay then," she said. "I can come to your party, and then we can go out for dinner together, and I can still go out with my friends in the evening."

It was an unusually hot afternoon. Without air conditioning and full-to-capacity, Louisa's Café was uncomfortably warm. A friend approached as I greeted people and signed a few books before the reading began.

"Why don't you take off your jacket?" she whispered. "Aren't you dying?"

"Can't," I said. "I think my blouse is see-through." We laughed like schoolgirls. I was all nerves.

It was only a lightweight, three-quarter-length sleeve, red cotton jacket, but still I was sweating. The air seemed to float in waves. I stood for a moment and let it wash over me as I looked around the crowded room. The table in the center was laid with fruit and cheese platters, bottles of wine, and flowers.

"I want lilacs," I'd told Tom. "Erin's given me her birthday for this. I want lilacs for Erin."

Erin was born with the lilacs nineteen years before. During my pregnancy we were renting a small, converted gardening shed on a large lot in what was once an apple orchard, now a residential neighborhood in West Seattle. We were surrounded by aging apple trees and sweet lilac bushes. The spring of Erin's birth, I spent many hours at a small garden table by the lilacs simultaneously dreaming of and terrified by impending motherhood. Three weeks overdue, I feared the lilacs would be gone before Erin arrived.

I finally went into labor in the wee hours of morning. Sometime during that long day, Tom scoured our large garden as well as the alleys and yards around the hospital to find lilacs still in bloom to bring to baby Erin and me the evening of her birth.

Nineteen years later, in 2008, the lilacs were still glorious in mid-May. Again Tom gathered an armload, and I filled several vases with blooms to place around the coffee shop. We arrived early to set up. It was afterhours for the café, and the owner had graciously given me her space to use for my event. I'd obtained a liquor license, bought wine, fruit, cheese, and chocolates. It wasn't much, but it was enough. Colorful tablecloths. Nothing serious or somber. The book had enough of that. I wanted to celebrate.

I'd chosen to launch my first book in the place where the bulk of it had been created, and I was thrilled to see the room fill with the supportive group of writers who'd heard so much of the early manuscript as I struggled during timed writing practice around these very tables. It felt right. I also saw friends, work colleagues, and students. What I didn't see were siblings, but then I didn't expect them. I hadn't even invited them.

It was time to begin. When I started to read, my hands shook and my voice quavered. I felt sweat trickling down my spine. I steadied myself on the tabletop lectern I'd borrowed from campus anticipating I'd be shaking too much to hold the pages in my hands. Nothing had prepared me for that moment. Years of teaching meant nothing. A few open mics in front of strangers couldn't prepare me for the launch of *The Thirty-Ninth Victim*, for reading in front of that room full of supportive souls. When it was over, I was rewarded by generous applause.

After the reading, I sat to sign books. I had no idea how to sign books. Earlier in the month, when I'd given copies to my former UW professors and writing partners, Jack Remick and Robert Ray, Jack pointed out I'd signed it on the wrong page. Still, despite his guidance, I struggled. I wanted to personalize each book, but I didn't know what to write. I worried about misspelled names, misspelled words, dedications that made no sense at all. It felt a bit like signing high school yearbooks, and I was never good at that either.

Then it was over. It seemed like forever. It seemed like a moment, a brief dreamy moment in time. But then, it wasn't really over at all. It was only just the beginning, the first in a series of readings and television appearances I'd managed to schedule. It was also the beginning of reconnections with old family friends, distant relatives, and high school classmates as well as messages from unknown readers in a manner I had not anticipated. I loved it. I continue to love it. But the launch was indeed over, and it was time to shift gears, time to begin another celebration, time to take Erin and her friends out to celebrate her nineteenth birthday.

❧ ❦

"Let's go for a drive before lunch. What do you think, Mom?" I said.

"Okay."

"We'll drive down to Tokeland and see the old hotel. Maybe we could even do some gambling at the casino."

"Oh, I don't do that."

"Me neither. What a waste of money! But some people have fun doing it."

"I suppose," she said.

Mom, Tom, Erin, and I crowded around my mother's tiny kitchen table eating toast and Cheerios and making plans for the day. I felt torn, as I always did when Tom and Erin were with me on these visits, between trying to have some fun with them while also focusing on Mom's needs. What would Mom want to do? Where would she want to eat? How much walking would she be up for?

Since Casey's death, her isolation was complete, her loneliness more intense. Without Casey, she was left with nobody to talk to, so she simply stopped talking. Even though Casey didn't talk back, at least she had been able to talk to him, pet, feed, and care for him. Now she was totally alone but for Doreen's and my weekend visits as well as lunches once, later twice, and finally three times a week with Eleanor. In one early phone conversation with Eleanor, I encouraged her to feel free to eat with Mom, convinced Mom would be more comfortable sharing a meal than being watched while she ate. I also wanted Eleanor to know we were happy to have her eat Mom's food.

"Thank you, but I don't cook Kosher for your mother," she said. "I usually bring a small lunch from home."

"Thank you," I said. "Thank you for being so good to her, to us."

After too many years of frozen dinners since Dad's death, the effects were obvious. Mom had lost too much weight. In my family, the more slender you were, the more attractive you were considered, so it took a ridiculously long time to realize that such obvious weight loss in an eighty-year-old widow was simply not a good thing. I was grateful to Eleanor for getting Mom to eat homemade meals again and for always leaving easy-to-reheat leftovers in the refrigerator for Mom to eat the following day.

In the beginning of Eleanor's time with my mother, when Mom still had a car, she and Eleanor would sometimes go grocery shopping together. But soon it became clear Mom should no longer be driving. There was the day she admitted to getting lost on the way home. Another day when she apparently backed into another car in the grocery store parking lot and drove away with the other driver yelling behind her – and jotting down her license plate number. Finally, when Eleanor had taken one too many rides with Mom driving, she let Doreen know she would be doing all future driving and wanted permission to drive Mom's car.

Doreen and I had talked about this moment, about getting rid of the car. We'd agreed the thing smelled so awful because of the endless hours Casey rode around in it with Mom that neither one of us was willing to try to clean it up enough to sell. We talked of donating it to charity. I don't know if Eleanor brought it up first or if Doreen did, but Eleanor wanted the car, and we were more than happy to give her a very good price for it. We wondered how Mom would react when she saw Eleanor driving it, but Eleanor assured us her son would be using it for a while, and by the time she drove it back into the yard, Mom wouldn't even remember it. Again, Eleanor knew more about these things than either Doreen or I did.

Still, every now and again, Mom seemed to have bits of clarity float through the fog that had become her memory. At breakfast that morning with Tom and Erin, Mom stood at the kitchen window and said, "That boy took it."

"What boy?" Tom asked.

"Took what?" Erin asked.

"He stole my car," Mom said, clear as could be.

"No, Mom," I said. "You sold it to him. Nobody stole anything."

"I did not," she said.

"Well, it's okay. I can drive today," Tom said, distraction being the best offense.

"That's nice," Mom said.

As time passed, a new routine developed. Eleanor would leave a grocery list on the refrigerator, and Doreen or I would do the shopping when we came for a visit. But there were always things we missed, or items needed between our visits, or visits that were missed due to inclement weather, conflicting schedules, or other challenges of life. Mom lost her credit card repeatedly until we finally established a hiding place in the back bedroom, a place that was out of Mom's reach, where we hid the card so Eleanor could use it for necessary shopping trips. That only worked until Mom began to struggle so much to sign the sales receipts it became uncomfortable for Eleanor to take her shopping. We needed another solution, and the obvious solution was to switch to cash. Every visit Doreen or I always checked the hiding spot and left enough cash for Eleanor and Mom to use for shopping and even an occasional outing. It worked like a charm.

After our morning drive to visit the old Tokeland Hotel, Tom, Erin, and I were sitting with Mom in a tight plastic booth of a little yellow café in Grayland waiting for lunch. Hamburgers for the three of us and chicken strips for Mom. The choices were limited, but then the only thing Mom ever ordered was chicken strips.

I heard the café door slam. Two people entered. A tall, large-boned woman in her late forties and a young man in his early twenties. Though we'd never met in person, I knew who she was as soon as she walked into the small café.

"Hi, Sally. How are you?" she said.

"You must be Eleanor," I said. "I'm Arleen. It's a pleasure to finally meet you in person."

"Lots of phone calls," she said with a hearty laugh. "It's good to put a face to your voice."

I introduced my husband and daughter as Mom watched, her face at work on a riddle.

"Here for the weekend, then?" Eleanor asked.

"Yes. I saw your shopping list on the refrigerator. I'll be sure to stock the kitchen before we leave tomorrow."

"Seems our little system is working good," she said.

"I think so. And Mom seems happy," I said as I gave my mother a big wink.

"Well, I promised my son lunch," she said. "Enjoy your visit."

She moved away from our booth toward her son who sat drumming his fingers on a nearby tabletop. When she was barely out of earshot, my mother leaned across the table and said, "Who's that woman?"

"That's Eleanor, Mom. She's the lady who comes to your house and cooks for you."

"No, she doesn't," she scoffed. "I don't even know her."

I glanced at Tom who only shrugged his shoulders and continued to eat his hamburger.

"She looks really nice, Nana," Erin said. "Is she a good cook?"

"I suppose," Mom said.

I could see the confusion in her eyes, yet I still wanted to believe that she was okay, that she could handle living alone. Later during the drive back to Seattle, I told Tom, "It was just seeing Eleanor's face out of context that confused her. Like when I see a former student in the grocery store or the post office. She'd know it was Eleanor in her own house, wouldn't she?"

"Maybe."

I ignored the doubt in his voice. "But she can still function in her own space, don't you think?"

"Maybe," he said.

̀̀ ∾

By mid 2008, Doreen and I began our search in earnest. We didn't want to face another winter of inclement Grayland weather. We didn't want to risk another week without power and the accompanying fear for Mom's well-being. Still, I was dragging my feet. I admitted, at least to myself, Mom was no longer safe living alone, but I had confidence she was all right as long as Eleanor was there to check on her. But Eleanor wasn't there daily, couldn't be there every day, and should we have another winter as rough as the last, Mom would be in serious trouble.

Doreen contacted an elder care organization in Seattle that provided assistance to families in finding appropriate housing for aging parents. The arrangement was a bit like that of a buyer's real estate agent. They helped locate a suitable placement and received a commission from the housing facility rather than from the clients. We were fine with the arrangement as long as we weren't pushed into something we didn't like or want, and we felt that together we could stand our ground. We figured it would be nice to get some direction from someone who had more experience in dealing with elder issues. We needn't have worried at all. Laura was a sweetie.

After visiting a few places on our own, Doreen and I had an idea of what we did and did not want. What we didn't have was a clear sense of whether we needed assisted living or dementia care. We narrowed our search to only those assisted living facilities that also offered dementia care. If we had to force Mom to leave Grayland, at least we were determined to make this her only move.

After months of weekends looking for places for Mom, we narrowed our choices to two facilities – one to the east of Seattle in Issaquah and the other to the north in Lynnwood. It somehow seemed fitting for Mom to return to Issaquah where she and Dad had raised their nine children. It was a pretty facility, a "cottage community." There were four or five assisted-living cottages with rooms for a dozen residents. The cottages lay along a small creek and were linked by covered pathways abundant with flowers and trellised vines. There were also three dementia-care cottages and one that was being converted into hospice care. If Mom was able to adapt to any type of care, this seemed like the place for her. Family-like, almost. Indoor-outdoor access. One level and small.

The first day we visited, Laura led us around the facility with casual ease, laughing and talking with residents and caregivers alike. We saw one old man sitting in a straight-backed chair smack in front of a television, his face a foot from the screen when we entered one of the cottages.

"Hi there. How are you?" Laura asked.

"I'm just happy to have another day," the old man said.

"A philosophy I need to live by." Laura joked with the residents, chatting and making them smile.

Our concerns about the place were that the dementia-care cottages were ringed by an ugly chain-link fence while the assisted living cottages were in an open yard along a quiet road with nothing at all to stop a resident from simply walking off.

"It's really not a problem," the director assured us. "Our residents are so busy and content, they don't want to leave."

"But our mother doesn't want to move at all," I said.

"And we're concerned about dementia," Doreen said.

"She'll be fine," the director said. "There's often some resistance and confusion at first. That's normal. We'll make it work for your mother."

The other facility, the one in Lynnwood, was closer for Doreen, but a bit more inconvenient to reach from my home. Also, it was exclusively a dementia/Alzheimer's care facility. Still we were impressed with the place. It was built with four wings, called houses, extending out from a central core. Within that center were two activity rooms, a nursing office, the kitchen, and the front entrance as well as several small seating nooks. Each house had fifteen bedroom units, each with a private bathroom, as well as communal dining and living rooms. It reminded me of a college dorm, the co-ed style. The entire facility was fenced with a tall, cedar fence, and a wonderful maze of garden areas and walkways wound around and between each house.

This too seemed a perfect place for Mom, but was her dementia bad enough? Did she really belong in a facility specializing in dementia care?

"Bring her in," we were told. "Let her share a meal with us, and we can assess her condition."

"She won't come," we admitted. "She refuses to move. It's hard to even get her to come to Seattle for a visit. This move is not going to be easy."

"We understand," we were told. "We've seen it all."

The weekend after narrowing our choices to these two homes, Doreen took color brochures with maps and activity schedules with her to Grayland to break the news to Mom and try to get her to consider a move, or at least to go for a visit.

"It's not working, Arleen," she said when I called. "She won't even look at the pictures. She's so upset with me now I don't know if she'll even come up for Thanksgiving dinner. I think she's afraid we're going to trick her into staying."

"Damn," I said. "This is going to be so hard."

"What are we going to do if she refuses to move?"

"Let's give it a little more time," I said. "Leave all the brochures and stuff there. I'll work on her again when I go down, and we can both mention it in every phone call we make. Maybe we can get Eleanor and Larry to start talking it up as well. And how about we use 'when' instead of 'if' with her from now on, okay?"

II

DECEPTION

SET UP

IN JANUARY MARLEEN planned a visit from her home in the Bay area. She and her husband had retired and planned to move back to the Pacific Northwest. She wanted a sisters' weekend or at least a sisters' dinner. When she called me, I told her I wasn't sure. Despite the one lunch together and a few emails, we'd never talked about what had happened the last time the sisters had gotten together.

"Why?" she asked.

"Are you guys going to beat up on me again?" I asked, only half joking.

"What do you mean?" she asked.

"I mean Alki Bakery. I mean I don't want to go through that again."

A silent pause.

"We were unfair," she said.

I said nothing.

"I'd just really like to see you. To see all of my sisters," she said.

"I'd like to see you too," I said.

A weekend gathering turned out to be too much, but a dinner was planned. Marleen and my next two sisters – Laureen visiting from her home in Istanbul and Charleen from the east side of the Cascade Mountains – stayed the night in a downtown hotel with Marleen. I agreed to meet for dinner but not to stay for the slumber party. Doreen did not join us at all. While the decisions we made were different, we shared our feelings of frustration and disconnection. We were both bothered that the other sisters could find time and energy to come together for an evening of fun but had rarely managed to visit Mom in the almost seven years since Dad's death. Maybe Doreen was just being more authentic than I was.

I chose to join my sisters for dinner. The last time I'd seen them together, they'd torn me apart for writing *The Thirty-Ninth Victim*. Now I was stronger. They couldn't hurt me now. Maybe Doreen's approach was more honest, but I was still willing to try to rebuild relationships or perhaps build what had never existed. At least that was how I approached the dinner.

I met my sisters at their hotel room. As I crossed into their suite, I was again the outsider. We made small talk.

"You look great, Arleen," Marleen said.

"Thanks," I said.

"Your hair's so curly. New perm?" Charleen asked.

"No, it's always been curly," I said.

"But it was straight before," Charleen insisted.

Before what? I wondered. Before puberty? When we were teenagers and I did everything humanly possible to have the long straight hair of the popular girls?

"Who wants a glass of wine?" Marleen asked.

"We better get to the restaurant or we'll lose our reservation," Laureen said.

"Sorry, I'm late," I said.

I was the younger wayward sister who'd made them late. I felt scrutinized and defensive. Lighten up, I told myself as we headed to the restaurant. Just listen. Just watch. Just see how this unfolds.

The tablecloth was crisp, heavy white, the napkins folded into mauve swans. Crystal wine and water glasses, delicate china, and the layout of silver that causes confusion and nervous laughter in some, haughty confidence in others. Laureen had chosen the restaurant. Once seated, she ordered the wine.

We wandered through dinner and trivia until Marleen asked, "So how's Mom doing, Arleen? I feel so bad. You and Doreen are doing so much."

"You'd know if you ever visited," I wanted to say. "If you ever called." Instead I said, "She's getting worse. Forgetting more. Doreen and I are looking into places."

"When I was in Hawaii for the holidays, Michael said he didn't think Mom even knew who he was when he called. What can we do to help?"

"Call her. Visit. Write," I said.

Charleen shifted in her chair, her discomfort rising. "I stopped calling her," she said.

I looked at her, saying nothing at all.

"It got too upsetting for her," she continued. "She got so confused because she didn't know who I was. She couldn't remember my name."

"She doesn't necessarily need to know who the call's from," I said. "She still loves and needs the attention."

"She needs to be around more people," Marleen said.

"She wants to stay in her own home," I said. "But she could sure use more attention."

"I don't think she should be forced to move. I wouldn't want anybody forcing me. If she wants to stay there, she should stay," Laureen said.

"Someday she'll have to be moved," I said.

"Why? Why not just leave her be?"

"Because she's reaching the point that she can't care for herself," I said. "Look, I agree with you, Laureen. I've always wanted to respect her wishes. But the day will come when she has to be moved."

"She probably should've been moved a couple of years ago," Marleen said.

"I'd say about four," Charleen said.

If you felt so strongly about moving her two years ago, or four years ago, why didn't you do it? I wanted to ask. I wanted to scream from the vaulted ceiling, swinging from the crystal chandelier of the plush downtown restaurant. Instead, I remained silent, knowing there was power in my silence. Just as there was power in Doreen's absence. Knowing Mom would be moved when Doreen and I made the decision to move her, no sooner and no later. Knowing Doreen was the only one who actually had the legal power to make that decision. Knowing that because of the monthly visits we'd both been making since Dad's death, because of the endless phone calls with

Mom and with her caregiver, because of the awkward conversations with the post mistress, the store cashiers, the neighbors, the doctor, we knew Mom and her needs better than any of our siblings. And we would be deciding when she'd move because they were not involved enough in her life to make that decision. But that didn't stop the opinions that flew across the table over crumpled linen and empty wine glasses, opinions based on shallow understanding of Mom, her condition, her needs, or her wishes.

❧ ❦

Earlier that same day, the day of the sisters' dinner, Tom and I helped move Erin into her third apartment in just over one year. She lasted in her first apartment, blocks from the University of Washington, only six months before the long lonely hallways and the homeless panhandlers on the street corners chased her back to West Seattle. I'm guessing the break-up with her first serious boyfriend also added to her loneliness.

She moved back to West Seattle still determined to live alone and rented an apartment just blocks from our house. Alone, but not isolated. "It's cheaper than another remodel," Tom said.

"True, but wouldn't it be nice if we had a little mother-in-law unit with a separate entrance?" I said.

"She wants her own place. This works. Let it be," he said.

So I did. Six months later Erin moved again. The appeal of an increased savings account and the possibility of travel those savings would allow if she could put enough aside convinced her to try sharing an apartment with a roommate. She lasted from January to June, another six months. The apartment was too small, one roommate was both too many and not enough at the same time. Erin decided to try a bigger place, this time with two roommates. Still, she stayed in West Seattle, preferring to live in the community where she grew up even if it meant a cross-town commute to school.

West Seattle has that kind of hold. It's a small town in the midst of a big city, connected by a high bridge that leads many to think it's just too far away and others to appreciate the gentle isolation. Erin grew up within walking distance of the small downtown area with a host of shops and restaurants where the owners and employees have known her since she was a child, refusing to sell her alcohol until she was twenty-one, even with fake ID. Recognition has a strong pull in this world of isolation. I didn't blame her for wanting to return, to stay, in West Seattle.

Erin's desire to be close to home, to come on a weekly, if not daily basis for a visit, a meal, a load of laundry, gave me deep pleasure and confusion. It was so very different, so wonderfully different from my own behavior and state of mind when I was her age. Even younger, at seventeen when I graduated from high school, all I could think of was how to put as much distance between my parents and myself as I possibly could, even when the loneliness became unbearable. It was what I'd seen my older siblings do. It was what I thought was expected – to become independent above all else. Even love.

But Erin was different. She no longer seemed to need to break away, to run as hard and fast as she could and leave us behind to sort through the chaos of shattered emotions, as she had when she was a high-spirited, young teenager. Instead, her apartments, her many moves, were her ways of experimenting with different living arrangements. Despite the frustration and just plain hard work of so much packing and hauling, unpacking and decorating, Tom and I were glad to help her out. So in early January, about a month weeks before moving Mom, we helped Erin move into her third apartment, a bit like a little Goldilocks still looking for a place that was just right.

❧   ❧

With our search narrowed to two facilities – Issaquah and Lynnwood – Doreen and I finally had to choose. I was haunted not only by the decision to move Mom, but also by the selection of where she might be most likely to adjust and find happiness. I believed that my sister was equally weighted by the decision. We needed reinforcements in the final decision-making process, so we took our husbands to see both facilities. Again, we walked through each like buyers and agents discussing the pros and cons of each place, always surrounded by a few curious residents listening to our conversation and watching our every move.

"But would she be happy here?" I asked in reply to Tom's assertion that it was nice.

"She's not going to be happy anywhere at first," he said. "But this place seems to offer everything she needs." We were sitting over a dinner of pasta and wine with Doreen and her husband in a tiny candle-lit bistro near the Issaquah facility. "And the food here is a whole lot better than anything you can find in Grayland."

We laughed a nervous laugh, relieved to have a decision finalized.

"I'll call them tomorrow, and we can start the paperwork," Doreen said.

"Okay. Let me know how I can help," I said. "I'm sure it's going to be a bundle."

"I wish I knew for sure Mom will be okay in assisted living. Maybe she really does need dementia care," Doreen said.

"I know what you mean. I keep going back and forth about that," I said. "But there's no guarantee either way, right? I mean, they're the experts, and they said they'd keep an eye on her 24/7 until she settled in. I suppose we just have to trust they know what they're doing."

In retrospect, I don't know if it was my inability to accept Mom's dementia that guided my preference for the Issaquah facility, or if it was the simple fact that it was in Issaquah, the town I still considered my own despite the sale of our family home and my parents' move out to the Pacific Coast decades before. Even in the various visits involved in making our final choice, each drive from Seattle, felt to me a bit like going home. I wanted Mom back in Issaquah despite my concerns about putting her into assisted living rather than dementia care.

It's true they also had dementia-care cottages, but Doreen and I had visited that area of the complex and disliked not only the chain-link fence surrounding it but the whole feel of the place. When it came to dementia care, the Lynnwood facility was definitely our first choice, but we were hoping assisted living was all Mom really needed – a place with regular meals, planned activities, new friends, and professional oversight. We made the decision, or I made my decision, unable to see behind the curtain.

ॐ ॐ

I've always prided myself on being an honest person – tactlessly honest at times, I fear – but I have not always been honest. I was not honest with my mother.

The deception began, of course, months, even years, before the seventh anniversary of Dad's death. I never told Mom point-blank she had to move, she could no longer live alone. I never told her it was unsafe. I never told her she had dementia, she was repeating herself, she was beginning to lose language. I never talked about what was happening to her. When she said things like, "My head doesn't work good anymore," I brushed it off with comments like "It's okay Mom, everybody gets confused sometimes." Did my own denial make Mom's acceptance of the inevitable more difficult than nature itself made it?

Even after Doreen and I had investigated a host of options and narrowed our search to two facilities, I was still avoiding the hard truth. Doreen took the brochures, the photographs, the activities schedules and menus to Grayland. Doreen and her husband spent numerous weekends arguing with Mom, using logic, trying to convince her of the benefits of a move. But I was a coward. I didn't want to make Mom mad at me. I wanted our visits to be carefree and fun. I wanted laughter and long beach walks. When I saw the piles of information Doreen had left with Mom from a prior visit, I said things like, "Hey, Mom, this looks like a really cool place to live." When she responded "I live here," I let it drop. We repeated the same exchange several times throughout my visits, but like Mom, I was clinging to a life that was slipping away from both of us.

The weekend after our dinner in Issaquah, Doreen and her husband were in Grayland once again taking the heat from Mom, and I was still being a wimp, still fearful of confrontation, still trying to respect my mother's need for independence. But we were stripping her of independence, leaving her exposed to a world that terrified her. Or, to be more precise, dementia was stripping her of the power to make sound decisions in an increasingly hostile world she no longer had the defenses to protect herself against. So much like raising a child, leaving her at day care or with a babysitter. The first day of kindergarten. The child alone and defenseless.

Doreen said she was once helping Mom dress or wash – things I had not yet done – and found Mom had put her bra on backwards, boobs in the back. I wanted to laugh. I wanted to cry. I imagined this confused old woman with small, sagging breasts struggling to dress herself, unable to get her bra facing the right direction, and yet unwilling to admit she could use some help on a daily basis. That she was horribly alone.

Children becoming parents. Daughters becoming their mother's mother. Role reversal I detested. I didn't like treating my mother like a child, stripping her of her autonomy, authority, respect. We were raised to honor our parents. When did that change? When were we given permission, even expected, to ignore that honor, to strip our mother of that honor?

On February 2, 2009, Dad had been dead for seven years, and I was still having nightmares of what had become of him. Did he know Mom had to be moved to assisted living, that he had left her alone in Grayland feeling determined, perhaps somehow obligated, to end her days as he had done? It was one anniversary I hoped Mom's dementia had stolen from her.

That morning I woke from a nightmare of terrorists dressed in black, faces covered, surrounding and attacking the Issaquah house, the house where I grew up. We were trying to escape, but somebody was missing. Mom? Maureen? I woke in a sweat, frightened and persecuted.

EXECUTION

ONE EVENING AFTER work, Doreen and I spent several hours in her Elliott Way office filling out forms for Mom. Some of it was relatively easy – photo permission, rules and regulations, medical release. Then came the likes and dislikes. Answering questions about Mom's preferences was harder. What kind of music did she prefer? What kind of group activities did she like? Endless questions. We laughed, we got frustrated, and through it all I was weighed down by a heavy heart and a deep dread of the coming weekend.

For a week my stomach churned, my intestines tied in knots. My back hurt, my shoulders hurt, my knee hurt. I was short-tempered at work and at home. Impatient with students and unwilling, unable to forgive my husband's minor flaws – the clothes on the floor, the water pooling around the kitchen sink, the dirty dishes in his studio. He was my punching bag. He suffered the brunt of the pain, frustration, and anger that was building. I had become my mother's mother. The approaching weekend I would strip her of her right of self-determination, an act that went against the very core of my being.

The previous weekend Doreen had spent two days arguing with Mom about the pending move. I hadn't even had the nerve to call her on the phone more than one hundred and fifty miles away. I feared confrontation. I feared rejection. I was ashamed of my petty fears. Ashamed of the power I planned to usurp from my mother. But still I couldn't call, couldn't tell her the truth about what lay ahead.

❧ ❧

Marleen flew up from California, and a carefully planned deception was put into place. The move would be on Sunday. While Marleen and I got Mom out of the house, Doreen and our husbands would go in and get the necessary clothing and furniture then head to Issaquah. Marleen, Mom, and I would take a long, leisurely drive while the van with a few of Mom's belongings rushed ahead. We'd rendezvous in Issaquah where, if all went well, Mom's room would be set up and ready for her to settle in and live happily ever after. In retrospect, it was absurd to think it would work out at all.

When Marleen got in Saturday morning, she and I drove to Grayland together. We arrived in time to take Mom out for a lousy lunch at a one of the few open restaurants at the Westport harbor. Then we decided to walk the beach. When we crested the last dune, we saw cars parked two rows deep at the water's edge, and tiny dark moving dots for as far as the eye could see. Clamming season. None of us had ever seen so many people on the beach. We walked down and back along the water, but the sun still hadn't set, and we wanted to see more.

Feeling naughty and breaking all my own principles, I agreed when Marleen suggested driving her rental car on the beach. We went in at the "T" in the road by Twin Harbors State Park and came out at Grayland State Park. The beach sand was packed and perfect.

Even at a snail's pace Mom was nervous, worrying the whole time about where we would get out. She suggested we drive out on each tiny walking path we passed. Still, I think she was excited and having fun. If nothing more, she enjoyed the fun Marleen and I were having and the overall silliness of the drive. That was her last view of her beach. She just didn't know it yet.

Later I made grilled cheese sandwiches for dinner as Marleen folded the last load of laundry. We pulled pictures off the walls and stuck pottery and bags in the car trunk all without Mom's awareness. I grabbed a few knickknacks from her bathroom, familiarities to warm her new home. We watched some television, and it was time for bed.

"You take the guest room," I told Marleen. I knew her back was worse than mine, and besides she'd had a longer day.

"And you sleep with me," Mom said.

"I'm fine here on the floor," I said. "See, I have my sleeping bag and pad."

"Oh no," she said.

"Sure. I'll be fine," I said as I scooted into my bag. "I'm a backpacker."

I didn't want to sleep with my mother. The stale air in her tiny bedroom with the door closed and the windows tight was too much. I just couldn't do it. Would it have been a comfort to her? Perhaps. Would I have been less sore the next morning? Maybe. But I still didn't want to sleep with my mother.

I was on the floor almost asleep when Mom came out with a quilt. She wanted to make me comfortable, wanted to try again, and yet again, to close the broken blinds so nobody would see me, wanted me to come into her bedroom and sleep with her. Again I refused. I was even a bit harsh. I just wanted her to go to sleep and let me do the same.

A little later I got up to use the bathroom. She'd left her bedroom door open, something she never did. As I began to close it, I heard, "Come on. Get into bed." I just wished her a good night and closed her door. I felt mean. I still feel mean as I write these words. But sleeping with my mother was not on my list of things I do. Not then. Not yet.

It was 7:21 Sunday morning, and I was awake. I couldn't sleep anymore. I had refused to sleep with Mom and the floor had trashed my back. I lay quietly for a while until I heard Marleen moving around at the back of the house. The scene was set, the deception in place, the show about to begin again.

～ ～

It just wasn't right. I could feel it from the moment we arrived, we being Mom, Marleen, and myself. Doreen, her husband, and Tom were already there, had already moved a few special pieces of furniture from the house into Mom's new room. I called Doreen's cell as we drove into the parking lot.

"We're here," I said.

"Okay, I'll meet you in the lobby," she said.

"How's the room?"

"All set up."

We met in the large lobby that doubled as an activity room. Where was the welcoming committee? Where was the activities coordinator or the caregiver we'd been told would help with the transition? Nobody greeted us, greeted Mom, or showed us to her room. It was Doreen who met us at the door and ushered Mom to her cottage. She showed her the room, pointing out her furniture, her bedcover, her clothes in the closet and dresser. Mom was confused. She didn't understand what was happening. I think she may have thought we were visiting somebody else.

"See Mom, this is your room." Doreen said. "This is your new home."

"No. I have a house," she said.

"Yes, and your house will be there. Your house isn't going anywhere. But you're going to live here for a little while," I said. Doreen said. Marleen said. In different ways. Repeatedly.

"No. I have a house," Mom repeated.

The caregivers seemed to appear and disappear, but no one stayed with us, no one was assigned to stick with Mom as I had expected. I was nervous, but then I'd been nervous for months and no longer trusted my own judgment. Maybe they're just giving us privacy, I told myself. They'll step in to be with Mom as soon as we leave.

We had arrived late and missed lunch. Food had been set aside for us in the small kitchenette attached to the cottage dining room, but nobody came to help us. We dug through drawers and cabinets looking for dishes and flatware, placemats and napkins to serve ourselves a family lunch. Our attempts at cheerful conversation fell flat. We were like a little lonely group in a school cafeteria after everybody's finished and left. I felt the other residents watching, but not joining us, not talking to us or to Mom.

By late afternoon it was time for us to leave. We sat with Mom for a while in the activity room. We were upbeat, promising to visit the next day. Some kind of activity was going on at a table at the far end of the large room, but nobody invited Mom to join. Finally, a caregiver joined us. She talked with Mom and encouraged us to leave. I relived Erin's tears the first day we left her at kindergarten, but this time there were no tears. Just bewilderment, confusion. As I look back now, I don't think Mom understood where we were or what was happening, and I am haunted by her feelings of abandonment, the feelings I imagine she had when we left her there, alone with strangers in the heart of winter, exactly seven years and six days from the day my father died.

ॐ ॐ

Tom and I headed back to Seattle alone.

"I need a walk," I said.

"How about that Bellevue greenbelt area?" he asked.

"I don't care."

We wandered in gray, wet silence. Dusk was falling when we got back to the car and drove home. We were making something to eat when the phone rang.

"Don't you ever answer your cell?" Doreen said.

"I'm sorry," I said. "I must've left it turned off or in the car or something. We went for a walk. What's up?"

"I got a call. No, I've gotten a bunch of calls. Mom tried to escape. She walked away. She just left. Walked down the street. Somebody, some lady driving by, found her and took her back. They didn't even know she was gone."

"Oh crap," I said.

"What are we going to do?" Doreen asked.

"What about the person who was supposed to be with her and help her through the adjustment period? Isn't that what they promised for the first day or two?"

"Yeah, but now they're saying it's our responsibility. They want us to hire somebody to watch her all night."

"Like a babysitter?"

"Exactly."

"I guess that's what we need to do then, right?"

"Yeah, I already gave them the okay, but I've got a bad feeling about this," Doreen said.

"Me too," I said. "Keep me posted if you hear more, okay?"

Tom watched in silence, understanding the gist of the call. As soon as I signed off, he said, "Look, you guys all have to be at work in the morning. I can go out there and spend the night with your mom. Better me than a stranger, right?"

We talked it over for only a few minutes before I called Doreen back.

"It's too late," she said. "They've already got someone arranged. Mom's tried to leave four times in the last two hours. They want to move her into dementia care in the morning."

"No way," I said. "That place is horrible. It looks like a prison."

"I know," she said. "I know."

∞ ∞

The following morning I headed to class riddled with guilt. I imagined Mom waking in a new place, a stranger watching over her. I imagined Doreen struggling to organize our next step.

The night before we'd made our decision. Mom was not going to live behind a chain-link fence. We needed a back-up plan if the Issaquah facility refused to allow her to stay in assisted living, and we knew we didn't want her in assisted living if it meant she could walk away unnoticed and be lost. If the Issaquah facility was unwilling or unable to help Mom in making the transition into assisted living, if Mom's level of dementia was such she did not belong in assisted living, we needed an alternative.

We'd planned our strategy the night before. First thing in the morning, Doreen would call the Lynnwood facility. She would explain what happened, explain that Mom tried to escape numerous times, that we would not allow them to move her into their dementia-care cottages behind an ugly chain-link fence, and that if Mom needed dementia care we wanted her in a facility specialized in that type of care. In short, we wanted her in the Lynnwood facility.

I called Doreen during a break between classes. "They'll take her," she said, her voice heavy with relief.

"When?" I asked.

"Today. This afternoon. I called Issaquah, and they wanted to move her into the fenced area today. I told them we'd be moving her out instead."

"Good for you. I bet they weren't too happy about that," I said. "Seemed like they had a lot of empty rooms in there."

"Definitely a renter's market. It's probably helping us get Mom into the Lynnwood place, too."

"Whatever it takes."

"We may not get our money back," she said. "It's going to be a total pain."

"I'm sorry you've got to deal with that, but the important thing is to get Mom in a good place," I said.

"Yeah, so we take her and her furniture to Lynnwood together this afternoon, okay?"

"Yup, I can get off at noon, and Tom can help. Let's meet in Issaquah at 12:30. We'll bring the van."

When I saw Mom, small and bewildered, I knew we had screwed up by choosing the assisted-living facility in Issaquah. It hit me like a punch to the stomach with the weight of seven years of denial behind it. Mom was not angry. She was not sad. She was simply very, very confused.

"Let's get you out of here, okay?" I said.

"Okay," she said. "Where are we going?"

"To a really nice place, Mom. A place you'll like." As I said those words, I didn't know if Mom would ever learn to like her new home in Lynnwood, but I knew she'd be safe in a dementia care facility.

We caravanned the long drive from Issaquah to Lynnwood with Mom's furniture in our big green van and Mom in Doreen's car. When we arrived, the facility director greeted us in the small lobby. "Welcome to Clare Bridge," she said. She spoke to Mom, to us, in a calm reassuring voice. After a few minutes of small talk, she called in the nurse on staff that day.

"Hello, Sally," the nurse said. "Will you go for a little walk with me?"

Mom looked at Doreen and me, the look of a child asking for permission, asking for reassurance.

"Go ahead, Mom," we said. "It's okay. We'll be right here. We're not going anywhere."

While the nurse informally assessed Mom's mental faculties, Doreen and I did paperwork and our husbands moved Mom's antique dresser into her new room. Later we made the bed, hung clothes in the closet, and arranged family photos around the small room.

Mom still looked lost and bewildered, but the constant attention of the caregivers, the smiles and touches, made all the difference. In only a few short hours, she seemed relaxed and settled in, holding hands with the nurse and working on puzzles in the activity room with other residents. It was almost dinner time, time for us to leave.

"She'll be alright," the director whispered to us. "Let's go out to the lobby now."

We gave Mom quick hugs and followed the director out through the locked door. She reminded us how to work the keypad, pointed out the riddle posted next to the door with the embedded code should we happen to forget.

"I'd suggest you give it three or four days," she said.

"You mean we shouldn't visit for three days?" I asked.

"Yes. We find it's best to give new residents a few days to settle in, get used to their new environment and caregivers without the family."

"Can we call to check on her?" we asked.

"Of course," she said. "And we'll call if there are any concerns."

The only call Doreen received the following day was to reassure us Mom was adjusting well to her new home. When Doreen told me the good news, I breathed a deep sigh of relief.

☙ ❧

Despite the reassurances from the Clare Bridge staff in Lynnwood that Mom was adjusting well, I couldn't sleep for three days. I spent a half hour after every meal flat on my back waiting for my digestive organs to talk nicely with each other. In short, I was a mess.

Doreen and I talked daily. She called the facility each day as well. I didn't. Doreen was the contact person, the one in charge, besides we didn't want to overload them with excessive calls. She'd talk with the care providers, and then update me. There was such calm it felt surreal, impossible to believe. Could this really have worked? Could Mom really be adjusting, not trying to run away, not in tears?

Tears? Of course not. My mother rarely cried. There would be no tears, just the stubborn determination that had characterized her behavior for the better part of eighty years. If Mom wanted something, you were lucky to know what it was, but somehow she made it happen. I'm not sure I'd go so far as to say Mom always got what she wanted. Instead she learned to keep her wants and needs simple and aligned. The one thing I knew she wanted more than anything in the world was to be allowed to live out the remainder of her life in her own home, and this was what we had taken from her. We had deceived her into making a move she did not want to make, that she had fought with silent fury using every fiber of her being. And she had trusted us. She got into the car in Grayland to go for a "nice long drive" and ended up abandoned in an assisted living facility in Issaquah. It made perfect sense she had walked away. She left without telling a soul. She left repeatedly because that's what made sense in her confused mind. She felt she didn't belong, so she simply left.

So how was it that in only three days she was adjusting to this new facility in Lynnwood? A difference in the care provided or resignation on Mom's part? Had she just given up the fight or had she already forgotten where she came from? Was the gray mist and ocean foam of the Grayland beach now a blur in the recesses of her memory, just as Dad's name had become? Could she already have forgotten the home she cherished just as she'd forgotten the man she'd adored for fifty years of marriage?

Or, were the caregivers lying to Doreen each time she made the call to check up on Mom? Were they painting a hopeful picture of adaptation when in reality Mom was suffering in misery? The situation demanded trust, and trust came to me in very limited quantities.

As I lay patting my knotted intestines, I puzzled these questions, trying to forgive myself, trying to convince myself we'd done the right thing. That moving Mom was right and necessary. That tricking her into the move had been essential. But was it? Any of it? What other choices were there? For I believe there are always choices. The challenge lies in making a selection from a list of less than desirable options, a selection I can most easily live with free from constant personal condemnation. So I listed the choices once again in my mind. I could only think of three, and we'd already opted for the third – deception.

The first choice, Mom's preference, would have been to leave her alone in Grayland. Perhaps we could have increased the level of home health care, arranged daily visits. But what about the fact that Mom no longer had a car, could no longer drive without getting lost? What if we heard again from neighbors that they had found her walking the highway lost and confused? And what about the winter power outages and the closed roads? I didn't want to face another winter like the one before when flooding prevented me from reaching her.

The second choice would have been to move to Grayland. Put simply, if Mom refused to leave her home, if she wanted to end her days in her own bedroom in the bed she'd shared with Dad for most of her long life, why couldn't I give that to her? The cost? My job. I couldn't teach in Seattle and live in Grayland. And what about Tom and Erin? What about my own family, my friends, my life?

As I write these words, I still feel a pang of guilt for choosing my own life preferences, my own priorities, over those of my mother. I was not willing to give up the life I had created for myself in order to care for my mother in her own home in the final decade of her life. I will have to live with that decision for the remainder of my own life. As I lay patting my colicky colon, I knew I had to learn to accept my decision and move forward. I also knew if Mom was truly adjusting as well as the caregivers insisted with each call Doreen made, then the acceptance of my role in forcing her to move would be just that much easier to bear.

I knew I had to see it for myself, and I counted the hours until I could make that first visit.

⨎   ⨏

I keyed in the code with clammy hands, Tom at my side. The door didn't open. "Here, let me do it," Tom said.

We walked in. I paused, unable to remember if Mom's hall was to the left or right. "This way," he said.

I followed my directionally challenged husband, knowing at this moment, on this day, he was more in control than I was. We walked the long hall. The air was heavy, but not unpleasant. The outer walls were lined with windows and doors opening to the garden areas between the four wings that extended out from the central core of the building. Even in the gray cold of February the gardens were attractive, the grass vibrant.

As we made our way to Mom's room, I saw her walking toward us, a tall, only slightly stooped, man at her side. Mom walked with quick, brisk steps – two to each of his long strides. He had a full head of wavy white hair and piercing blue eyes. The similarity to my father in his later years was undeniable. The same description could have been used for both men.

"Who's that?" Tom asked.

"No idea," I said.

"Looks like your mom's got herself a boyfriend."

"It's only been three days," I said. But as I watched, I had to admit there was a certain intimacy in the way they walked together, the way they chattered. We approached unnoticed. "Hi Mom," I said.

She stopped and stared for a moment, a wave of confusion washed over her face as she tried to place my own. I was a ghost from a life she'd left behind only a few days prior. For a moment, she could not remember who I was.

"Hi Mom," I repeated. "It's me, Arleen. I'm your middle daughter."

"I know that," she said. Then she turned to the man standing at her side and said, "This is my sister."

"This is my husband, Tom," I said. "We came to visit."

"That's nice," she said.

"Are you going for a walk?" Tom asked.

"Yes," she said.

"Who's your friend?"

Mom looked back and forth between the two men, unsure, unable to respond.

"Will you show us around, Mom? Maybe show us your new room?" I asked.

"Okay. This way," she said. She turned around and started walking, leaving the old man standing in the hallway alone as we headed in the opposite direction.

"What about your friend?" I asked.

"He's okay," she said.

We passed the two connected activity rooms, one large, the other small. A chubby woman with a wide smile approached. "Hello Sally. Who is this?"

"My sister," Mom said.

"Daughter," I said. "Arleen." I extended my hand in greeting. To my surprise, this woman wrapped me in such a tight hug I gasped.

"I'm a hugger," she said when she released me. "Your Mom didn't want a hug the first time, did you Sally, but she does now." Sure enough, Mom seemed to relax into the woman's arms like a sleeping baby in the arms of a loving mother.

It took my breath away. My mother was not a hugger. My mother did not express her emotions physically. I could not remember a full-body hug with my mother. Ever. And here she was, day three in dementia care, hugging a stranger. Who was this woman who looked like my mother, who possessed my mother's body, but who clearly was no longer the mother I knew?

"Are you showing them around?" she asked Mom, and turning to us she said, "By the way, I'm Gwen. I'm an activities coordinator, and I just love your mother. I'm so glad she's here."

"Okay," Mom said. And she headed out the door.

"Which way is it?" I asked. "I can't remember the hall."

"Cottage Place," Gwen said. "That way. Last room at the end on the left. Enjoy your visit."

We headed down the hall to the end, and Mom pushed open the door. "This is my room," she said.

"Very nice," Tom said.

"This is my bed. This is my dresser."

"And what's in here?" Tom asked, knowing exactly what lie behind the door.

"Bathroom," Mom said. Then she giggled, embarrassed and silly.

Who is this woman? I thought. And what have I done? All these years of respecting her wishes, honoring her repeated, determined claims that she wanted to stay in her own home, that she would not move. Yet three days in dementia care she was brimming with laughter and hugs.

Maybe I had been wrong. Maybe we should have forced the move sooner. Or maybe this was a honeymoon period. It might last or it might not. Either way, I was happy to see my mother's smile, hear her laughter. Even if only for a day.

III

AFTER THE LAST MOVE

2009

I QUICKLY LEARN the toughest part of visiting Mom in dementia care is figuring out how to pass the time. I always complained it was a struggle in Grayland, but at least there were a few distractions – the beach, the harbor, the antique shops, even television and puzzles. Dementia care is different. Now is different. Now is a bit like meditation or yoga, and I've never been very good at either. The focus of both is on the art of breathing: five breaths in, five breaths out. Then six. Then seven. Or, simple observation of the rhythm of breathing. Observe the air as it enters and leaves the body. I can't do it. I panic. I cannot empty my monkey mind. I see Maureen struggling for her life as her killer strangles her to death, her young body deprived of the breath needed to sustain life. I see my father sitting in his recliner in T-shirt and shorts, fever raging, gasping for breath, refusing medical care as his lungs fill with fluid, as he allows death to take him.

The mindful breathing of meditation and yoga challenge me beyond the limits of my mental control, but now my mother offers me a new form of meditative or mindful practice. Now I must learn to be in the present to be with my mother because my mother no longer has a past and future is no longer a concept that makes sense to her. To be with Mom or rather to be at peace with Mom and enjoy her company, I need to give myself to her, to the present, in a way I never learned to do with anyone, including my daughter.

When I look back through the years – Erin as a toddler, a four-year-old, an eight-year-old – my greatest regrets hinge on my inability to stay in the now that is required to play with a young child. Instead of playing, I was teaching, shaping, planning. I wasn't in the moment, and the years flew by unattended, leaving only fragments of memory in their wake. I was too absorbed in my own tragedies, my first family tragedies, to begin my own family and to be the engaged mother I might have been. I did not, could not, be in the present and play the simple games of childhood. Children know how, Erin knew how, to be totally present in her games. Neither the past nor the future was of interest, simply the now.

Later, as an adolescent and young teenager, Erin became part of the now generation created by technology – instant messaging, email, cell phones, My Space, Facebook, chat rooms. There seemed an underlying inability or unwillingness to plan, to commit to a plan, because something better might come along. I was still so busy shaping, teaching, lecturing, so busy correcting her past mistakes and planning her future, I was rarely just with her, enjoying her, being present with her.

I didn't have a second child, that opportunity to rectify the errors made raising the first. Instead, I have my mother. In an odd and unexpected way, my mother has given me another opportunity, another practice, another way to learn to be in the present. Now I am learning to mother my mother as she slips backwards into childhood.

Because it is still a struggle to be in the now, because I still have much to learn in early 2009, I fill those early visits with outings, convincing myself that it is good for Mom to get out, to leave the facility, to see a bit of the neighborhood.

I take my mother to the mall, only blocks from her new home. It's her first outing. "I live here now," she tells me as though I didn't know, didn't play my role in making it happen, didn't force her to move against her will. "My house is gone, sold," she tells Erin. I do not correct her. I'm happy she has created a new story that gives her comfort. I give Erin a look, and she knows not to correct her grandmother's mistake.

We walk the mall just as she did years before in Aberdeen with Dad – holding hands, looking in shops, watching the people. Mom is tentative, perhaps a bit frightened. She clings to my hand. I am gentle, fearful of bruising her, breaking a bone. I remember the many times my father would squeeze too tight when he held her hand. I remember how she pulled away and gave him a playful punch. "That hurts," she'd say. Now I feel fear in her hand.

"I've been here before," my mother says one moment, referring to a mall I know she has never set foot in. A moment later, "Where are we?" she asks in the voice of a child, timid and fearful.

"Marcella. Marcella," I hear a voice calling an accented version of my mother's full name. I turn to see a beautiful dark face smiling at my mother.

"Marcella, how are you?" the woman asks.

My mother looks to me in confusion.

"I am Cella. Our names almost same," the woman says, almost sings in melody and smiles. She bends to wrap my mother in a gentle hug.

"Good," Mom says, hesitant, but returning the hug.

"Do you know my mother?" I ask, more than a bit incredulous.

"Oh yes," she says. "I am Cella, too. I work Clare Bridge. I love Marcella. So sweet lady."

I look at this vibrant, young African woman, her arm still around my mother's shoulders. I look at the tiny, frail, white woman who is my mother. And I am holding an image I would have denied possible ten years before.

"We all love Marcella," the young woman says.

Once again I wonder who this Marcella is I do not know, this woman who is my mother, this woman who is now living only in the present, the past lost, the future unknown.

As we continue our walk, I remember another mall, another time. Erin is still very young, maybe four or five, but already she is putting together her own outfits for preschool each morning. Already she has strong opinions about what she will and won't put on her small body, what she likes and doesn't like. Already setting out clothes for her to wear is a wasted effort.

We're at the mall, or maybe downtown, the flagship Bon Marche with the elegance of years gone by, now another Macy's. We are in a tiny cubicle together because at four or five Erin still wants me in the fitting room with her. By eight or nine, I'm banned, left to wait outside until she finds something worthy of showing me. But at four or five I am still with her, trying hard to keep my hands locked behind my back as she pulls clothes on and off again. She does not want my help except, perhaps, to put the rejects back on hangers.

"Only one dress," I tell her. "One spring dress for Easter dinner at Nana and Boppa's house."

As a child myself, I always looked forward to spring, to Easter Sunday. The new dress was always the most important part. I carry the tradition forward and squish into the corner of the fitting room as Erin tries on dresses.

"This one," she says.

"You look great, Sweetpea," I say. "Are you sure that's the one you want to buy? You've only tried on a few. Maybe you should try these on, too."

"No, I want this one."

"These are really nice, too. Are you sure?"

A nod of her little blond head, a look of determination and decision in her eyes tell me she's done shopping. The child has always known how to make a decision.

"Okay, then," I say. "Take it off now, and we'll go pay for it."

"No. I don't want to. Can I wear it now? I want to wear it now," she says.

"But it's for Sunday dinner with Nonna and Boppa."

"I know," she says.

"It won't be new and special if you wear it now." Again, determination in her eyes tells me it's not worth the fight. "Okay," I say. "Let's go."

I'm not sure when that started, when my daughter first decided she was going to wear the new dress, pants, shoes home from the store. Maybe it began during the horrible Christmas rainstorm a few years before when we bought her a sweater at the Public Market to stop her shivers. Or maybe it was a child's understanding and appreciation of being in the moment, of loving the feel of that new dress, of not wanting to let go of pure and simple pleasure.

Now, we sit in a different mall, Mom and Erin and I. Now Erin is an adult, and Mom is a child.

"Look Nana," Erin says. "Look at that little girl." She points to a child dressed in a bright red fluffy coat, her short legs clad in white tights, black patent Mary Janes on her tiny feet.

Mom smiles and holds Erin's hand. "Like you," she says.

"I really love her," Erin says as we climb into the car for the drive home. "She's so nice, so sweet and funny. She was never like that before."

My daughter's words please me. And they break my heart. For twenty years she has not connected with her grumpy grandma. Now, as my mother edges toward the point when she will no longer recognize who we are when we come to visit, my daughter forms a fragile relationship, the connection she has needed throughout her young life. A grandma. A funny, fun-loving, upbeat, sweet grandma. A grandma with easy hugs and kisses. A grandma without a word of criticism.

"I thought for sure she'd say something about your jeans," I say, pulling at the threads hanging from the tattered hole just above her left knee.

"Yeah, me too," she says. "But she didn't say anything about the holes. She didn't say anything mean at all. Why's she so different?"

"I don't know. Maybe she was under more stress than we realized. Now she doesn't have a thing to worry about. Maybe she's found some peace and comfort with three meals a day and no locks to check and double check every evening."

"Yeah, and everybody gives her hugs. It's like, I don't know. It's like she's just so happy."

"Almost like a kid again, right?"

"Yeah, like a happy kid. But not really 'cause she's still my Nana. She's just nice now."

"And what a flirt," I add with a laugh. "Did you see her with those guys at dinner?"

"Yeah, but it's kind of sad. She doesn't even remember Boppa's name anymore."

"And soon," I say, "soon, she won't remember us either. Do you think she knew us when we got there?"

"She knew we were there for her," my daughter says.

"But she didn't know our names. And then she called me her sister. She always calls me her sister. Do I look that old?" I ask. A feeble attempt to lighten the mood.

"Why do you think she calls you her sister?" She ignores my plug for a compliment. "At first I thought she'd lost the word daughter. But now I think it's more than that. I remember she used to tell me, years ago when she still had her memory, she used to tell me I reminded her of her sister, Grace, because I made her laugh like Grace. It's odd, you know. I've never even met my aunt Grace."

"Really? How can you have an aunt you never met?"

"Well, I guess I met her as a kid, you know, when I was really young. But they always lived in the Minneapolis area, and we've always been out here. We never traveled much as a family – with nine kids, how could we? Maybe I met Grace in South Dakota when we were visiting Nana's parents on one of those family car trips, but I would've been a little kid."

"That's so weird."

"Yeah, I suppose it is, isn't it?" I fasten my seat belt and slip the key into the ignition. We pull out of the parking lot and head for home. I smile, pleased that maybe, finally, after almost twenty years, my daughter might be able to build some positive memories of the grandmother who has played such a minimal role in her young life.

As I begin to drive, I'm lost in thoughts, in memory. It was my father who first called me the meat in the sandwich. I preferred cheese. Melted cheese. At least that way I was a bit connected, melted together, part of the Big Kids, part of the Little Kids, but still the middle child. That was my identity. That was who I was.

When Maureen was murdered in 1983, I lost that identity. I was, I am, no longer a middle child. At twenty-nine I still had no idea who I was. At thirty-five I became a mother. For ten, fourteen, eighteen years my role was defined. Erin was the center of my life: an obsession, an absolute joy, a complete terror.

Now as both my daughter and my mother gather years, I am once again the meat in the sandwich. I hear my father's words. The jovial laughter of his younger, happier years. My mother will be eighty-five in September, my daughter twenty in May. I will be fifty-five in October. Twenty … fifty-five … eighty-five. The symmetry isn't perfect. I gave birth once at thirty-five. My mother gave birth nine times. I was her fifth child, born when she was thirty. What do all these numbers mean? Only that my mother and my daughter have found common ground. My mother at almost eighty-five is the woman she once was when she was twenty, and that is the woman my twenty-year-old daughter has fallen in love with – a jolly grandmother with ready hugs and happy smiles.

I am again in the middle watching my daughter and my mother bond in a way that was not possible before dementia stole the anguish of memory from my mother. Denial did only half the job. Dementia is more complete. Or perhaps it's true that dementia strips a person to the bare essence of their personality. Perhaps Mom was once this carefree, loving soul she has again become, who I am now fortunate to know and with whom my daughter has connected.

I am, once again, in the middle – watching. And loving what I see.

                                        ∾ ∾

It is my third visit in the two weeks since my sisters, our husbands, and I took Mom from her home. Each time we begin the visit with a tour. Each time my mother shows me her room, her bathroom, her closet, her window, her heater.

"It's hot in here," she says.

"It sure is," I agree. For as long as I can remember, Mom has complained about being cold. Now she's too warm.

"It works like this," she says, turning the dial of the small wall heater farther into the red zone.

"Maybe it should go this way, Mom. Blue is cooler. Red is hotter."

"Okay," she says.

She shows me each framed photo on the shelf and the dresser. "This is my family," she says.

"Yup," I say. "That's Doreen and Michael. And there's Dad." I rattle through the names of our large family, pointing, reminding. Trying to retie the fragile string of memory and give her back the names and relationships she struggles to grasp.

"And this one is my dad." She holds a photograph of my father.

"Ray," I say. "Your husband. My dad."

She returns the frame to the dresser and pokes around her room for a few minutes.

"What else do you want to show me, Mom?"

"Will you be warm enough?" She gestures toward the window.

"Sure. Let's go outside."

The winter sun is bright as we walk the long semicircle sidewalk surrounding three-quarters of the building. Only the front entrance lies beyond the security of the solid wood fence that encloses the facility.

"It's so beautiful," I say. "It'll be even prettier when the bushes and flowers begin to bloom this spring."

"There's lots of cars," she says. "Up there." She points to the parking lot of the adjacent building on the hillside above.

"Yes, but the fence keeps them out."

"And the gate," she adds.

"The gate keeps you safe."

"It doesn't open," she says. She shakes the gate with both hands.

"That's right. It keeps you safe," I repeat.

We reach the end of the semicircle and turn to retrace our steps in the opposite direction.

"And my house?" she asks.

I freeze. Here it is. The beginning of trouble. "It's okay," I say.

"Is there a sign?" she asks, struggling to find the words.

My thirty years of ESL teaching serve me well. I complete her thoughts, her sentences, when words escape her. "No, Mom. There's no sign."

"I mean, is it ..."

"Sold? No, it's not sold."

"Is there anybody there?"

"No, Mom, nobody's there. But, I'd like to use it sometimes if that's okay with you."

"You can have it," she says. "I live here now."

A small table stands in the middle of the large activity room. Sunlight shines bright through the tall windows. White tablecloth.

Folded washcloths. Colorful caddies of nail polish, cold cream, and hair curlers. Chairs form a wide circle around the table. As the clock inches toward 2:00 p.m., these chairs fill, one by one, with residents. Some roll in seated in their own chairs, others enter with walkers, and still others, like my mother, walk with brisk, confident steps. All come with the curiosity of young children, not fully understanding the words: Spa Day. But willing, even eager, for the attention.

This is Mom's first Spa Day. My mother has never, in all her years, visited a spa. Throughout her life, her many years of work and mothering, her nails were short and efficient. Her hair was cut, and at times permed, only to make it easy to handle. With nine kids, anything that simplified life was important.

Was she always this way, my mother? Was there a time in her high school or college days, as a young nurse, as a flight attendant, when she gloried in her beauty, when she pampered her skin, her hair, her nails? When she preened her natural assets?

Who was my mother before she became my mother and slowly lost herself?

It's Mom's turn at the spa table. A headband holds back her silver hair as a young volunteer massages cold cream into her wrinkles.

"Where's my daughter?" I hear her ask as I walk through the open door.

"She's gone to your room for a minute, Sally. She'll be right back."

"I'm here, Mom," I say, a hand on her shoulder. "I was putting your coat away in your room."

"Do you know where my room is? I can show you."

"You showed me, Mom. It's okay. I put your coat there."

"That's good," she says.

She looks up into my eyes, the cold cream glistening in the winter sunlight, her own eyes unshielded by glasses. I see trust and love and confusion.

"Thanks for the nice walk, Mom, but I need to go back to work now." I lie. An innocent lie, I tell myself. A lie that allows me to leave while she is fully occupied, distracted by cold cream and gentle fingers.

I wonder what it would be like to massage cold cream into my mother's face, to feel her skin under my fingers without the plastic surgical gloves worn by the volunteer. Would it make a difference to her? My skin against hers? Would she even know now that my skin, my fingertips, are of her, from her?

I take my mother's hands in mine. Small, birdlike bones. I feel each of them under paper thin, dry skin. Delicate, easily bruised skin. Transparent skin. I remember years before, when I was living in Venezuela, I was called *La Rana Platanera* – the banana frog – a tropical species with such transparent skin that the inner workings of the body are visible to the naked eye. Or so I was told. My blue veins showing through thin, white skin earned me a nickname that I now gift to my mother's hands. The hands of a *rana platanera*.

I feel her small hands in mine, and I remember the pudgy soft hands of my daughter. Now that she is an adult, my daughter and I don't hold hands. Now her fingers are long and slender, no longer the pudgy, chubby fingers of a toddler. Now she has rounded, sometimes polished nails, no longer the French acrylics of her early teens.

I've never seen artificial color on my mother's nails. Trimmed short in her years of nursing and mothering, these ten nails have now grown long and hard, almost claw-like. A novelty for a woman who never had nails. Difficult to cut and file. The chore had become overwhelming for her, and yet she would not allow me to do it for her or to take her for a manicure.

Now it is different. Now it's spa day. Now my mother has long pink fingernails.

"This is my sister," she tells the volunteer, who continues to massage cold cream into her skin.

"Your daughter?" the volunteer responds.

"Yes," I say.

Then I lean forward and wrap my mother in my arms, fearful of hugging too tight, of bruises and broken bones. "I'll see you soon, Mom," I say. "I love you."

"I love you, too," she says.

I hurry toward the exit and enter the code that allows me to leave, fearful her comfort level is temporary, that at some point she'll decide she's tired of this game and want to go home.

But then, maybe not. Maybe she's relieved. Free of fear, surrounded by warm, gentle caregivers, no longer bearing the weight of responsibility.

Maybe her words in the garden an hour earlier are her new truth.

᠊ᜌ   ᜌ᠊

I key my way into Mom's new home in the early afternoon of an unusually warm, early spring day. I walk the wide halls encircling the center square of the single-story building. The doors to each of the four houses are blocked open to improve air circulation. I make my way to the large activity room expecting to find a semicircle of residents engaged in some type of game or activity, singing or maybe just watching a movie on the large, flat screen television.

But as I enter the large room, I find it empty, not a single elderly soul to be seen. I move on to the next room, a smaller gathering room with long tables for puzzles, cards, bingo, crafts. There I find a handful of women with one of the activities coordinators, but no Mom. I retrace my steps. I check the dining room and the small sitting room. Still no Mom. When I reach her room, I give a gentle rap and try to turn the knob. Locked. I didn't even know the doors locked. Later one of the caregivers assures me they can easily open any of the doors with a straight pin or nail. But at that particular moment, I am surprised and concerned. After a few more tries and a few louder knocks, I feel those little hairs on the back of my neck, the alert of panic. Where the hell is my mother?

And then the door opens. My mother stands before me in a long-sleeved, bright-red fleece sweater smoothing her hair with one hand and rubbing the sleep out of her eyes with the other.

"Oh," she says.

"I'm sorry, Mom," I say. "I didn't mean to wake you. I didn't know."

Know what? That my eighty-four-year-old mother naps like a two-year-old every afternoon between lunch and dinner? I wonder how long she sleeps. I wonder if she dreams, what she dreams, where her mind goes when she is asleep. I wonder if she has the night terrors that haunted my own two-year-old so long ago.

"It's okay," she says.

"I was wondering if you'd like to go out for a drive, Mom. It's a beautiful day," I say as I walk into her stuffy bedroom.

"Okay," she says. "But I have to go to the bathroom."

"And you probably need a short-sleeved shirt. It's warm out there."

"Really?"

"Yup."

"But I'm cold."

"You won't be outside." I pull a shirt from her closet and hand it to her as she enters the bathroom. "Put that on, Mom. You can put a sweater over the top if you get cold."

A few minutes later, she's ready. "Let's go have an adventure," I say.

"Do you have a car?" Mom asks.

"Sure do."

"I don't have one."

"Well, it's a good thing I do, then." I dangle the keys in front of her like a dog treat in front of a hungry hound. "What'd you think? Do you want to go out for a drive?"

"I don't have a car," she says.

I take her hand, and we walk out to the parking lot.

"I'm hot," she says.

"Yup," I say with a laugh. "It's a hot day in Seattle."

"Is this your Dad's car?" she asks.

"Nope, it's mine."

"Did I tell Mom where I was going?"

"Yup, they know we're going on an adventure."

I head toward the small waterfront town of Edmonds thinking she'll enjoy the familiarity of the beach, the waves rolling up the sand and the gulls overhead.

"Do they know where I am?"

"Yup, we told them we'd be back by dinnertime."

"Okay."

After several false turns, I find my way into Edmonds and pull into a parking spot facing the beach. The spring sunlight dances on the cold water of Puget Sound as a ferry docks at the terminal. We count cars as they stream off the large boat.

"Did we tell them?"

"Yes, Mom. We told them. Are you ready for a cup of tea?"

She looks confused. "Tea? But I don't have any."

"That's okay. We can get some."

"But I don't have any." She pats her pockets, looks at the floor of the car and around her seat.

"Money?" I ask.

"Yes."

"No worries. I've got money."

"But I don't have anything."

"It's my treat."

I maneuver into another perfect parking spot just across from a corner coffee shop and the beautiful little Edmonds water fountain. As we settle into a cozy corner with warm tea between us, I know the time is right. I know I need to try one last time to understand this woman who is my mother. With a deep breath, I begin.

"I'm writing another book, Mom," I tell her, knowing full well she has no memory of the first book I wrote or of the conversation we had a few years before in the Westport pizza restaurant when I told her I was writing about Maureen.

"That's nice," she says.

"It's about you."

"Me? Why me?"

"Well," I stammer. "Because you're my mom, you know, and because I like to write."

"Okay," she says. My confusion seems to satisfy her, so I forge on.

"I was wondering, Mom, what's really, really important? What should I be sure to include in this story about you?"

I know I can't ask her what she remembers. I can't use that dreaded word. Instead, I stick to *important*. "What's important to you, Mom," I repeat. "What's been important in your life?"

I watch as her expression changes, as a distance enters her face. She is far away from me, from the little coffee shop. She relaxes into the high-backed, velvet chair, her head tilted back, her eyes to the ceiling.

"Oh, I don't think about that." There is a long pause before she continues. "I don't know. It's been a good life."

We sit in silence for a long while enjoying those few words, the warmth of our tea and the spring sunshine, the faint sounds of water flowing in the fountain beyond the window, and the rich heady fragrance of freshly ground coffee. She stares into the world above her as I wait in silence, unsure if she will say anything more and unwilling to interrupt her thoughts.

"Did we tell Mom where we were going?" she asks.

"Yes, we told them we'd be back by dinner." And I know, in that moment, we will never again speak of this story I am writing.

"Where's the car?" she asks as I help her from her chair.

"Right there, at the curb."

"The red one?"

I look up and down the street. There's no red car anywhere to be seen. "Nope," I say. "The green one. Or is it blue? What do you think, Mom? I never know what to call it."

"Blue," she says. "Blue's my best color."

"So, now we have to figure out how to get back," I say as I hold the car door and she sinks into the seat, clinging to the window for support.

I drive out of Edmonds and head north on Highway 99, but somehow I forget the cross street. Is it 188th or 148th or 128th? Numbers. I think of myself as numerically challenged, but as I struggle to remember names as well, I fear I am becoming my mother. I push the thought from my head and arbitrarily take a right turn on 148th. After numerous false turns on endless residential streets that seem to curl back onto themselves, I pull to a stop and look at my mother.

"I have no idea where we are. I think we're lost."

"Lost," she echoes.

"Yeah, but it's all part of the adventure, right? I know if I keep heading this way, we'll hit Interstate 5, then we'll be able to figure it out." I consider pulling out my phone and using the GPS to get us back on track but decide against it. Meandering seems like much more fun.

"Okay," Mom says. "You're a good driver."

"I had good teachers."

"Who?"

"You and Dad taught me, remember? In the riding ring."

I realize my mistake before the word is out of my mouth. Like a slap in the face, I used the word *remember*. I tested her memory. She clams up, desperately trying to remember. I keep talking, determined to explain away her confusion.

"I drove around and around and around in circles in the horse riding ring at the first Issaquah house. Sometimes I drove with you and sometimes with Dad until I was good enough to go on the road. Crap. Should we go left or right? What'd you think?"

"That way," she says, a finger pointing to the left. "Did Dad teach me to drive, too?"

"Maybe," I say. My heart is heavy with the knowledge that my dad, her husband, her dad, my grandfather, have all become one in her muddled memory.

"Now we're really lost," I say.

"Oh good," she laughs.

"I hope you don't miss dinner."

"I'm not hungry," she says. "You make me laugh."

"Good. Now if I can just find a way out of here."

Just then, I see the interstate crossing over the road ahead of us. "Hoorah! Now I sort of know where I am," I say, and Mom claps her appreciation. "North or south? Are we too far north or too far south? I guess we'll head north."

"Okay," she says.

"Wrong again," I say a few minutes later when the large green Everett sign looms overhead. "How'd we get this far north? I could've sworn we were too far south."

"I don't know," she says. "You're driving."

I steal a glance in her direction as I stop at the foot of the off-ramp and prepare to make a U-turn. She is smiling, a huge mischievous grin painted across her wrinkles. A few minutes later I take the correct exit and, in moments, pull to a stop in front of her building.

"Home, sweet home," I say.

❧   ❧

I am alone in Mom's house, tired after spending the better part of yesterday sorting and cleaning. I barely made a dent in one room, her bedroom. This is a huge, sad job. There is so much here to sort – charity, trash, storage – all layered with memories. Fifty years of marriage. Eighty years of life for Dad, eighty four and counting for Mom.

It feels intrusive digging through Mom's underwear drawer, her closet, deciding which pile or large black plastic bag her possessions belong in. But she is gone; the woman who lived that life in this house, is gone. She will never return to this house. She does not remember the physical possessions left behind. And, of course, they no longer matter.

How much do I do here? How many decisions do I make without Doreen? I see myself trying to make this place my own, making it clean and comfortable for myself, and that's dangerous. Tom and I may not be able to buy it. We may not want to buy it. So for now, I turn it into a bare, clean vacation home – ready for rental, though likely never to be rented. A place for any of the siblings, not just me, to come and spend a weekend at the beach, though I know I am the only one with any strong interest in doing so.

This means clearing out all the old junk, the accumulation of old clothes, linens, and kitchenware as well as what is just plain trash. At the same time, most of the furniture will be left where it stands. Then there's the how. How to remove truckloads of charity items and trash? Can I do this alone? I don't want to ask for help. I wish Doreen were coming alone to join me, but I know she will come with her husband, and I realize this will not be a sister-bonding process. It's just work to Doreen, and she has other things she'd rather be doing. She has no desire to spend weekends in Grayland this summer, or ever.

I want the space, the house, the beach. I want to spend hours, weeks sitting here writing. Where would I set up a desk? Maybe no desk at all. Maybe just the kitchen table at the beach until the house must be sold. Spring 2010. That's what Doreen's got in mind for a sell date. One year to decide if Tom and I want or are able to hold onto this place, to decide if the emotional attachment is worth the investment, if it could become the writing retreat and artist studio Tom and I would both love to own. One year to determine what we want and what we are willing and able to spend. I see a summer of split weeks: Monday to Thursday here. Friday to Sunday in Seattle. Weekends in Seattle so I can go to writing practice at Louisa's Café on Fridays and the Uptown on Sundays, and because Tom and Erin might have time off. Maybe sometimes they'll join me here at the beach, and I won't go home at all. I lose track of time here alone. The sun rises and sets in silence, and it hardly matters at all. There are few clocks in the house and fewer that function. The windows are open to the late winter chill, and the air carries the smells of salt and sea. I feel no desire to leave.

I lie in bed, in what was my mother's bed, and I remember all the visits, seven years of visits. Every evening we would watch a Hallmark Hall of Fame movie, eat our bowls of ice cream, and go to bed. Mom would fuss with the thermostat and check the doors twice, three times. I'd be in the guest bedroom, window wide open to the November rain, the December gales off the beach. I'd read and wait, a half hour, sometimes an hour, until I was certain Mom was asleep. Then, I'd sneak out of the bedroom and down the hall to the thermostat without making a sound. With a tiny backpacker's flashlight, I'd readjust the thermostat. I'd be tempted to move the lever from far right maximum heat where Mom would leave it, too far left. But I never did, never could. After all, this was my mother's house. Instead, I'd lower the setting to a reasonable seventy degrees and tiptoe back to bed. By early morning I'd awaken in an oven. I'd get up to find the thermostat back up to the max and know Mom had beaten me at my own game. Did she really get so cold in the night? Did the cold of a seventy-degree house awaken her? Or was she simply unable to sleep and once awake and wandering her tiny home in a thin nightgown, she'd grow cold and push up the thermostat before returning to bed – a bed heavy with multiple down comforters? My sister and I would debate this, unable to decide if we were being cruel in lowering the house temperature each night. Mom would deny ever touching the thermostat or even getting up at night, so trying to get to the bottom of the question was a useless waste of words. It is a riddle without an answer.

Now Mom lives in a small room at the end of a long hall of small rooms. She still has a thermostat that she often pushes too high, but now she complains of being too hot. Today my mother eats three meals a day and can no longer fit into the clothes we took with her when we moved her into her new home. Now she has a new wardrobe to accommodate her growing girth. Now my mother doesn't walk the halls at night checking that the doors and windows are locked. Now my mother feels safe.

I wonder sometimes if we waited too long, if we should have forced her kicking and screaming to move sooner. Well, not kicking and screaming. That was not Mom's style. Simple stern refusal was her style. Or denial. When we finally made the move, we tricked her. We were deceptive. Did we wait too long? Did we leave her fearful and cold and stubbornly determined for too long? Perhaps. But then again, how does one judge the progress of dementia and how much sooner would she have been accepted in her new home? If we'd forced her to move sooner, would she have adjusted with the grace she has shown, would she have found the peace and happiness she now enjoys?

Just as the riddle of the late night, early morning thermostat changes will never be solved, the question of the perfect moment for Mom's last move has no answer.

While cleaning out an old file cabinet the night before, Doreen's husband found Mom's nursing school diploma as well as a letter regarding a furlough from United Airlines dated January 1945. The offices would be moving to Denver headquarters. Would Mom be returning?

I want to keep both documents and who knows how many more that are now in secure storage. I want to read and process and understand the lives of these people who were my parents. Who were they before they had nine children? Who did they become when we grew up, left home, and were gone from their lives?

So many pieces of memory – photographs, letters, jewelry. This house is full of memories. Does Doreen trust me to be here with these memories? Does Doreen know I will write of these memories? I remember the compromise we reached when we agreed to disagree about my decision to write memoir.

"But you need to know I will continue to write," I said.

"I don't want to know about it," she said.

So I do not talk to her about my writing, about the publications that followed *The Thirty-Ninth Victim*, about this manuscript.

It was my idea to open the file cabinet last night. She was ready to leave it here. Her concern, her responsibility as Mom's power-of-attorney and executor, was the cataloging and packing of all valuable items for future sale or distribution.

As we pack, Mom is alive so this talk feels strange – to be discussing estate before death. But I believe it is essential. What can be sold to support her, if necessary? The value must be assessed, just as it must be for this peaceful, quiet little shambles of a house. But what is the value of letters, photographs, documents?

I need an escape. I have to get down to the beach before I leave. I have to walk and smell and see. I have to say hello to Maureen.

~ ~

There was a time in the early 1980s, just after my sister's disappearance, just after wandering for the better part of the prior decade from California to Venezuela, Hawaii to Mexico, that I taught at a private English-language school in Seattle. There, during my last month of employment, I met Claudia. A former student, we have been friends ever since.

It was Claudia who first discovered The Pink Door on Post Alley just above Pike Place Market, and introduced it to me. An Italian restaurant with an outdoor dining area and a tiny bar with exposed red brick walls and bistro tables, it reminded Claudia of her hometown in Switzerland. On summer evenings the overhead trellis on the deck was strung with tiny colored lights and a soft sea breeze floated up from Elliott Bay. We could see West Seattle and the islands in the distance.

Married and living on the other side of the country, Claudia has visited often through the years. Her daughter, Rebecca, was born only a year after Erin, and from the time they were toddlers, we've taken "our girls" to The Pink Door and regaled them with stories of our long-ago adventures. What has been a favorite of mine for years has become my daughter's as well. So, it's no surprise that in early May, when I ask Erin where she wants to celebrate her twentieth birthday, she says, "The Pink Door."

A week later, Tom, Erin and I enter the restaurant from above, descending the steep stairwell into another world. We sit at a corner table in the eclectic, candle-lit room, the ceiling so high an aerial acrobat performs above us. The warm, old-world style sienna walls are covered with sepia photographs, heavy oils, mirrors in gilded frames. A fountain of concrete cherubs claims the center of the dining room challenging the aerial acrobat for air space, and the fragrances of Italy waft from the kitchen – oregano and thyme, garlic and tomato.

My baby is twenty years old today, and I am filled with relief. I know my fears have been unfounded and perhaps pathetic, but they plagued me for twenty years. Maureen was murdered just before her own twentieth birthday. For twenty years, especially the last five or six, I was haunted by a deep, irrational fear, a constant reminder. Like most mothers of teenage daughters, I hoped that she would make safe decisions, gather supportive friends, and meet decent young men. Unlike other mothers, I feared my daughter would make some inconceivably stupid mistake, the kind of mistake Maureen had made, one that would lead to her death.

But now I lift my glass to my daughter to toast her twentieth birthday and a heavy weight lifts from my shoulders. I sprout wings and fly. She has survived. She is safe. She is not Maureen.

જ ૯

Mom sees us walking the hall toward her. There's a slight wave of her hand, a bit of recognition, I think. Or perhaps just a natural response to my own wave. She disappears into the dining room. We are only a momentary interruption. Someone else has her attention. We follow her, but there's nobody there, the dining room is empty but for my mother. What shadow, what ghost has she followed?

"Hi, Mom," I say. "Look, I've brought you a surprise." I see confusion in her eyes and pull my niece closer to my side. "This is your granddaughter. Remember your oldest son, Robert? This is his daughter." I hear *remember* slip from my lips again and curse myself. I can almost see a physical reaction.

"Of course, I know who she is," she says as my niece leans over, her long slender arms encasing her grandmother in a tight hug.

"Hi Granma," she says. "How are you?"

My mother steps back and turns to me. I see the confusion that remains in her eyes. "Robert's daughter. She's all grown up now, isn't she?" I say. I give her the name.

I remember Erin as a baby, a toddler. I remember naming the objects, the people, in our small world. Giving her words to repeat, to learn, to store in her lifelong memory. I give my mother her granddaughter's name again knowing I will need to repeat it again and then again throughout our afternoon together.

"Will you show us your room?" I ask.

"Okay," Mom says.

I take Mom's arm and turn her in the appropriate direction. As we walk, we pass a man clearly lost in his own anger.

"Isn't that your new friend, Mom?" I ask.

"He's mad at me," Mom says.

"Why?"

She shrugs her shoulders, a slight gesture of confusion and resignation.

"Did something happen?" I push a bit more, but Mom remains quiet. I remember my last visit when the two of them were walking the hall together talking in opposite directions, but still talking, a certain familiarity and comfort between them. This man now stomping past, muttering his angry muddled thoughts, seems like a different person. I feel as confused as Mom.

We continue our slow walk and arrive at Mom's room. Again, the show-and-tell routine: her bed, her closet, her family in photographs along the wall. This time I find clothing that is not Mom's on her hangers and in her drawers. I find a man's wedding ring that does not belong to my father on her dresser. I accept that clothes, towels, photographs float from room to room in a dementia care facility like germs in a hospital, but the wedding ring I slip into my pocket to leave at the front desk. It must be returned to the family of the owner now unaware of both its emotional and financial value. I don't realize then, don't make the mental leap needed to consider the two rings on my mother's fingers.

We stand for a moment, three of us in her tiny room with nothing more to see. "April showers bring May flowers, right Mom? I guess we can't go for a walk outside. Can you show us the activity room? Maybe we can work on a puzzle."

Again, we pass the angry, muttering man in the hall. He is wearing bedroom sleepers and is wet from having gone out in the rain without coat or shoes. His face is contorted from what looks like a lifetime of anger. I cannot understand what happened to the gentle smiling man I saw only a week earlier.

"He's mad at me," my mother repeats. But I am at a loss to understand what could have happened to cause such a change, what Mom could have done.

We enter the activity room and find a few residents at a long table working on puzzles, struggling with the large child-sized pieces just as they struggle with lost words and memories.

"He's mad at me," Mom repeats in a soft voice, heavy with sadness and guilt.

"I don't think so Mom," I say. "It looks like he's just mad at the whole world. At life itself."

"No, it's my fault," she says.

My niece puts her long arms around Mom's shoulders and redirects. "Do you want to do a puzzle, Granma?"

"Okay," she says.

"Give me a minute," I tell my niece. "I saw someone in the nurse's office. I'll be right back."

I hurry down the hall and poke my head in the door of the small office and dispensary. "Can I have a word with you?" I ask an on-duty nurse who I do not recognize.

"Sure, I'm Nurse Colleen," she says.

"I'm Sally's daughter, Arleen. I'm also a college teacher, so I understand the legal limitations on what you can and cannot tell me about my mother and the other residents, but clearly something has happened here in the past week, and it's affecting my mother."

"What do you mean?" she asks.

At that moment, the disheveled, angry man could be seen walking through the garden in the rain. "Only last week, Mom and that gentleman were walking and talking and laughing like old buddies. Now he's stomping around in an angry stew, and Mom can't stop repeating, 'He's mad at me.' She feels totally responsible for his change in behavior. I need to know what happened."

"Nothing happened," Nurse Colleen says. "Nothing has happened to cause your mother to feel responsible for his behavior. It's just who she is. Both of them, all of the residents, play out past memories and patterns of behavior."

"So nothing specific happened to make Mom feel she caused the change?"

"No, nothing your mother is responsible for," she says.

"Then I need help convincing her of that because she is swimming in a sea of guilt right now."

"Okay, I'll see what I can do to assure her she's not responsible, and I'll get all her caregivers to do so as well."

"Thank you," I say. I walk back to the activity room unsure as to what, if anything, I've achieved. I wonder if it's true, if Mom is playing out long-learned patterns of behavior. If so, how many times did she take responsibility for Dad's bouts of anger and depression throughout their fifty years of marriage?

I think about my own relationships with Tom and Erin. Like Mom, I often feel responsible, feel as though I've done something wrong, if they are grumpy in the early morning or in a foul mood at the end of a long day. I think about how often, when I ask them what's wrong, I assume their anger is directed toward me.

As I walk into the activity room, I see my mother and niece sitting next to each other working on a puzzle, Mom's blouse buttons pulling tight across her rounding belly, and I feel a surge of love.

I hold a new awareness, a gut-level awareness that I have to learn what my mother never learned – to allow others their range of emotions without assuming I am always responsible for their behavior.

ॐ ॐ

I am alone in Grayland, only my second visit since we moved Mom. My big plans for spending the summer here, for making this little house my summer writers' retreat have not materialized. No decisions have been made yet, but the writing is on the wall. I cannot deny that writing or the emotion it carries. I remember the conversation with Tom only a few days before.

"It was their dream, your mom and dad's dream," he says. "It's not our dream. We need to build our own dreams."

"I know," I say.

"And I don't want another project, another house to fix up and maintain. That place is a mess."

"It's not so bad. We could just keep it as is for a while."

"Until it crumbles around us? No way."

"Stop exaggerating," I say.

"Look, I know the beach is important to you, but ask yourself this: if it weren't your parents' place, is it the house and location you'd choose?"

I think a lot about Tom's question, but it's hard to separate the two – the house from the memories, from the need for connection. Even a fragile connection is better than none at all. I don't give in right away, but I do limit my visits, unwilling to allow myself deeper attachment, knowing that with each visit, I will want to hold on tighter.

Now, I sit in my mother's kitchen and let my imagination fly. The blue would have to go. I'm not a big fan of blue décor. The blue carpet and blue patterned linoleum and blue countertops would be replaced, the walls repainted. In fact, this wall, the wall between the kitchen and the living room could be taken down to create a bar separating the two small areas. New, bigger windows in the front and maybe French doors from the bedrooms into the large backyard.

He's right. He knows it would be another huge project. A project we cannot afford. A project he doesn't have the time, energy, or interest in pursuing. We must choose, and this house is not my husband's choice. But is it mine? That's the question I struggle to answer as I sit at the kitchen table sipping morning coffee, my manuscript spread before me, like the house, a feeble attempt to understand the past, to cling to a past, now gone, carried out by the morning tide.

After several hours of writing, I spend the remainder of the day emptying closets, cupboards, boxes from the attic. I find a long family history in letters, pictures, and childhood mementos of my parents' nine children and extended family. Old, tattered papers that carry the must and decay of many years. There are nine piles on the hearth, one for each of my parents' children. I sort through the memories my mother has saved – baby books, report cards, school photos, pottery handprints, construction paper silhouettes. I place each item in the appropriate pile. Laureen's report cards and baby book on her pile. Robert's letters from Hawaii, held together with now-brittle rubber bands, on his pile. Photographs of both Charleen and her children go onto her pile.

I move slowly. I do not read the letters, though I am pulled by powerful temptation, the temptation of an archeologist choosing not to disturb a sacred burial site. The temptation of a writer. I know I have no right to invade my siblings' privacy so I only glance at the letters and cards each of them sent home through the years, scan to find a name, nothing more. A lifetime of letters and cards I never imagined my mother had saved. Fifty years and nine kids' worth of memories, moved from house to house. How many times? Five, six houses? Six moves?

And if I am confessing here, I also need to say I do not allow myself to read all these bits of memory, of family history, these letters and cards, because I know if I give myself permission, if I let my hand reach into that cookie jar, I risk losing all self restraint, and without setting some limits for myself, the writer will take over, the writer will tell my siblings' stories. Stories I have no right to tell.

ॐ ॐ

The front door swings open at about 9:30 Sunday morning. Erin, pillow under her arm and tears in her eyes, pushes her way into the living room.

"Hi, honey," Tom says. "What's up?"

"I can't stand it anymore," she wails.

We sit in the living room, tears tracking Erin's soft cheeks as she tells of her roommate problems, of waking at 4:00 a.m. to voices on her porch trash-talking her in slurs, of cigarette smoke wafting through her bedroom window. She tells us she waited in her bedroom until the apartment was quiet and then she snuck out, passed her roommate's friends crashed on her fold-out sofa in the living room. "My apartment is trashed from their all-night party," she cries.

We listen to our daughter and help her formulate a plan for dealing with the situation, and all the while, in the back of my mind, I hear that tiny voice telling me I'm a fraud, an imposter. I pretend to be a good, solid, grounded mother with not only comfort, but also good advice to offer. But what do I know? I always lived alone or with a man. I never shared an apartment with girlfriends. Only once, my first year in college at Seattle University, I shared a tiny dorm room with three other girls. But I discard that memory. It doesn't count. I was too lost, too much a loner, to share more than the basic words of necessity with those girls. I don't even remember their names.

This is different. Erin's roommate is a girl she considers a close friend. I want to wrap my twenty-year-old daughter in my arms and comfort her as I could when she was two, but now the problems are more complicated, and she needs to find her own solutions. Now I can offer little more than my love and her old bedroom to crash in until her lease ends next month.

A few weeks later, I sit in the downtown Medical Dental building. Erin's been taken in for oral surgery to remove all four wisdom teeth. I wait and worry. She's been terrified and grumpy since I woke her at 6:35 a.m. Her first words: "No, I don't want to." She was sleeping in her old bedroom, Churchill at her side. I didn't realize my daughter still sleeps with her stuffed doggy from childhood, now threadbare from love. A companion through all her pains – physical and emotional – Churchill has given her years of comfort. Before Churchill there was a series of smaller pound puppies. Tom and I tried to keep two around, switching them out when they needed to be laundered or when we lost one, so Erin was never without. I can still see my baby girl, right thumb in her mouth holding her pound puppy by the ear, rubbing the soft plush under her nose. The comfort of textures and smells, a sponge to absorb her tears. Today Churchill has a big job. I hope his powers are strong.

Two weeks pass, but I'm not paying attention, I'm not watching as closely as I need to watch, thinking my daughter is no longer a child, no longer in need of a mothering, watchful eye. Only when we return for the two-week post-op, when Erin repeats that the lower left side of her face still hurts as she has the day before and the day before that, only when the nurse comments on the slight swelling which I am embarrassed to admit I have not observed, do I see her pain.

I see it in the tension in her face and shoulders when the oral surgeon tells her she has two choices: another week of amoxicillin to see if it will control the infection or reopen the wound and flush out any debris that might be causing the infection.

"What's the best?" Erin asks.

"Well, there's no guarantee the antibiotics will control the infection if there is foreign matter caught under the healed skin," the surgeon tells her.

"So, you mean I could come back next week, and you'd still have to open it, and I'd be on a third week of antibiotics?" she asks.

"Yes," he says. "There's a good chance that could happen."

"Then do it now," she says.

When the doctor turns to talk to his nurse, Erin searches my face for approval. I nod in agreement to assure her I support her decision. Just get it over with – a philosophy we share. Erin has never had a cavity, never had an injection of Novocain. I know the injection is going into already sensitive swollen tissue. I know my daughter is hypersensitive. I know it will hurt like hell.

I wait in the outer office my stomach in knots, my own jaw in pain. Twenty, thirty minutes later, Erin pushes her way out, eyes red, tear-stained make-up smudges at the corners. I stand to embrace her, and she pushes me aside. She has pulled inward, her defensive wall high. A fortress of protection, of self-preservation that has always pained me as I feel shut out and unable to help even while I admire her ability to garner personal strength. We stand, side-by-side, not touching as we make another follow-up appointment, checking my work schedule against hers to find a time when I can come with her. As the receptionist hands Erin the appointment card, I see the tremor in my daughter's outstretched hand. We head to the underground parking lot of the Medical Dental building.

"It hurts so bad," she whimpers as soon as the elevator door close behind us, and we are alone. Like my mother, my daughter is unwilling to show emotion before the curious eyes of strangers.

"Isn't it numb?" I ask.

"No. He gave me like four shots. But I still felt everything."

I cringe, remembering my own nightmare of dental work, my own resistance to Novocain. I remember learning, finally, to request extra injections and to demand that they wait long enough for the medication to take effect. My daughter didn't have the body of experience she needed to ask for another injection or more time. Meanwhile I was sitting in the waiting room doing nothing to help her. I feel like the worst mother in the world.

"Can we get my medicine first, Mom?

"Of course," I say.

She waits in the car as I wait for Vicodin and Amoxicillin. The week before, she vomited Percocet after cutting her leg open on the corner of a mirror while moving into yet another new apartment. But Vicodin she knows. She tolerated it six months earlier after a car accident. An accident she walked away from with little more than some serious bruising and back pain, to the surprise of firefighters and tow truck drivers alike. She knows Vicodin works.

My cell rings as I stand in line at the pharmacy counter.

"Mom, it hurts."

"I'll be right there. Hold on, Sweetpea." I rush out of the store with a water bottle and painkillers. She pops one in the car on an empty stomach.

"Mom, I'm starving, but I can't eat."

"How about some soup at Lee's?"

I see us seated at the restaurant. I watch the tremor in her hands as she holds the menu, the tension in her face, the tightness in her shoulders. And I watch the transformation. I see the Vicodin take hold, her shoulders relax. The tone of her skin seems to change. She eats a warm bowl of wonton soup, and we go home where she crawls into bed to sleep away her suffering on a cloud of Vicodin. As I go about my afternoon chores in silence, I wonder about pain and my own inability to protect my daughter from the inevitability of pain, all kinds of pain, she will face in life.

∽ ∾

With a six-pack of blooming pink and lavender petunias in hand, I visit Mom. A project. Something to do together, to remain in the now. It's hard to have a conversation with someone who has no past. How can you give a family update? Tell about Tom's job, Erin's new apartment, the curriculum writing project that's monopolizing every working moment of my life? How can we talk about my siblings, her children, who she no longer remembers? A husband she doesn't recognize in the photos that line the walls of her tiny bedroom at the dementia care facility she now calls home, no longer remembering the beach home she fought so long against leaving.

So I take my six-pack of petunias in one hand and my mother in the other and lead her to one of the raised gardens adorning the patios. Raised to the perfect height, built to the perfect width for those whose aged joints no longer allow kneeling or bending.

My mother digs tiny holes and dutifully plants the tiny flowers. "Right here?" she asks.

"Perfect," I say.

"Is this okay?"

"Looks good to me."

"No more," she says. She pats the dirt around the last plant and drops her shovel. Then, she lifts the black plastic container, turns it upside down and gives it a shake to be sure.

"No more," she repeats and wanders away from me.

It isn't the "No more" of younger, earlier years. Years when she was the kind of mother who said little but who got our attention with short two-word commands. Years when "No more" meant do it again and there'd be trouble. I never knew what kind of trouble. Not until much later, as a young adult, as I began to understand what trouble meant and how my parents responded to trouble. No, these words my mother utters now are not the words of the mother she once was. Instead, they are the words of a confused child. More a question than a statement. Certainly not a command.

I stand for a moment and watch. I don't see the gray hair and chubby, short body of my eighty-four-year-old mother, but the blond curls and tiny body of my daughter at two as she wanders away from the flower garden we are planting in search of other adventures in the large garden of our tiny rental home.

And I see a clay tennis court, hot and dry, built into the Oaxacan hillside with wide stone on both sides to serve as bleachers. The ever-present bougainvillea trails the stone walls that wrap the ends of the courts to catch wayward balls. I see Dad and Mom in pale blue and white, my mother with a visor shielding her eyes from the bright sunshine. I hear my father cheering me on each time I slam the ball to the line, and my boyfriend fails to return it.

My parents are visiting me in Mexico City. We've gone on a weekend trip to visit Mayan ruins. I'm playing tennis with a boyfriend, and I beat him. Dad thinks it's great, but then I wasn't beating him. He hates the role this boyfriend is playing in his visit with me, so my beating him is a bit of pleasure he relishes, laughing his head off at the boyfriend's loss of macho pride. The game ends. Dad slaps the boyfriend on the back. "Come on," he says. "I'll buy you a beer."

My mother pulls me aside as we all walk back to the hotel lobby for cold drinks. I remember it as clear as if it were yesterday. Crystal clear because it is the only advice my mother ever gave me about boyfriends, about boys, love, sex, or anything remotely related. Her voice is soft, almost a whisper. "You have to let him win sometimes," she says.

I scoff, full of young arrogance. "No way. If he can't beat me, it's his problem. I'm not going to let anybody beat me just to make them feel good."

I don't know if the boyfriend hears my words. In my arrogant insensitivity, I don't care. In the end, it doesn't matter. The boyfriend abandons us in Guadalajara less than a week later without so much as a goodbye. I am heartbroken. But I still disagree with my mother's advice. I know it is the clandestine immigration trail from Nicaragua through Mexico to Florida that causes this abrupt departure, not my beating him at tennis. But that's not the point either.

The point is that once, just once, my mother ventures to give me some advice, and in my young arrogance, I squash any chance of further communication. I don't honor my mother or her opinion, and as a result, the lines of communication are severed. I suppose one could argue she is the mother and I am the daughter, that it's too little, too late as I am already in my twenties. Still, it remains a memory of the one time Mom tries to talk to me, and I shut her down. I show her no respect. A regret, I suppose. A regret of no value and no resolution because now my mother has no memory of anything at all. I am the keeper of the memories that remain. The memories of the life we have shared. Now we plant petunias in a garden belonging to neither of us.

⤜ ⤛

I throw my overnight bag in the backseat. My backpack and laptop. I head south on Interstate 5 for my third and final visit to my parents' Grayland home. I will meet Doreen and her husband at the beach house. The house has sold as is, furniture and junk included, but still we must decide what we want to keep, what to put in storage for the day when Mom is gone and the final distribution of her belongings must occur.

It's Saturday morning. Tom is working again, always working, so I go alone, knowing I need to be alone for a while. How long I don't know. I need to be away from Tom. It's easier I tell myself. Later I tell him. It's easier to be lonely alone than lonely under the same roof of a shared home. So, I climb into my old Subaru with tears in my eyes, thinking I'm leaving for the weekend, knowing I have no reason to return, no time limit, nothing pressing to attend to until fall quarter begins in mid-September.

I leave Seattle in plenty of time to get to Grayland and have a few minutes alone in the house with the spirits of my father and the woman my mother once was. But I dawdle, as is my custom, my history on every drive to Grayland, every visit I've made for the past seven, now closer to eight, years since Dad's death. I stop at Top Foods in Olympia. I need gas. I want a latte. I buy some fruit for the house. "The refrigerator isn't working, so don't bring a bunch of food," Doreen has told me. I buy three bright, scented candles that are now in the bag for charity in my living room, the bag full of items from my mother's house. I buy these candles to dawdle, nothing more. The scent, sickly sweet, is overwhelming.

I drive another hour, a headache forming from the candle scent. I stop again, this time in Aberdeen. For seven years this is the stop I have made. Ross Dress for Less. I shop. I buy something I don't need. Something I would usually return on my next drive to Grayland, but there won't be another drive. The Nike Running top is mine to keep. Later, I wear it on the beach, collecting stones and sand dollars, saying goodbye to Maureen and Dad.

I move the scented candles into the trunk and drive the final half hour to my mother's house. The front gate is open, my sister's car already in the driveway. I park and enter the house to find her and her husband deep in conversation with Larry, the neighbor who has purchased my parents' home.

"Looks like a done deal," Doreen says, a wide smile of relief spreading across her face.

"You came alone?" Larry asks, craning to see behind me, to see if Tom is with me.

"Yup, just me," I say, trying to find some happiness to inject into my voice, trying to block the rising sense of sadness and loss that hits me like a Pacific wave.

"Should all be finalized soon," Larry says. Perhaps he misinterprets my expression. I don't know. I can't stomach the celebratory tone. I nod and walk down the hall with the pretense of putting away my bags. Alone, the tears erupt. I lean against the hallway wall, listening to their final arrangements. As power-of-attorney and executor, Doreen makes the decisions Mom can no longer make. The house must be sold to pay for her care. I understand this. The house is not a house I would want to buy if not for the emotional ties. As Tom says, it was my parents' dream not ours. We have no desire to leave Seattle, to live in an isolated community on the Pacific Coast. We are spoiled by our specialty markets, quality restaurants, theaters, bookstores, museums. If we were to buy another property, it would be a vacation get-away, nothing more. It would be on the beach, not a block away with no view. Or, at the very least, it would be a two-story cabin with a view of the beach from a lanai large enough for table and chairs. And it would not be on a beach designated a state highway that allows car traffic.

Grayland was Mom and Dad's dream, their retirement, not ours. No, it is not the house or even this beach I mourn, but the end of an era, the end of a generation. It is a connection that is no longer, a connection to the beach that carries my sister's ashes, a beach my parents loved. It is a beach that will someday claim the combined ashes of my mother and father if their wishes are respected in the years ahead.

Larry leaves and Doreen finds me in the hallway wiping tears from my cheeks. "Are you okay?" she asks, unable to hide the surprise in her voice.

"Yeah," I say. "It's just hard, you know."

"Oh, Arleen," she says as she wraps me in an awkward hug. "You shouldn't have come."

"No," I tell her. "I need to be here. I need to say goodbye." But I don't think she understands. Her life story is so different from mine. Four years younger than me, she never left the Seattle area, was never disowned or disconnected from our parents. She never disappointed them, never caused them the pain I caused. Unlike me, Doreen doesn't seem to have holes, wide and gaping, in her relationship with Mom and Dad, in her understanding of these people who were our parents. And where there may be holes, she seems to be able to accept them in a manner I envy.

Doreen and her husband don't stay the night in Grayland. Together we spend Saturday sorting and organizing, but by 10 p.m. they are ready to return to Seattle, eager to wake Sunday morning in their own bed with a day at home stretched out before them.

We still have nine piles on the fireplace hearth, the hearth that no longer holds a wood-burning stove. After one complaint too many from Mom about the mess my father always made building fires, Dad ripped out the stove and moved it to the sun room. The beautiful brick hearth remains bare, a metal picnic plate over the hole that once held a stove pipe.

The nine piles, begun on an earlier visit, now grow and are replaced by boxes, each box labeled with the name of one of the siblings. As we sort through photos and memories, as we remove pictures from the walls, as we read inscriptions on the stacks of books my parents were given through the years, we add to these boxes. That is our decision, our process. We will return everything that pertains to, belongs to, or came from each of the eight living siblings. Anything specific to a sibling – family photos, letters, gifts once given to my parents – must now be returned. Everything else, all the memories, all the history will go into storage for as long as Mom is alive. All else – furniture, linens, dishes, utensils, tools, ladders – is to be sold with the house. I am relieved there will be no need to empty the place, to bring in a dumpster for trash, to carry loads to charity. We do not need to make renovations – get rid of dry rot, put on a new roof, paint. The new owner will do all of it. Now we must only make decisions about what will be saved. Later we'll need to figure out what to do with the items we put into storage. Without a detailed will, with a will that states "divided equally among our eight living children" how do we decide? Who will get Mom's wedding ring? Will the collection of Irish Belleek be broken up? The Galway crystal? The antique tea cups from our great grandparents? These decisions can be left for now.

I push these thoughts away and focus on the nine boxes for nine siblings. Doreen's focus is on the big stuff, the few furniture pieces from our paternal grandmother we've decided to keep. Will the storage unit be large enough? I watch as she and her husband remove the sign that hung above the garage door for decades – *Ray and Sally Feeney* – burned into wood in my father's distinctive handwriting. But I am drawn to the piles and piles of photos and letters we find in closets and cupboards throughout the house. As I sort through years of family history, I label more boxes, but not with family names. These I mark by decade. A box for the 1990s to present, another for the 1970s to 1980s, another for early family stuff from the 1940s to 1970s. And then the really old stuff, the letters and albums and photos of people, faces unknown to me.

I try to organize my work and focus first on the living room. Pictures, then books, checking for gift inscriptions. "With love from Marleen" into the box labeled with her name. No inscription? Leave it? Pack it? Doreen wants to leave behind as much as possible, the house needs to look lived in, ready to move in. She wants the extra funds offered for the lived-in look, another few months of expenses for Mom in dementia care. Every dollar counts, I understand, but still I'm not willing to leave behind more than necessary. I don't want to sell or donate the objects of my parents' daily life, the things that filled every home my parents ever lived in. The dining table and chairs, the matching china hutch and serving cart, all from my childhood. Pieces my parents collected one by one because they could never afford to buy a complete dining set all at once. High-quality Early American maple furniture none of their children have expressed a desire to keep, so Doreen and I must decide. Sell it with the house or put it in storage?

For a brief hour, I desperately want Dad's chocolate brown leather chair and ottoman, a gift from Mom at a time when they could scarcely afford such luxury. Once a graceful, stately chair, now so old the leather is cracked, the nail studs tarnished, and the sunken seat filled with a pillow. A chair I can't destroy or sell because by losing it, I fear I'll lose the memories of my parents' early life as they struggled to build a home together. A time when each purchase meant the world to them, when purchases were supposed to last a lifetime. But where would I put the thing?

"You're driving me crazy, you know," Doreen says. "There's no place in the storage unit for it. You can't take it now. That's not fair. Someone else might want it. We have to leave it. The house has to be furnished. What do you want it for? It's ugly. It's old. It'd look like hell in your house. It's not Dad. It's a chair."

She's right on all counts. But still it's hard to let go. We save our grandmother's dressers, but not Mom's china cabinet or Dad's ratty old recliner. I wonder what antiques from my mother and father will be in my own house someday that Erin will have to sort through. Which of my own objects will my daughter decide to keep? Which will she feel guilty or sad about donating to charity? I'd like to find a way to avoid all this for her, to keep her from ever having to make the decisions my sister and I have to make. But maybe the objects won't mean so much to Erin. Maybe the memories themselves will be strong enough, powerful enough to make the physical objects nothing more than old stuff that once filled the corners of her parents' home.

I finish sorting the living room and start on the boxes from the attic. Doreen and her husband finish loading valuables for safekeeping and return to Seattle. I stay on alone. Another day or two, I think. Enough time to get everything sorted and boxed. Enough time to get some breathing space away from Tom. Odd really, the problem between Tom and me these days is that he's working so much I never see him. Resentment builds. I came to Grayland knowing I'd stay as long as I need, for Mom and Dad and Maureen, but also for me and my marriage.

Sunday I discover more boxes of memories in the laundry room, in the bedroom closet, in the garage. In those boxes I find bunches of old letters. I find letters between my grandparents – the grandfather who joined the merchant marines during WWII and died shortly after the war ended. I find letters between my parents when they were still dating – Mom in nursing school in Minnesota and Dad working at Todd's Shipyard in Seattle. These letters I cannot resist. I read of a time when Mom was here in Seattle, alone with five young children while Dad was on a job in Ketchikan, Alaska. A letter when Mom suggested a trial separation. A response from Dad asking her to come for a visit, check out the schools. She was on a plane the day after Dad sent the telegram. These letters I read in Mom's chair at the kitchen table. I drink tea and lose myself in my parents' history of intense and not always easy love.

Tom calls and says he wants to see me. I tell him of my loneliness, of the sad, hopelessness that engulfs me. He comes on Monday, stays until Wednesday. We walk the beach and talk of our own dreams for the future, dreams that were not my parents' dreams. When he returns to Seattle on Wednesday, I know my marriage is solid despite the recent strains.

I'm still not ready to leave when Tom goes back to Seattle. There's no reason for me to go back until I'm ready. He understands this, and I am grateful. I can stay as long as I want, as long as I need. At some point I will stop sorting and packing. I will just be in the house and on the beach. I will say goodbye.

When I wake on Thursday morning, Tom is gone, and the house is silent. What have I learned by being here, I ask myself. I've learned Mom and Dad loved each other passionately. Their love is evidenced in a lifetime of cards, letters, and photographs. I also realize how much I missed from 1972 to 1984, the years between the day I left home for university and the day I returned from another lifetime in Mexico.

A new family dynamic had developed that I was not a part of while I was gone for those dozen years. During that time, Doreen and her husband were an integral part of Mom and Dad's life, here and at their winter home in Arizona, a home I never visited. I came back wanting to be part of a family, wanting to slip right back into a family that, in many ways, had moved forward without me. I should never have expected anything different. For all those years, Doreen was there for Mom and Dad. She filled the void caused by loss. I never realized the role she played in their lives or how much of an intrusion my return must have been.

The weekend turns into a week. Gray-green water, gray-blue sky, gray-brown sand. Days of overcast skies and fog that lasts from sun up to sun down. Other days of sunshine and higher temperatures than I've ever known on the Pacific shore. Long days of sorting volumes of letters, cards, and photos – history dating back to the mid 1800s. Family history going back five generations to my great, great grandfather from Ireland. History I sort and box.

I feel I'm getting close to being able to say goodbye and leave Mom and Dad's home forever. I know I am fortunate to have had the time to piece my history together, and perhaps my heart as well, by fingering so many mementos of personal and family history now sealed in boxes headed for storage.

The car is packed, the house organized, lists made. I am ready to say goodbye and return to my own life in Seattle confident my parents' home is ready to hand off to new occupants.

But before I leave, I walk to the beach one last time. I head down the street and along the right-of-way trail at the edge of two properties. I climb the first dune and catch a glimpse of the Pacific. Unlike the day before when there was a dark bank of clouds along the horizon, today the narrow band is clear blue white, blanketed from above by dark clouds.

I drop between the dunes, long green dune grasses tickling my bare legs, and climb the second dune. The unobstructed view of infinity never fails to take my breath away. My feet sink into the soft sand as I make my way toward the harder surface at the water's edge. To my surprise the beach is lined with thousands of pelicans, seagulls, and other seabirds I've never learned to identify.

I head north into the wind. *If you always begin facing into the wind, the return is easier.* A lesson from my father. I walk slowly, unwilling to disturb the birds, getting as close as possible to watch, angry at the two cars coming up behind and startling them into flight. I stare into the horizon. "I have to go now, Maureen," I say. "But I'll be back each year. I'll stay at the yurts. You'd have liked the yurts at the state park. I'll be back."

As I walk, the sky opens. I feel the light before I see it. I stop, stunned. The dark clouds have parted, revealing the full globe of hot white sun, the kind of sun that looks like a full moon. A sun without a trace of yellow. I stand and stare at the brilliant sky, grateful to Maureen, to Dad, and to the inexplicable power of nature and life itself. A thought unearths itself the way a hermit crab digs to the surface of the sand. "Is it okay, Maureen?" I ask. "Is it okay for me to write the Triple Morrigan, to write about Mom and Erin and me?"

The sun glows above the gray-green water, and I know I am not alone. In that brief moment, I know I've found my place in the world, and I know Maureen and Dad and the mom who was and the one who still is, will always be with me. Then, the clouds close like a curtain over the sun. If I hadn't been there to witness nature that day, I wouldn't have believed it.

I continue my walk stuffing my pockets with beach stones and cradling sand dollars in my left hand. I didn't plan to collect, only to walk and say goodbye. But goodbyes and hellos, past and future meld together, and I want to share a bit of Grayland heaven with my writing sisters, the talented writers I share my Sunday mornings with each week.

Light is fading as I return to the house. There is one peach, beautiful and ripe, still setting on a plate where I left it the day I arrived the week before. I slice it into pieces and walk from room to room with plate in hand. To the guest bedroom I shared with Tom and with Erin since her first visit at only a few months of age. To the garage where Dad spent endless hours on projects. In my parents' bedroom, I see them lying back, heads propped up on pillows reading their books. Now you know, they tell me. And I know. I understand their love and their pain. I can accept the life they gave me.

I wander through each small room – the sunroom, the living room, and finally the kitchen where I put the plate in the dishwasher. Then, just for Mom, I wipe the sink dry with a paper towel, just as I know she would have done.

As I drive home, my thoughts wander. I am grateful the little house at the end of the dead-end street will not suffer the indignity of a For Sale sign waving in the stiff Pacific winds. It will not be violated by looky-lookies, as Dad called them, city folks searching for a good deal on a second home at the beach. The house will not be invaded by slick realtors with stern instructions on improvements and staging. In fact, the little house will never be stripped of her furniture, never left bare, empty, forlorn.

Since my father's death, Larry had used two of my father's garages to store his excess vehicles and construction equipment. It was a good arrangement for all. Larry had a place for the junk that no longer fit on his own oversized lot a few houses down the narrow beach road. Mom still had the garage connected to the house for her car, and she gained some company, a neighbor coming into her large lonely yard on a regular basis to use her garages and share a cup of microwaved Lipton's in her tiny kitchen. And Doreen and I had someone we could count on to check on Mom and make sure she was okay. This had been crucial in the winters, those long gray beach winters when gale winds took out the electrical and phone lines for days at a time. Mom never learned to use the cell phone Doreen gave her and service was unreliable at best.

I didn't realize then what I know now. I didn't know Larry was more than just a neighbor. Through the years while Dad was still alive, Larry had become a younger friend who was just down the street. He was always ready to help Dad with projects he could no longer do alone, and later he was there to help Mom. It's odd to realize the depth of this friendship in my parents' lives only years later, only when the parents and most of the neighbors and friends are gone.

I think about Doreen as I drive home for the last time. I remember all she has done for our parents. As their power of attorney, the fate of the little house fell in her lap once we finally moved Mom into her new home. She approached Larry to let him know the house would be going on the market and he would need to remove his junk, though I doubt she used that particular word. The garages needed to be emptied. Larry's response stunned her. "When you're ready to sell," he said. "I'd like to buy the place."

At first we only laughed and held our breath, certain Larry would not be able to come up with the financing to buy the place at the price we asked. But looks deceive and judgments make fools of us all. Larry bought Mom's little house, bought it furnished. Mom's tables and chairs, china cabinet and loveseat still in their places. The butcher block and bookcases Andrew built in high school shop class. Dad's tools still hanging from nails in the garage. The lawn mower and rusted posthole digger in the tilted, sinking shed in the backyard. Mom's untended roses, overgrown vegetable garden, and blueberry bushes gone wild. Even Dad's brown leather chair and ottoman with tarnished nail heads in front of a television too heavy to lift. I think of all of these things as I drive home this last time, and I worry. Did Doreen and her husband remember to remove the huge stained glass window – white dogwood against a green background – Dad's grandest work? What else have we forgotten, sold to Larry by the simple fact it was left behind? But I choose not to think in those terms. I choose to think that what was left behind was left to the house itself, the tiny little beach house, the last house Dad built in a stream of eight houses he built in his lifetime, that Mom and Dad occupied in their fifty years of marriage. The tiny house on the beach, Dad's final resting place, Mom's final home is the only logical, reasonable place to hold their history, to leave their belongings intact. And I choose to never return. I don't want to see the changes that will, without a doubt, be made. I am not so naïve as to think Larry and his wife won't make their own alterations and arrangements to the little house at the beach.

Leaving the house and beach behind me, I smile, remembering the phone conversation with Doreen the night before. She called to check up on me, to make sure I was okay alone there, but the conversation wandered as these things do, taking on a life of its own.

"God, that fur coat is awful," she says. "It stinks. I mean really stinks. Every time I open the closet, it knocks me over. I wish I'd just left it there. It smells like a rotten animal."

"Well, I suppose it is one, in a way," I say. Not at all helpful.

"I wish we could just get rid of it. Who's going to want the awful thing? I'm going to have to find some kind of air-tight plastic bag to seal in the smell."

"Can't you just put it in the storage unit?"

"So, you don't think I can just get rid of it? Who'd want the thing? You couldn't wear it."

"Laureen might," I say with a laugh, Laureen being the only sister of six who's ever worn fur. "Seriously though, we should keep it. I don't know if Laureen or anybody will want it, but it's too soon to decide."

"I know," my sister says with a hint of resignation in her voice. "It's just so damn stinky."

"Get it out of your house," I tell her, but my mind is far away. I see a petite woman with a wide smile, joy written on her tired face. My mother is dressed for a rare evening out, glorious in the bear skin fur coat Dad had brought home for her from Alaska. My mother smiling in deep, dark, warm fur. A beautiful luxury for any woman in the 1950s, but even more so for a woman who had little luxury in her married life. A luxury at a time when fur was still worn, when women did not risk attack for wearing Alaskan fur for an evening on the town. I have no idea where my parents went that evening. Into Seattle to visit old friends? Dinner? Dancing? Theater? All I know is that it was a special event, rare enough to snap a photograph at a time when developing a roll of film was costly, each photo a careful consideration.

I shake away the memory as I realize Doreen is still talking. "Okay," I hear her saying. "I'll put the stinky old thing in storage. Another thing we'll have to figure out what to do with."

ॐ   ॐ

"They're blue, Arleen. Sort of a gray-blue."

"That was Dad. He always had those vibrant piercing blue eyes. Mom's are green, aren't they? Sort of a gray-green now."

"Nope," she says. "They're just gray now."

I let it go, having long since learned not to argue with Doreen even though she's my younger sister because she's usually right. Detailed, meticulous, and right. But for some inexplicable reason I've convinced myself I have my mother's eyes. So I talk to myself on my next drive to Lynnwood. Pay attention, Arleen. Be observant. Don't be afraid to look her in the eye. What is it about eyes, about looking people in the eye, about remembering eyes that has always eluded me?

I know people who can close their own eyes and see the eyes of another – the life and expression in those eyes painted on the backs of their own eyelids. I am not one of those people. I close my eyes and I cannot see my father's eyes. I cannot even see the love I know is clear as day in my husband's eyes. I cannot see the intensity in my daughter's eyes.

My daughter has my eyes and those of my husband. Green. But she was not cursed with my lazy eye, crossed at birth. She has not worn glasses since her second birthday as I have. We laugh that my farsightedness was counter-balanced by Tom's nearsightedness, so Erin was born with perfect vision. Though now, as a young woman, she has reading glasses.

Perhaps it is the glasses I've worn since the time I hid them in the backyard sandbox that have cursed my ability to see the eyes of others. Despite all these years, I still feel a barrier between my own eyes and those of another – a thick wall of glass. Thanks to advances in technology, the coke-bottle thickness of the lenses has been shaved in half. But the barrier is still there, like looking through a window at the rain instead of standing outside the door.

I drive to Lynnwood coaching myself on the fine skill of observation. How can I be a writer, I scold, if I'm a lousy observer? Good writers are outsiders with keen observation skills. The outsider part works well for me. The observation skills need focus. I walk into Clare Bridge determined to pay attention to detail, to see, really see the color of my mother's eyes.

"She's in the activity room," I'm told at the front desk, and I'm pleased they know her precise whereabouts without my prompting.

"Will I be interrupting?" I ask.

"Not at all. They're watching a Shirley Temple movie. It's almost over."

I code myself in and walk the hall to the activity room. Air-conditioning and open doors, but still the air is heavy with age and institution. I pause at a door open to one of the patio areas and breathe deep.

I find my mother in a straight-backed vinyl and stainless-steel chair, sitting behind a row of three wheelchairs, her attention held by the singing and tapping of a tiny blonde surrounded by the blackened faces of a large male choir. I am appalled. She is transfixed. I wonder for the briefest moment if those curls remind her of Maureen or if I'm alone with my memories of my little sister's ringlets.

I sit in the empty chair beside her and am warmed by the recognition and pleasure that flows over her face when she feels my touch on her arm and looks in my direction. I look into my mother's eyes and confirm what I already know – that Doreen is right. My mother's eyes are gray now. Does that mean my memory is as flawed as my sight? I want to see my mother's old driver's license. I want proof her eyes were once green. That green was once her favorite color because it brought out the color of her eyes. That despite the height, pale freckled skin, and dark hair of my father, I have my mother's eyes. For apart from her eye color, or the eye color I claim she once had, I have little in common with my mother. I am not stoic or silent. I refuse to use denial as a defense mechanism. And I do not want her dementia. So I cling to green eyes, to my memory, regardless how flawed it might be, of my mother's green eyes.

I sit next to my mother and look into the watery gray depth of her eyes, and I'm not sure what I see in them.

"Oh, it's you," she says.

"Hi, Mom. Good movie?"

"I don't know," she says.

"The end," I say, as the credits begin to roll.

"Is that all?" asks a woman in front of us.

"Yup, that's the end," I say.

"I want to see more of that little girl," the woman says, and her attention returns to the large flat screen on the wall in hopeful anticipation. I am reminded of a dog hoping for a second milk bone.

"Do you want to go for a walk, Mom?" I ask.

"Okay."

"You might want to take off your sweater. It's really warm outside today."

"Oh no," she says, and then, as though she doesn't want to offend, she struggles to find the zipper tab to the heavy fleece stretched tight over her now bulging belly. "I'll open it," she says.

We walk out into the unusually warm September sun. We've gone no more than fifty feet when Mom says, "It's warm."

"Yup," I say, wanting to add an I-told-you-so. Instead I say, "Here, let's take off your sweater." I help her out of the winter polar fleece, pull it through my heavy purse strap to carry it for her, and continue walking.

I am concerned by how slow and unsteady my mother has become. She is eating better and is more relaxed than she's been since before Dad's death, but she is not getting the exercise she got living on her own in Grayland. She needs daily walks, and I don't think that's happening. I make a mental note to talk to the staff. Could they form a walking club? Another structured daily activity? Or am I just trying to deny the inevitable effects of age, the changes that seem to come faster and faster with each passing year? I remember my father's words: *the older you get, the faster it goes.* Is that what I bear witness to with each slow step?

Mom seems tired, so we find a bench in the shade, and I struggle to make conversation. I tell her of the news I've received about the declining health of both her sister's husband and her old nursing school friend. "I'm healthy," she says.

Stay in the present, the now, I remind myself. "Look at those pretty fingernails," I say as I take her hand in mine. "You must have had spa day this week."

"No, I have bad hands," she says, pulling her hand away and curling her fingers into a small fist.

"Your hands are great, Mom. They're strong, hardworking hands."

"And bad skin," she says. She struggles with the buttons on her long-sleeved blouse, pushes up her sleeve to show me her arm. The skin is parchment thin, dry and flaky.

"You've always had dry skin, Mom. We all do."

"Not you." She rubs the skin on my bare arm. "Your skin is good."

"Not really. My skin is just like yours, I use gallons of lotion. Every day, after every shower, I coat myself in lotion."

"Really?"

"Yup. Just like you taught me to do when I was a little girl. Do you have any lotion in your bathroom?"

She shrugs.

I smile as we walk inside. I have my mother's skin.

When we reach her tiny room, I check the bathroom. Two large bottles stand next to the sink. I wonder how often she confuses the liquid soap and the lotion, or how often she uses either.

"Look what I found, Mom. Come, sit with me." We sit on the edge of her bed, and she dutifully rolls up her sleeves like an obedient child. I gently massage lotion into the fragile skin of her hands and arms.

"Are your legs dry, too?" I ask.

"I don't know," she says as she pulls up her pant legs and pushes down her socks. I lean over and begin to massage lotion into her flaky legs.

"Ouch," she says.

"I'm sorry," I say. I wonder if I'm really using too much pressure, or if she is simply so unaccustomed to human touch it feels odd to her. I continue rubbing, and she does not pull away from me. I am surprised by the sturdy roundness of her lower legs. The firmness and strength of her leg muscles compared to the softness of her arms. I continue to massage her legs, wondering if I could get her to take off her clothes so I could rub lotion into her entire body, wondering if I am ready for that.

"That's enough," Mom says, as if in response to my unspoken question.

Later, as I retrace my steps from my mother's room to the exit, I peek into the open doors of the other residents. I see two, maybe three, residents lying in bed, oxygen tanks close at hand. I feel surrounded by death. In the past year I have lost three wonderful women in my life, all to cancer: a work colleague, a writing sister, and a friend with whom I shared my years in Mexico.

My mother appears to be a content, chubby version of the woman she once was. But who is she really? And where has the woman she once was gone? Is loss of memory little more than walking death – living, breathing death – with no past or future? That's too harsh. She still finds pleasure in each day, in the bright sunshine, in the colorful petunias we planted in the raised beds, in the hearty meals she is served three times each day, and in the smiles and hugs of her caregivers and visitors. My mother is not dead, but still I feel a profound loss. The loss of a past. The loss of sense and meaning and history. Or maybe it is only my exaggerated need to understand the past. Perhaps I need to learn to turn my back on the past, pay attention to the present, and look to the future. But in my mind, to deny the past is to deny those we have lost, and I am no more willing to deny the blessings of the friends I have lost this year than I am to forget my sister or my father, or the woman my mother once was.

I am under a blanket of melancholy as I drive home to West Seattle. I need to shake it off, hang it out on a line to air. I need to get on with life, with writing, with living, with loving, with appreciating every single breath I pull into my lungs.

≈ &

Mom sits at the head of a long table pulling at the elastic band of the cone-shaped birthday hat perched on her head, the bright ribbons trailing down her back like colorful, curly hair. She is surrounded by her children and grandchildren. I'm not sure Mom, or any of the other residents for that matter, has any real idea what all the excitement is about, but I believe they feel it, they know it's a party, and they're eager for cake and ice cream.

As I carry the large cake past the smiling, wrinkled faces to the adjacent room and set it on the long table where Mom reigns supreme, my steps are punctuated with a loud, off-key rendition of *Happy Birthday*. Two large candles flicker atop the cake, an 8 and a 5.

"Happy birthday dear Mom, Nana, Grandma, Sally ..." We each choose the name, the relationship we cherish. Then a family chorus of voices encourages her to blow out the candles.

"For me?" she asks, bewilderment written across her face, her eyes full of wonder.

"Yes, Mom," I whisper in her ear. "It's your birthday. We're all here to celebrate your birthday."

"How old am I?" she asks.

"Eighty-five. See the 8 and the 5 on your cake."

"Really? So old?" she asks, turning to my eldest sister seated to her left for confirmation.

"Yes, Mom," Marleen says. "You're eighty-five today."

"Blow out the candles, Mom," I whisper into her ear.

"Come on, Nana," sings the chorus of children and grandchildren around the table.

She puffs up her cheeks like a five-year-old and blows out the tiny flames atop the wax 8 and 5 with all her might. A shy, girlish smile of pure pleasure brightens her face as clapping, cheers, and laughter fill the room.

I laugh to myself as I carry the cake, now coated with the gentle germs of my mother's breath, back to the serving table where two employees in plastic gloves are waiting to cut the large cake and scoop the ice cream. Rules are rules and food must be served wearing sanitary gloves. Doreen, Erin, and others carry plates to the family as well as to all the residents seated at the small tables in the large activity room.

"I want some," says an unshaven man in slippers.

I recognize him as the man who befriended my mother when she moved in, the man who had become angry. I am glad my mother no longer seems to remember him or take responsibility for his behavior. "Okay," I tell him. "Go ahead and sit down, and I'll bring you a piece."

"He's a walker," one of the caregivers says.

"Oh," I say and hand the man a piece of cake which he eats as he circles the tables, leaving a trail of cake crumbs and dribbled ice cream behind him.

Conversation flows around the long table the staff set up for our family in the adjacent room at the opposite end of the large activity room. There, six of Mom's nine children crowd together with spouses and children. Andrew and Michael flew in from Hawaii the day before. Marleen and her family are up from California, now moving back to the Pacific Northwest. Charleen and her husband came over the Cascades from Ellensburg and are joined by their adult children. And, of course, Doreen and her husband are here as well. Siblings and cousins in cone-shaped party hat, some seeing each other for the first time since Mom's eightieth birthday at the Tokeland Hotel, reconnect around the yellow table and bright flowers with colorful streamers overhead. Red punch in plastic cups and empty cake plates scatter the table.

Will there be a ninetieth, I wonder as I sit at the far end of the table, determined to observe, to remember the events and conversations of the day. I visit with a sister, a nephew and his new wife, and I wonder when I'll see them again, wonder what, if any, family gatherings we will have when Mom is no longer the catalyst. And I realize we are back in the same family place as we were before *The Thirty-Ninth Victim*, but not quite because now I know that if they are aware of my writing career, my blog, my short publications, my readings or even the work on this manuscript, they are choosing to ignore it. And in doing so, they are choosing to ignore a large part of the woman I have become. They say nothing about my writing, and I do the same, accepting the limits of the established familial bonds.

"Time to open your presents, Nana," I hear my daughter say. From the opposite end of the table, I watch Marleen at Mom's left and Doreen at her right, handing Mom cards to read, gifts to open. Marleen stands and walks to the counter along the far side of the room, now piled high with colorful packages and passes them to the table. The pile in front of my mother grows.

"For me?" she asks. "Why for me? It's too much."

"Open the card first," someone hollers.

From the far end of the room I see Mom's confusion, the way she looks to the left and right, twisting her body to see if anyone is behind her, if the call out is to someone other than herself. It is as though the memories, the understanding or awareness comes and goes, a bit like hot flashes or chocolate cravings, but far more elusive.

Doreen hands her a card, and Mom struggles to read it. "It's from Charleen, Mom. See right there, it says Charleen."

"Who?" Mom asks.

"Your daughter Charleen. Hey Charleen, wave."

"It's me, Mom. I'm number four," my sister says and waves her hand.

"Oh, that's good," said Mom.

Before I left home earlier that afternoon, I promised myself to stay back, observe. But as I watch my mother's growing confusion, I see a young child overwhelmed by excitement at her own birthday party, and I can't remain on the sidelines. Marleen gets up again from her spot next to Mom. The chair is empty, and I take it.

There are a number of open cards in front of Mom and one in her hands. I read it aloud, slowly, clearly, using my ESL teacher's voice. She hands me another, and I read it aloud as well. Then she hands me a third. With each card, she asks, "Who's it from?" I call out the name, tell the person to wave, and Mom responds with her own little wave to the appropriate family member. A curled finger wave of a child. I am reminded of the many visits to the Grayland house, of Erin in her car seat, twisting her tiny body to wave goodbye to her grandparents as I pulled the gate closed behind us.

There are moments when Mom appears lucid, aware of who we are, who she is, what's going on. At the table, she seems to know we are family and we are celebrating her, but she does not see herself as the eighty-five-year-old matriarch of all who share the table. Instead, she is a young woman, carefree and happy, surrounded by people who love her. Not a bad way to spend an eighty-fifth birthday, I suppose.

"How's Nana?" Erin asks the following weekend when I return from another visit.

"Oh, I don't know, honey. Not so good this time."

"What's wrong?"

"She just wasn't happy, you know. When I got there, she was walking the halls and when she saw me she asked if I had a car because she wanted to go home."

"That's so sad."

"Yeah, it was the first time I've ever heard her say anything about going home."

"What'd you do?"

"I told her how much everybody would miss her if she left, and then I distracted her with all the pictures I had of her birthday party I had on my laptop."

"Did she remember?"

"The party? Not really. And she didn't recognize herself either. She really doesn't know who she is or how she looks anymore. She kept saying, 'Oh, that's not me!'"

"Poor Nana."

"The worst part was that she didn't want to do anything. There were these two little girls there. I think they were one of the caregiver's daughters. Anyway, they were playing chair volleyball with a balloon, you know, tossing it back and forth in circle. But Mom didn't want to participate at all. She finally went for a short walk with me around the gardens, but I practically had to drag her."

"Well, Mom. You can't expect her to be upbeat all the time. I mean everybody has a bad day, you know."

"I suppose you're right. I just wish I'd been smarter. In retrospect, I should've taken her for a drive, even just for ten minutes might have helped. When I told her I had to leave, she wanted to walk me to the car. I was really worried, but I let her come outside to the parking lot with me to show her my car. I told her she could help me put my big bag and computer in the trunk, and then I'd walk her in. She wanted to wave goodbye to me from the sidewalk like she used to do in Grayland, but I walked her inside instead."

"You had to get her back inside the locked doors, right?"

"Exactly. Lucky for me she decided she had to go to the bathroom and forgot all about the car. So I walked her inside and just kissed her goodbye and left."

"How sad."

"You know, it reminds me of the time Mozart nipped me because he didn't want to get out of the back of the station wagon. Do you remember that?"

"You were so upset."

"All I needed to do was drive around the block and Mozart would have been happy. He wouldn't have known it was only a few minutes, and he would've jumped right out of the car when I stopped. I should've done the same thing with Mom. It probably would've brightened her day and only taken a little more time out of mine. I just wasn't thinking. Or, to be completely honest, I was thinking about myself, about being at home, about enjoying this gorgeous day with you and Dad."

"Don't be so hard on yourself, Mom. You spend a lot of time with Nana. Every visit isn't going to be perfect."

"How'd you get so smart?" I say. I give her a tight hug, grateful to have her in my life.

ও ক্ষ

"I need to do some shopping, Mom. Just a few groceries. Do you want to go with me?" We're sitting on the edge of her bed. Once again I arrive midafternoon to find her napping. She smooths back her soft gray-white hair with both hands and rubs the sleep from her eyes. "We'll go to Trader Joe's," I say. "It'll be fun."

"Okay," she says. "But I don't need anything."

"I do. Will you help me find a few groceries? If I don't get some coffee, I won't be able to wake up for work tomorrow morning."

"Okay," Mom says.

A few minutes later I help her pull a jacket over her bright red Christmas sweater, and we head to the door. "Do you have a ...?" she asks.

"Car?" I say, supplying the word for her. "Yes, I have a car. Do you want to drive?" For a split second I fear she'll say yes and then what will I do?

"Oh no," she says.

Trader Joe's is just a few miles away. In only minutes, we pull into the crowded parking lot.

"Lots of cars," Mom says.

"Yeah, but we're lucky. A perfect parking spot."

"Good," she says.

We enter the store. I push the cart, and Mom clings to my side like a young child. I fantasize about putting her into the child seat. I imagine hoisting her up, getting her legs through the slots, only to find her hips and belly won't fit in the seat.

The store is busy with pre-holiday shoppers. Thanksgiving and Christmas merge into a single month of excessive consumerism. I struggle through the holiday extras, searching for staples.

"Coffee," I say. "That's what I came in for. Stay close, Mom."

I try to read the labels and make my choice while Mom pokes around, wandering up and down the narrow crowded aisle. Coffee in hand, I grab her arm and pull her around the end of the aisle to the grinder.

"Too many people," she says.

"Just a minute, Mom," I say. "I need to grind this before we leave. Can you wait a little longer?"

"Too many people," she says again.

"I know. Only a few more minutes, okay?" I open the can and pour the beans into the grinder, choose my setting, and start the machine. My phone rings. It's Doreen. "Yes, I'm visiting her right now," I say. "We're at Trader Joe's."

I'm distracted for what? Fifteen, twenty seconds? When I look up, look around me, Mom's gone. "Crap," I say. "Gotta go. I've lost her."

I never lost Erin. In all the years of her early childhood, I never let my mind wander, never let her stray from me in a public place. I'd witnessed the panic of other mothers, the mothers of lost children, fearing the very worst as they frantically searched for a young child who'd wandered off. I'd heard stories of abductions, and I made certain I would never be one of those mothers. My fear for Erin was so intense, I never relaxed my guard.

But here I am in Trader Joe's, waiting for the coffee grinder, talking to my sister, and I've let down my guard. I feel the fingers of fear crawling up my spine. "Crap, crap, crap," I say as I stick my phone in my pocket, cap my coffee, and search the adjacent aisles. No Mom.

I head to the exit, terrified she may have wandered out to the busy parking lot trying to escape the crowd in the store. Then, I hear a voice. Male. "Is this who you're looking for?"

I turn to see my mother clinging to the arm of one of the store clerks. "Mom," I say. "Thank goodness. Where did you go?"

"I don't know," she says.

"She seemed a bit confused."

I look at the bearded young man. "I bet," I say. "Where did you find her?"

"Just over in Produce," he says.

"Thank you," I say. "Thank you very, very much." I want to give him a hug. Instead, I hug Mom, and she gives me a look that tells me she has no idea what the fuss is all about. "Come on, Mom," I say. "Let's check out now and get you home for dinner, okay?"

"Okay," she says.

Later, driving home alone, I think about Mom's confusion and my own fear at Trader Joe's, and I wonder about taking Mom on outings. I remember a conversation I once had with my mother-in-law, a woman who took care of her own mother through memory loss to Alzheimer's. It was shortly after we'd moved Mom into her new home. I mentioned it was located near a large mall and theater so there were lots of great places to take her. "You know," Lucy said, "the time will come when the outings will be more for you than for her."

I think about the events of the day, and I realize that time has arrived.

2010

I DISTRUST MY memory. The volumes of journals, date books, and saved emails cluttering my workspace attest to that distrust. I write because I fear becoming my mother and losing my memory. I document life, but still I cannot be certain my details are always a hundred percent correct. It's akin to not remembering or not realizing that a last time will be the last time until it is too late. Like the last time I saw my sister, Maureen, at the airport in Mexico City. I had no idea I would never see her again, so I let the moment slip from memory until I recalled it through writing. And now, I cannot recall when I took Mom on her last outing from Clare Bridge. For a while I was convinced the fiasco at Trader Joe's was it. But now I know I was wrong.

It's January 2010. My eldest brother's wife comes to help their daughter move from Portland to Seattle. My niece moves in with a friend only blocks from our house, and my sister-in-law stays with Tom and me. Erin is living in an apartment, so her bedroom is available.

I take the two of them to visit Mom. Erin joins us as well. I try to prepare my sister-in-law. "She likely won't recognize you," I say. "She doesn't really know Doreen or me either. Only that we are connected to her somehow."

"I understand," she says.

We drive to Clare Bridge and urge Mom to give us a tour of her home. Then we invite her out to lunch at the mall. We walk together through the post-holiday mall madness, the decorations looking as worn as the people making their returns and exchanges. Mom is nervous, but excited. She holds my hand, then each of our hands in turn. She holds us together as she holds herself together.

I see a kiosk selling board games. Tom and I have never been big fans of New Year's Eve. Instead, we've bought a new board game each year throughout Erin's childhood and spent the evening at home – just the three of us, sometimes with friends – playing silly games. I buy a special edition Planet Earth Monopoly game, something I think Tom will like. Years later the box remains unopened, the tradition dying as Erin begins making her own New Year's Eve plans.

We settle on a restaurant, one with a model train running around the room on overhead tracks. A distraction, something in the present to point at and talk about with Mom. We have our meal and take Mom home.

I remember another meal out as well. This time just with Erin and Mom. We go to the Red Robin near Clare Bridge. I ask for a quiet table, and we're seated in a back corner near the service station. Each time a waitperson passes to or from the kitchen with plates of food, or stops to fill a water pitcher, pick up or return a coffee pot, or calculate a check, Mom startles and Erin distracts her with stories of her UW classes, her latest apartment, her friends.

When were these restaurant meals, memories that float through my mind unwilling to settle on a calendar number? I am certain my sister-in-law's visit began just after Christmas and extended into early January. She became ill, her throat so raw she could barely whisper, the visit extended until she was well enough to fly home to Hawaii.

And the Red Robin meal? When was that? Later that year when Erin and I celebrated Mom's eighty-sixth birthday or just another visit when Erin was hungry and needed a solid meal? The point is that despite my copious journals and day planners, I cannot remember the exact date of Mom's final outing, the last time I took my mother outside of the fenced and locked confines of dementia care. I cannot remember the day her world was reduced to the four television lounges and four dining rooms in the four hallways, to the two activity rooms, the fenced garden walkways, and to her own bedroom and bathroom. It terrifies me that something so profound escapes me, just as the early and incremental signs of my mother's dementia escaped me. I suppose my terror lies in selfish concern that I will also miss the early signs of my own memory loss. Already I wonder what it means when I can't remember the names of colleagues I've worked with for over twenty years, when I confuse the letters "b" and "p" and the words "hamburger" and "pancake" or when I type the letter "k" when I need "d." Are these signs of dementia or just stress? Or, as my doctor has told me, just the hormonal changes of menopause messing with my mind?

So Trader Joe's was not Mom's last outing with me, and I will continue to write my stories with the memories I can hold for as long as I can hold them, for I know that even if the exact dates are a little off, the essence of the memories – their emotional truth, my emotional truth – is accurate. And emotional truth is what I value most. I do not doubt I will again make waves in my family with the publication of another memoir, and there may be certain repercussions. But perhaps it will be different this time. I know my fear of their rejection has weakened. I can only hope the conditional love that has so tragically marked my family is also dissolved.

I sit with my sister-in-law over cups of hot tea at the kitchen table, and I remember her email from the previous summer, an email expressing gratitude to Tom and me for hiring her daughter on a temporary project and letting her come up from her home in Portland and stay with us. It was in that email she also apologized to me for "jumping on the anti-Arleen bandwagon upon reading the manuscript" of *The Thirty-Ninth Victim*. I remember my relief that it seemed to be over. Each of my siblings, in their own way, was showing me they were no longer angry and they did, indeed, still love me.

At home one evening my sister-in-law says, "I get it now. I understand why you did it."

Later, alone with my journal, I write those words along with these: "And as Robert becomes more like Dad – a recluse of minimal words – she understands I was not vilifying Dad, but humanizing him. Because we all deified him for so many years, the fall was hard."

A few days later, again with warm tea, or perhaps a glass of hearty red wine, we sit together and talk of family. "You've got quite a treasure trove to write about, don't you?" she says.

"Yeah," I say. "Lots of memories. And I'll try to do it without pissing everybody off again."

᠗ ᠗

It's February 2010, my mother's first anniversary in dementia care. Mom no longer greets me when I arrive for visits, no longer recognizes me at all. This time when I arrive, Mom isn't in the activity room. She isn't in her own room. I ask a caregiver, and the walkie talkies are activated. She's in Country Lane, I am told. I find her wandering that hall, not her own.

"Hi, Mom. Going for a walk?" I see confusion in her eyes. "Arleen," I say. "It's me, Arleen, your daughter." I take her hand. "Let's walk together, Mom."

"I ... a little problem." Her free hand reaches to the back of her pants. "I'm wet," she says.

Oh, damn, we've come to this? I think. "A little accident, Mom?" I say aloud.

"I don't know," she says.

"Should we find your room and get you some dry clothes? I've brought you some pretty new shirts, too."

"Okay," she says.

I lead her to her room like a small, docile child, the kind of child who is just too obedient. There I find a pair of clean pants with an elastic waistband and clean underwear. I hand her these along with one of several new tops I've brought for her. "Do you want help, Mom?" I ask as I open the bathroom door for her.

"No, I can do it," she says.

The bathroom door closes, and I wait. I search her closet and drawers for signs of other accidents, other problems, relieved I find nothing. Five minutes later the bathroom door opens. Mom stands before me, the new shirt tight, much too tight over her bulging belly.

"Too small," she says.

I laugh and give her a quick hug. Then I quickly grab an old favorite from her closet – the off-white sweater with the Navajo motif. "How about this one?" I say.

"I like it," she says. She takes it from me and closes the bathroom door again.

One year ago today – fifty-two weeks, three hundred sixty-five days – we moved Mom into dementia care. At the time I thought she looked good, maybe a bit thin, but strong and healthy. The doctor told us she was undernourished. Now she can't fit into her clothes. A woman who always wore small, petite sizes, except perhaps during her many pregnancies, cannot wear the women's medium polo shirts I've brought for her. Lost in thought, I hardly hear the door open a few minutes later. I look up to see Mom's chubby round body and the twinkle in her eyes. I see contentment, the simple comfort of clean, dry clothes.

I look into the bathroom and see Mom's dirty clothes folded in a neat pile on the floor in the corner, reminding me of the mountains of clothing and cloth diapers she folded for her large family until my sisters and I were old enough to help with the task.

Mom stands before her mirror, hairbrush in hand. She brushes with her right hand, smooths with her left. A gesture I recall from childhood.

"This hair," she says.

"It won't stay back, will it?" I say from the doorway. I enter the bathroom with a cloth hairband in my hand, having already noticed the trouble Mom was having with her hair. She has not had a perm since moving into dementia care. The stylist has suggested letting it grow into a simple blunt cut, but the grow-out process is taking time. "How about if we try a hairband? Here's a pretty blue one."

"Okay," she says.

"Turn this way, Mom. Now up it goes." I slip it over her head and try to pull it up over her face to hold back her wayward bangs.

"Ouch," she says.

"Sorry. I got your ear. Here, is that better?"

"I can do it." As she slides the band behind her ears, I remember the years my young daughter spent trying to grow out bangs and wonder just how long the blue hairband will stay on my mother's head before she decides it isn't comfortable.

"Better?" I ask.

"Okay," she says.

Mom no longer walks me to the door when I leave, just as she no longer greets me with a little wave when I arrive. I remember how she used to stand at the front door of the Grayland house as I backed the car out of the driveway at the end of each visit just as her own mother stood at the door of her childhood home in Herried, South Dakota many decades before, as I now stand on my own doorstep waving goodbye as Erin leaves on weekend trips to visit friends on the far side of the Cascades. As I ponder these departures, my heart yearns for Grayland. I miss the gray-blue skies, the gray-brown sands, the long, long beach. I miss walking along the water's edge, waves crashing beside me drowning all sound with their power. I miss picking shells, sand dollars, and agates from the shore. I miss the flocks of tiny birds that lift in unison from the sand as if on command, that swoop and rise and fall in patterned perfection. I miss the clumsy gulls and the graceful herons. I miss the strong cold wind, the wind that never stops even in the summer. The wind that carries my sister's ashes.

I miss running free. Running the beach, my younger, stronger self with more muscle, less fat, and no metal pins in my knees. I miss walking the beach with my mother, the young healthy woman who loved the beach, collecting and sharing everything but words.

I remember the day we decided to walk the beach to Westport. An ambitious all-day hike. The sun was high. The sky a glorious blue that only the Northwest knows, a deep dark blue reflecting off the Pacific. Not a cloud to be seen. Just Mom and me and the long open beach. This was before cell phones, before instantaneous communication, when people still had to make plans. We calculated the beach distance, the mileage, the hours we thought it would take us, and we planned the time and place where Dad would meet us for a ride home. We joked we'd stay in a Westport hotel if he didn't show up. He'd be on his own for dinner. Then we set off, this time remembering to put plastic bags in our pockets to hold the treasures we were sure to find along the way. I was in my mid thirties; Mom in her mid sixties, a spry, healthy woman, full of energy, full of life, despite the tragedies she'd already endured, ignorant of those yet to be suffered. For one glorious day we walked the beach and collected treasures. I have no memory of conversation, of what we may or may not have talked about beyond the simple comments on the unique beauty of each other's finds. But I do remember the gentle peace I felt walking at my mother's side on a shared adult adventure.

We reached the state park, our planned meeting place. Dad and Casey were waiting. "I thought you'd never get here," he said. "Thought I'd have to send out a search party."

"Where are you taking us for dinner?" Mom said.

My cell phone rings, interrupting my memories. I know I shouldn't answer while I'm driving, but I do anyway. "I'm at the store," Tom says. "Do you have any ideas for dinner?"

I start laughing so hard at the odd synchronicity of memory and reality I have to pull to the side of the road.

>> <<

Today I am wearing my mother's wedding ring. I have given myself this gift, this temporary, short-term gift of my mother's wedding ring, now on my left ring finger up against the band of gold that represents the bond I have with my own husband.

This ring of my mother's represents almost sixty years of love that bound my parents so tightly there were no fault lines and hardly enough space left for their nine children. For almost six decades my mother wore this ring, the gold worn thin by long years of hard work. How many times I remember my mother pulling her small hand from my father's large tight grasp, her "Ouch" loud and clear. My father, not knowing his own strength, would squeeze her hand so tight the gold would bend. As kids, my siblings and I would have hand-squeezing contests to see who could illicit the same response Dad got from Mom. My father, a man of few words and strong emotions, showed his love of my mother by grasping her hand so tight he bent the delicate gold of her wedding ring, by hugging her small body so tight against his own she'd gasp for air.

Now I wear my mother's wedding ring. For one week. A week-long reminder of my parents love for each other. A love my mother no longer remembers because she no longer remembers the man with whom she shared her life.

We are in Mom's tiny room. She is rubbing her hands together, still wet because she's left the bathroom without drying them completely. She rubs them on her pant legs. The gesture of a child. She twists her wedding ring on her left ring finger. "Too tight," she says as she pulls it from her finger and tries it on her other hand.

"Here, let me see," I say. I take the ring and slip it into my jeans pocket. "Come on, Mom, let's go get some cake and ice cream." Together we head to the activity room for the Bunny Hop social, the ring forgotten. As a precaution, I slip off my own wedding ring and add it to hers snug in my pocket. I'm unwilling to risk the off chance my ring reminds her she is missing her own, that when we hold hands she senses something is missing.

I feel the thief. I have deceived my mother. So easy. Her innocence so simple to manipulate to my advantage. I have considered this moment long and hard. I have heard my sister's words, "She's lost her sapphire ring, Arleen. The one we gave her for her birthday. It just makes me sick to my stomach. Really, just sick."

"It's only a ring," I hear myself say, but I'm overwhelmed with sadness. I remember the afternoon at Doreen's house. I remember Erin helping us hide the ring box in a bag of mini Snickers – Mom's favorite candy bar. I remember my mother's surprise and my young daughter's delight when Mom dug into the plastic bag to offer us each a candy. "There's something more in there, Nana," Erin said, unable to contain her excitement.

"I know," Doreen says, interrupting my memories. "But it's such a loss."

It's more than the monetary value she's referring to. I know the fact that Mom and the other residents can't distinguish between gaudy Mardi Gras beads and diamonds or sapphires is the real heartbreak.

We talk of Mom's wedding ring, of her diamond earrings, of the risk of more loss. "The earrings have screw-on backs," she says. "I'm not so worried about those. But her wedding ring … She's always playing with her rings."

She's right, of course. Mom has developed a habit of removing her rings, of trying to find a finger that offers a better fit. In the years since Dad's death, she's lost and regained over twenty pounds, her joints have swollen, and her rings no longer fit as they did in earlier years. And yet we moved her into dementia care with no thought of the possibility of Mom losing the most treasured jewelry she's ever owned. Or, when we thought about it in passing, we were reluctant to take more from her after already taking her home.

Now the sapphire ring is gone and the wedding ring is on my finger, a reminder of deep lasting love, a reminder of loss. I will wear this ring for a week, and then I will give it to Doreen for safekeeping until the distribution of my mother's belongings must be decided.

"Where's Nana's ring?" Erin asks as she watches me take off my watch and pull the earrings from my ears one evening a week later.

I've just come from the supermarket laden with organic ground beef, whole wheat buns, lettuce, tomatoes, avocados, and potatoes for the hamburger and homemade baked French fry dinner my daughter requested. "I have to change before I start dinner," I tell her, buying myself some time. She watches me, observant, aware of details that escape many.

"Where's Nana's ring?" she asks again when I come out of the bedroom in comfy sweats, my hair pulled back in a ponytail.

"I put it away," I tell her.

"Why?"

"I gave it to myself for a week. Remember? That was all."

"Why? Nobody knows or cares. Were you afraid something would happen to it?"

"Oh, I don't know." I stall.

"But why not wear it? It looks so good with your wedding band."

"I don't know, Sweetpea. I guess I just don't want to get too attached, you know? It's not mine. It may never be mine. I gave it to myself for a week. That's it."

I don't tell her how close it makes me feel to my mother to wear the ring she wore for so many years, how wonderful it felt to imagine my father as a young man slipping the ring on her finger. I don't tell her how badly I'd like her to have her grandmother's ring someday or how powerless I feel about the decision-making process that will someday be required to determine where my mother's ring finds a new home. I am the middle child. I have always felt I have no voice. I cannot tell her of my fears that it could be claimed by the eldest daughter or by the daughter with the first granddaughter. My fears swirl at the very thought of someday having to determine what will be done with my mother's few remaining possessions, most of little value, monetary or sentimental, except for my mother's wedding ring, her diamond earrings, and the sapphire ring she has already lost.

The week after I pocket Mom's wedding ring, Doreen slips a new ring on her finger, a cheap piece of costume jewelry she's picked up as a replacement for the two rings Mom has lost, the wedding ring I took from her and the sapphire ring missing somewhere in Clare Bridge, likely on someone else's finger or in some other room. I still wonder about the diamond earrings. Doreen tells me not to worry. She reminds me they have screw-on backs and Mom doesn't even notice them anymore. I'm not concerned about the potential loss. They have no emotional value to me at all, and Mom is beyond the awareness needed to care. But my sister, I worry about. She was so upset about the lost birthday ring I worry she'll be devastated despite or maybe precisely because of her conviction that Mom won't lose them.

My daughter watches as I begin to make the hamburgers, pulling my own simple gold wedding band from my finger and shoving my hands into the bowl of ground beef, chopped garlic, and chives clipped fresh from the garden.

"Yuck," she says. "I think I'll go see what Dad's doing."

"Okay," I say. I chuckle to myself, happy my once-vegetarian daughter now eats meat as long as she doesn't have to help cook it or even watch the preparation.

"Don't forget your ring," she says as she walks from the kitchen.

ॐ ॐ

Mother's Day Tea is scheduled for 3:00 p.m. on a Tuesday afternoon. I still can't figure out why they decided to do this on a weekday given how difficult it could be for family members to attend. I suppose having early afternoon weekday events is their priority – no weekend overtime pay and early enough in the day to not mess with the evening routine. Still, how many family members, adult children of the residents, are able to leave work early enough to be with their loved one for a holiday event on a weekday midafternoon? My afternoon schedule is flexible, more so than most, definitely more so than Doreen's, so I go.

I walk out of a meeting early and leave campus with time to spare. Arriving at Clare Bridge, I find the parking lot overflowing. I realize I'm not the only one who's left work early, unwilling to allow their mother to be alone at the Mother's Day celebration regardless whether the mother even recognizes them. Or maybe these adult children are, in fact, retired. The place is milling with people, family groups collecting at springtime bright tables. Quiche, tea sandwiches, fruit plates.

"Where's Mom?" I ask Jamie, the events planner, busy directing folks to their pre-assigned tables.

"You'll be sitting there with Mary and her daughter. But Sally? Let's see." She pauses for a moment trying to remember where she last saw my mother. "She's right down the hall, napping," she says.

Sure enough, I find Mom sound asleep in an upright armchair tucked away in one of the sitting alcoves off the main hallway. I approach, kneel at her side and touch her arm. "Hi, Mom," I whisper. "How are you?"

She opens her eyes and fails to recognize me.

"It's Arleen, Mom. Your daughter. I came for the Mother's Day Tea. Happy Mother's Day."

Confusion fills my mother's eyes. Confusion tinged with fear.

"It's okay, Mom," I say. "Did you have a good nap?"

She straightens in the chair and rubs the sleep from her eyes with the backs of her hands. I see Erin at two, waking from an afternoon nap, her tiny fists rubbing her eyes.

"I fell asleep," she says, in halting jagged words, as though picking for each word individually from a cluttered pile.

"Did you have a good dream?"

"Oh, I don't know," she says. She reaches out her hands to me in greeting. When I lean in for a kiss and hug, I notice the ring on her right hand. The missing sapphire ring. The ring we'd searched her room trying to find and then reported lost. The ring Doreen had cried tears of regret over for not having removed it from Mom's hand before it was lost. The sapphire ring is again on the ring finger of my mother's right hand.

I take her hand in mine and massage her joints. The ring is tight. "Does that hurt, Mom? Maybe we should take it off?"

She begins to work the ring, pulling but unable to get it over her swollen joint.

"Wait a sec, Mom. I think I've got something that will help." I take some L-Lysine lip balm from my purse and smear it on her finger.

"Look," Mom says as she hands me the ring.

"It slid right off, didn't it?" I say with a laugh.

"Good," she says.

"I'll keep this for you, okay?" I say.

"Okay." She holds her hands out to me again, this time for inspection. "Bad skin."

I rub lip balm on the tops of her outreached hands. "Rub them together like this," I say, and I show her how to rub top of hand to top of hand, a trick she had taught me years before. A trick I've passed on to my own daughter.

"Good," she says. "I didn't do it this way."

"Feel better?" I ask. She nods. "Ready to have some Mother's Day tea?"

"Tea's good," she says as she pushes herself from the chair. "My ring?" she asks.

"It's safe, Mom. I'll keep it safe for you."

"That's good," she says, and we walk to our table.

"Do you remember the missing ring I mentioned a few weeks ago?" Probably not the best starter. The poor gal at the desk had no idea what I was talking about. I tried again. "Two weeks ago Doreen and I both reported Sally's sapphire ring was missing. We searched everywhere."

"Oh yes, I remember."

"Well, it's reappeared on her finger."

"Really?"

"Yeah. Do you have any idea where it was or who found it?"

"No, I'm afraid not," she says. Her shoulders gave a slight shrug.

"Okay, well, I'm glad it reappeared."

"Yes, things do seem to move around a lot. Do you have the ring now?"

"Yes. Safe in my pocket. It's going home with me."

"Good."

"Next we'll have to take care of those diamond earrings."

There's a vigorous nod of agreement. "We don't want any valuable jewelry here."

"They just don't understand the difference between diamonds and plastic beads anymore, do they?"

"No, I'm afraid not."

With a sad smile, I sign out and walk to my car. I slip behind the wheel and dig deep into my pocket to find Mom's ring. I stare at it for a long time lost in memories of Snicker bars and birthday parties before slipping the ring on my finger.

Then, I pull my cell phone from my purse and scroll for my sister's number. An answering machine. "Hey Doreen, get this. I'm just leaving the Mother's Day Tea thing and surprise, surprise, the sapphire ring has reappeared. Hallelujah. Next challenge is the earrings. Call me." I end the call and start my car, hoping I've missed the worst of the rush hour traffic, knowing it's an idle wish.

A few days pass without a word from my sister. Odd, she hasn't called, but I figure she's just busy. The phone rings while I'm cooking dinner Saturday night.

"I'm guessing you thought you left a message, but all I got was 'I'm leaving Clare Bridge.' I figured if something was wrong you'd call again. Life's been so hectic around here," Doreen says.

"Nothing's wrong. Just good news. Mom's ring made a reappearance."

"I meant to tell you. Sorry. She had it last weekend. I didn't notice until right when we were leaving. It was another spa day. When I saw it on Mom's hand, I asked Jamie about it, and she told me she had discovered it on another woman's hand. Go figure, right?"

"Yeah. Things really do float around that place, don't they? But, did you want her to keep it? I hope not because I took it. I have it now."

"No, that's good. I just couldn't figure out how to get it from her. I'm glad you've got it."

"Next the earrings."

"Yeah, that might be tough."

"Maybe if you tell her they need to be cleaned or something."

"Yeah, as long as I can unscrew them. They were really tight last time I tried."

"Well, at least we know they won't be disappearing," I say. "I'll bring you both rings for safekeeping when we meet for lunch, okay?

"Sounds good," Doreen says.

৵ ৶

Erin and I stand at the smudged glass counter of the downtown Claire's. I feel my daughter's frustration like a pot ready to boil over. It is her twenty-first birthday, and she spent the better part of the morning at the DMV getting her new driver's license. Finally an adult, she was given a horizontal temporary to replace the vertical license given minors in the state of Washington. Her new license will arrive by mail. Her old license was perforated to show it had been replaced. She has given both of these driver's licenses to the clerk at Claire's.

"You have to show two pieces of valid ID," the salesgirl says. "These aren't valid."

"What'd you mean they're not valid?" Erin asks. "I just got this one this morning."

"We have to have two pieces of ID."

"You've got two pieces," my daughter says, trying to stay calm. "In fact, you've got three. Here's my credit card."

"But this one's paper and this one's got a hole in it."

"You mean I can't get my ear pierced because my license is new?"

The clerk only nodded, more a shrug than a nod. A dismissive shrug.

"But if I were sixteen I could get my ear pierced. Now that I'm twenty-one I can't?"

"Looks that way."

"You really mean you won't accept my new license even with a credit card?"

"It's paper."

"Of course it's paper. It's a temporary. I got it today … on my birthday."

"It's not valid."

"Of course it's valid. SPD accepts it. The state patrol accepts it. Any bar in the city accepts it."

"Sorry," she says in a voice that expresses no sympathy, no empathy, and a whole lot of power-tripping attitude.

I step up to the counter. "I'm her mother. Just pierce her damn ear, alright? It's only one little hole. It's not even a new hole. It's just grown closed on one side. I'll buy a pair of good earrings."

"I can't," said the clerk, now losing just a fraction of her attitude. "She's twenty-one."

"But you just said you can't accept her ID, so maybe she's not twenty-one. Maybe she's eighteen. I'm her mother. Let's just pierce her ear, okay?"

"I can't."

"I'd like to speak with the manager."

"I am the manager."

"Come on, Mom. Let's get out of here," Erin says.

At this point I think she's afraid I won't be able to keep my cool as well as she can. The girl's got an amazing ability to stay calm, or at least to appear calm, despite her frustration. We aren't even out the door when the rant begins.

"How can they be so stupid? I mean she was just plain stupid."

"They definitely just lost any future business from us, didn't they?"

"I don't want anybody that stupid touching my ears," she says.

"No worries," I say. "We'll find someplace else."

"There's no other place downtown."

Of course, she's right. After a few inquiries it's clear Claire's holds a downtown monopoly on ear piercing. A shame. I'd promised Erin the re-piercing and a pair of earrings for her birthday. Now our plan is foiled by meaningless stupidity.

After a little downtown wandering, a new pair of shoes and a little travel purse, we head toward The Pink Door to meet up with a small gathering of family and friends for a birthday dinner.

"Hey Erin," a voice calls as we cross First Avenue. We turn to see Marleen's son.

We go through the back and forth greetings of family who live in the same city but rarely see each other. Then I hear Erin say, "Yeah, it's my birthday."

That's the cue I need. "Do you want to join us for dinner?" I ask. "We're on our way to The Pink Door right now."

Together we cross First Avenue, enter Post Alley and walk down the stairs into the restaurant. Prosecco is ordered for a birthday toast to the young woman who has filled my life with meaning and joy for the past twenty-one years. The baby turned woman. All grown-up and ready to embark on a journey of adventures of her own making.

"Can I see your ID?" the waitress asks.

Erin pulls out her new license, the one the clerk at the Claire's wouldn't accept, and passes it across the table.

"Happy Birthday," the waitress says with a smile. "What can I bring you?"

"The prosecco will be fine," Erin says.

I smile and remember our discovery of prosecco on a recent family vacation to Venice. I remember my many visits to this restaurant, an old favorite from before my marriage. I remember sitting in this very room only a year before celebrating Erin's twentieth birthday, just the three of us. It seems like yesterday. Now the table is crowded with a scattering of brightly wrapped gifts and surrounded by friends and family.

"To Erin," we say as we lift our glasses in unison.

"And to Maureen," I say in silence. "Thank you."

A few weeks pass and graduation day arrives. Again Erin has chosen a backyard barbecue celebration, just as she did for her high school graduation. Again, Tom and I spend May and June doing more yard work than we've done in the intervening years since the last graduation. By graduation day, we both need massages for our aching muscles. The gardens are overflowing with flowers, a new trellis adorns the backyard fence line, and the trees and vines are pruned to perfection. Even the fish seem happy in the sparkling water of the corner pond. The weather cooperates with bright Seattle sunshine and a deep blue sky.

Tom borrows a huge propane BBQ and sets it up in the front yard. Tables with umbrellas and chairs fill both sides of the backyard. The refrigerator is packed to capacity. There's a cooler full of soft drinks and a keg under the new trellis. The party is ready.

The day before we sat, just Tom and me, in a large auditorium at the University of Washington and watched our daughter graduate. Erin did not want to participate in the day-long, university-wide graduation in the football stadium. Instead, she walked the Political Science departmental graduation stage and received her diploma. Later we asked a stranger to snap a photo of the three of us beside the bronze husky guarding the entrance to the building. Erin was a university graduate.

Now, as the garden fills with friends and neighbors, cousins and aunts, I am the proud mother, overcome by joy. I watch the young people in particular. I am fascinated by how they gather and talk. I see them, a row of five or six adult children sitting in a tight line on the foot-high wall of my new vegetable garden. In my mind's eye, I see four-year-olds sitting on the edge of a sandbox. How have the years passed so quickly? What comes next in the lives of these young adults? Whatever it is, I know I will always be a part of my daughter's life, and that bone-deep knowledge makes me smile.

֍   ֍

Mom is wandering the halls and mumbling about going home when Erin and I arrive. But what is home in her muddled mind? A vague concept floating somewhere between the simple beach house she shared with Dad, the house she grew up in Herried, South Dakota, or her tiny room at the end of Cottage Place hallway?

"It's so sad," Erin says. "Poor Nana. It's like she thinks she's going to get in trouble or that her parents are worried about her."

"Yeah. Distraction, distraction, distraction. That's what they do here. They try to keep her and the other residents occupied and distracted each time they start worrying," I say. But I know my daughter is right.

We're walking the halls together with Mom humming along between us when one of the caregivers approaches. "Sally tried to escape an hour ago," she whispers in my ear. I motion to Erin to walk ahead with Mom on her arm to give me a moment with this news.

"Escape?" I whisper as soon as Mom is out of earshot.

"Yes. She got out the gate. She said she wanted to go home. She was anxious and scared when we found her at the front door."

"She seems okay now," I say, confusion fogging thought. "We were just going out for lunch. Is it okay?"

"Sure, it's okay. She'll be fine."

I catch up with Mom and Erin at the door and code in our own escape.

Later, after we return from lunch, after the congested drive back to West Seattle, after hours of thinking about what the caregiver told me of Mom's attempted escape, I draw my own conclusions. This is how I see it play out as I lie in bed that evening. Mom is walking along the garden paths. The bright red emergency exit button on the gate catches her attention and draws her like a moth to a light bulb on a warm summer night. And like a moth that gets too close, Mom touches the red button. The gate swings open. It is a simple act of curiosity. She wanders through the open gate, which closes tight behind her, and she finds herself in unfamiliar, frightening territory. There are large parking lots and cars racing along a busy street just below the hill that holds the building and fenced gardens Mom has just left behind. She has no idea where she is or where she should be. She continues to wander following the outer walls of the building, her anxiety mounting. Finally she is found by a caregiver alerted by the alarm that sounded when Mom inadvertently opened the locked gate.

"I want to go home," she tells the caregiver who then assumes Mom has master-minded an escape. Mom says she wants to go home, but home is the safety of her room at the end of Cottage Place hallway. Her Grayland home with Dad, and even her childhood home with her parents, are long forgotten or merged into some kind of vague conceptual memory rather than any clear reality.

She is, of course, anxious and scared when she is found. She is locked outside, lost in a new and frightening environment, and she doesn't know how to get back inside. She doesn't know how to get *home*.

An interesting phenomenon in elderly care in America today is the vast number of caregivers who are immigrants to the United States. According to the Direct Care Alliance, a national advocacy group for workers who provide care for America's elderly and those with long-term illnesses and disabilities, 21.8% of all nursing home aides and 27.1% of home health aides in America today are foreign born. I would venture to guess the numbers in Seattle and at Clare Bridge in Lynnwood are much higher. And while I have yet to encounter a caregiver whose English skills are not remarkable – far superior to the foreign language skills of the vast majority of native-born Americans – as an ESL teacher, I know there are times when language, when individual words, are taken too literally by second-language speakers. I believe this is what happened in the case of my mother's attempted "escape." When Mom used the word "home" it was misunderstood to mean something other than the concept my mother was struggling to express with her own increasingly obvious loss of language.

I don't know how accurate these interpretations might be. I also don't know if these ideas went anywhere after I shared them with the Clare Bridge nurse. I do know the bright red emergency exit buttons have been altered on the gates in such a manner as to avoid inadvertent exits resulting from the curiosity of childlike brains. I also know I am satisfied with my own understanding of the events of that day, and I do not fear for my mother's well-being.

A few weeks later, I visit Mom again. Again, we walk in the gardens. When we reach the end of the walkway that dead-ends at one of the gates, Mom points to the bright red button, now encased in a plastic security box. "Don't touch," she says.

আ ্ড

Aunt Lilly is my mother's youngest sister. She and my uncle Wesley have lived in West Seattle since the 1940s. Still, they played only a minor role in my childhood. Mom and Dad moved out of the city and raised their nine kids, myself included, in what was then the rural farmland of the Issaquah Valley. Even my aunt and uncle's purchase of an adjacent plot of undeveloped land did little to bring them into our lives. My two cousins were almost strangers to me. Then, at seventeen I left home and soon after left Seattle.

When I returned to Seattle in the early eighties just after Maureen's disappearance and before her confirmed murder, Aunt Lilly and Uncle Wesley offered me the rental of a tiny house across the alley from their own West Seattle home atop Genesee Hill. A few years later, Tom painted clouds on the storage room ceiling and made a nursery before our baby's birth. In another two years, we were able to purchase our own home, only blocks from the rental, but contact with my aunt and uncle returned to sad infrequency despite our physical proximity.

Like my parents, by the nineties my aunt and uncle spent half of each year in Arizona. At the same time, my own life was consumed by my daughter, my work, and my writing. Barely able to keep track of my parents and siblings, apart from the annual Christmas card, I lost contact with my extended family once again.

Then, Dad died, and Mom was alone. My aunt and uncle, who also had a small vacation home near my parents in Grayland, visited her almost every summer. When we finally moved Mom into dementia care, Aunt Lilly called me every so often to see how her sister was doing. That's when I learned of Uncle Wesley's failing health, the reason for their continued year-round residence in Arizona.

Now it is summer time, and I get a call from Aunt Lilly. They're in Seattle and want me to come up the hill for a visit. My cousins are home as well. We set a date. I'm nervous. I find it hard to visit with family I feel I should know, but don't. And yet with Aunt Lilly and her daughters it only seems to take a few minutes of small talk before they find my comfort zone. It's their questions, I think. The questions they ask about my life and my writing make me feel they really care. I learn they have read *The Thirty-Ninth Victim*, and they believe I have written a good book, a book that is balanced and honest, a book with social merit. When Aunt Lilly asks if my siblings have read it, I am honest. I tell her I don't know. Grateful to be able to talk about my writing with family, I feel validated.

When Laureen comes to town a few weeks later, we are again invited for a visit. Again, we sit around the dining room table with tea, coffee and cookies: Laureen and her youngest daughter, Aunt Lilly, one of my cousins, and me. Uncle Wesley is resting in another room. They ask about Laureen's teaching in Istanbul, about my niece's life in Bellingham, about their plans for the future. We talk of childhood and family and Mom. Somehow the conversation turns in my direction, and Aunt Lilly, in that wonderful way she has of putting it all on the table, says, "She's a really good writer. Have you read her book?"

"I have," my niece says a bit too quickly as though wanting to fill the air space, wanting to cover for her mother.

Aunt Lilly continues to look directly at my sister, waiting for her response. It's not a challenge. Just her natural curiosity. I could've jumped across the table and kissed her for doing what nobody in my immediate first family, myself included, is willing or able to do – address the elephant in the corner.

"I don't have a copy," my sister says.

"I can give you one," I say. Fortified by my aunt's question, I find myself stronger, unwilling to give an inch.

"That's okay," Laureen says. "I want to read your other book. The Amazon one."

"That's not a book," I say. "It was only a contest, and I didn't win. So no book. Only a manuscript."

"But it's fiction, right?" she asks. "A novel?"

I nod. I look at the silent faces around the table and take a drink of my warm tea.

"I want to read that one," my sister repeats.

"Maybe. Someday," I say. "When it's published."

There's no conflict, only a sister unable to face her own family history in black ink on white paper on the printed page. I can accept that. In fact, I can accept it more easily than I can accept the truth of the situation – that the conversation would never have occurred, that my writing life would never have been mentioned, without Aunt Lilly's intervention.

It's just after the visit with Aunt Lilly that Laureen and I formulate a plan to visit Charleen at her home in Ellensburg. The following weekend we drive Interstate 90 over the Cascade Mountains. Charleen, the sister who comes between Laureen and me in age, has moved with her husband to a farm in the far shadows of the mountains. I have never seen the place, never made the drive, never felt I was welcome since the release of *The Thirty-Ninth Victim* even though the move was several years before. With Laureen and her daughter, I feel stronger, able to invite myself along without fear.

I haven't seen Charleen since Mom's eighty-fifth birthday party at Clare Bridge, and yet I am welcomed with open arms. She shows us around the house, the preschool, the barn, the garden, the apple orchard. We make garden fresh vegetable and local cheese sandwiches, and we talk of nothing at all.

"Let's go see the site," Charleen says after lunch.

"Site?" Laureen asks.

"Yeah, the Habitat house," Charleen says.

"But I'm not dressed for a construction site," Laureen says.

"How do you dress for a construction site? And who cares? The workers aren't going to care. Or is that the problem? Do you want them to care?" I love to tease Laureen, our only unmarried sister.

"Come on, Mom. It'll be fun," her daughter says.

"Alright, but I have to use the bathroom first," she says. "And I'm not swinging a hammer."

"I suppose we all should," someone says.

"There's two, Arleen. You can use the one in our bedroom," Charleen says.

It's odd how at times the human eye is drawn as though by some invisible thread to what the mind most needs to know. I need to know if I've been forgiven, if Charleen, like my other siblings and my sister-in-law, has come to terms with my violation of family protocol, if she's forgiven me for having published *The Thirty-Ninth Victim*.

In the hour or two of conversation since our arrival, no question has been asked about what I'm up to, what's new in my life, what matters most to me. We talk about Charleen's new life in Ellensburg, we talk of our kids, we talk about Mom, we talk about the Habitat for Humanity work she and her husband are involved in, but my writing is not mentioned. I don't have Aunt Lilly here in Charleen's kitchen to bring up the unmentionable, and because it is not mentioned, I still don't know if I've been forgiven.

Then, I walk into my sister's master bedroom on my way to the bathroom, and my eyes fall to a low bookcase running the length of the far wall below a large picture window. Over half the bookcase is hidden from sight, but several feet are still visible just beyond the foot of the bed.

Perhaps my eyes always go to bookshelves when I'm in someone's home for the first time in the way some people used to gravitate to the LP collection, and later to the CD tower. Now, with MP3 players, how do you size up a new friend's musical tastes? With the onslaught of recorded books and digital readers, will the day arrive when walls are no longer lined with the books that tell the tale of personal passions?

My eyes graze my sister's bookshelves, and there at the very end of the bottom shelf, front cover in full view, my eyes rest on *The Thirty-Ninth Victim*.

I stand in silence. I want to go over, pick it up, page through in search of a folded corner, margin notes, a bookmark, of any evidence the book has been read. But I am frozen in place.

"Come on, Arleen, let's go." I hear the call from the other room. I use the bathroom and rush out with only a fleeting glance at the book that tells me at least Charleen has cared enough to buy a copy. I'm guessing that unlike my sister Laureen, Charleen has not only bought the book, but has also read it.

I still wish we could talk about it, about the book, about my writing life, about this new manuscript about Mom I have spent the last few years creating as well as the novel I've started. I wish I could invite my siblings to readings of new works and send them copies of new publications, but as long as I write memoir, I know this is unlikely, for I feel certain these gestures would be unwelcomed. Or, maybe I just need courage.

જ ન્

I stand in the doorway to the Clare Bridge dining room, my niece at my side, scanning the room. Tables are scattered throughout, white tablecloths and harvest decorations. The number of chairs at each table corresponding to the number of guests planning to join each resident for this early Thanksgiving dinner.

I recognize the sweater before I recognize my mother's face. It's a face I don't know. A hairstyle that is new to me. In all the years I have known my mother, from childhood to middle-age, I have never seen my mother as Jessica Tandy in *Driving Miss Daisy*. The sparkle of her eyes holds me, pulls me across the room. I've never seen her eyes so gray-blue, her cheeks so pink, her hair so styled.

"You look gorgeous, Mom," I say.

"Me?"

"Yes, you. Was it spa day today?"

She pats her hair, unsure what I'm talking about. Not remembering the afternoon of make-up and makeovers, the special pre-Thanksgiving dinner activity.

My niece gives her grandmother a hug, and we settle at our table by the window. Mom is cold and my niece offers her wool shawl, draping it over Mom's shoulders. I'm snapping a few photos with my cell phone, cursing myself for once again not having my camera when I need it, when Gwen, the activities coordinator, approaches with a camera and offers to take a few shots of us.

"Sally, you're so beautiful," she says, smothering my mother in a tight hug. "You're all beautiful. Such a beautiful family."

For such compliments, even I am even able to put up with extra hugs. My mother is indeed striking. For the first time I catch a glimpse of the beauty, albeit faded, but still alluring of the woman my father fell deeply in love with so many years ago. I'm given a peep hole into the past and am grateful to the staff for showing me my mother, showing me the woman my mother once was, the beauty she was, the beauty she still is at eighty-six, even in her confusion, even in the sweater with the Navajo motif she's worn since the years when she and Dad drove each autumn to Arizona to escape the winter cold of Seattle. There they stayed in the comfort of a small home Dad built on the Arizona/Mexico border just outside of Why, Arizona. "Why?" read the T-shirt I once made for Dad. A joke. But maybe not. So many whys haunted my relationship with my parents. With so many unanswered questions, their choice of Why, Arizona just seemed to make sense.

But I'm not thinking about Why, Arizona, or even of Dad as I sit with Mom and my niece for Thanksgiving dinner. I do wonder why we're having Thanksgiving dinner on November 2nd, but mostly I find myself pondering my mother's beauty, how the pinkish purple sheen of eye shadow makes her eyes sparkle gray-blue, and the touch of eyeliner darkens them just so. I study how the color on her cheeks and lips seems to make her glow. And how her hair pulled up and back from her face gave her a polish reminiscent of the nursing school graduation picture that stands on my writing room bookcase.

I am happy, thrilled, to have a glimpse of Mom's beauty. Saddened to accept I am seeing it only now, so late in life, at a point in my mother's life when she no longer recognizes the beauty in her own face, no longer recognizes my face or my niece's face as faint reflections of her own.

≈ ≈

I key myself in and head down the hall. Another visit. I pass the baby room, a room vaguely reminiscent of so many infant/maternity rooms where Mom worked through her long career as an RN. There's a large viewing window where a new parent could stand to see the babies lined up in tiny cribs just beyond the glass. But this room holds only one large crib, not rows of infant bassinets, and the two babies lying in the crib are anatomically correct babies of plastic and cloth. Mom loves the baby room. I often find her there, leaning over the side of the crib tucking in the babies.

But not today. I keep walking. "She was here a few minutes ago," Gwen says when I stick my head into the activity room. "I think she was headed to her room." So, I walk the hall of Cottage Place, knock softly on her door, and push it open. She sits on the edge of her bed, her feet barely touching the floor. She seems lost in a difficult decision.

"Hi, Mom," I say. "They told me I might find you here. What are you doing?"

"I don't know," she says.

"Taking a nap?"

"Maybe."

"It's getting close to dinner time. Tough decision, right? You don't want to miss dinner, do you?"

"Oh no," she says.

I sit down next to her on the bed and put an arm around her shoulders. As if in slow motion, she relaxes her weight into me, and together we roll back onto the bed with a gentle laugh. Then we lie in silence for a moment.

"This feels good, doesn't it?" I say. Never a back sleeper, I roll over onto my side and pull my knees up. Mom remains flat on her back beside me, her legs dangling over the edge of the bed. I lie at her side on the narrow bed, my hand resting on her soft belly. I stroke her smooth, white hair with my other hand. My mother has become the child Erin once was. She has returned to the innocence of childhood. And like a child, she enjoys the moment, relishes the touch, feels my love.

There's so much I still do not know about this woman who is my mother. So much I'd like to know, but will never know. When she introduces me as her sister, is it because she's truly confused and thinks I'm Aunt Grace? Or, does she introduce me as her sister simply because she struggles for words and the word *daughter* evades her – a woman who gave birth to six daughters?

I cannot fathom looking into the beautiful bright eyes of my own daughter and failing to recall the word *daughter*, failing to remember the day she spoke her first word, the day she screamed on Santa's lap, the day I caught her shoplifting, the day she graduated from university. But my mother remembers none of those milestones in my life. I wonder if she ever did, even then, even when I was the child and she the young mother. How can you remember the first word of the middle child of nine kids? There were other, far greater concerns to deal with like getting food on the table and making sure the older kids got off to school on time, the younger kids had their diapers changed.

Indeed, there is much I do not know about my mother. And will never know. But what if I'd had the nerve to ask before it was too late? What if I'd tried to interview my mother? What would I have asked and what, if anything, would she have told me?

I'd like to know if she felt she'd lost herself in her fifty years of marriage to my father. Or, did she truly believe in her heart she had gained more than she lost?

I'd like to know if she and Dad talked, really talked about what was in their hearts, about their pains and their joys. Did they share and support each other on an emotional level?

I'd like to ask my mother why she allowed Dad to disown my sister, Laureen. I'd like to know if her love for Dad was greater than the love she felt for her children. And if it was not, how could she come to terms with the kind of sacrifice that meant losing her daughter and two granddaughters? I'd like to know which way the balance tilted between love and dependency in their marriage.

I'd like to ask my mother how a woman comes to terms with the vicious murder of her youngest daughter. How did she survive, whom did she talk to, with whom did she share the agony in her heart?

What happened to the friends my mother had as a young woman? Did that young woman and those friends simply disappear when she married Dad, had nine kids, and raised her family on a farm in the Issaquah Valley? Who did she talk with, who did she share her secrets with when the pain was unbearable? Did she ever want to just give up, walk away, die? What in the hell kept her going? Her love for Dad? Her obligation to her children?

What about before, when she was the child? Did she share her innermost thoughts and dreams with her own mother? With her father? Either of her two sisters or her brother? And if she did, if she learned to speak and share with these people in her life, how could she leave it all behind and become my father's stoic shadow? And now, if she could look back, if dementia had not stolen her memories, how would she assess her own life?

I lie beside my mother, my hand resting on her belly, feeling the air, the life force, enter and leave her body, and I am engulfed in love. When I relax, she relaxes. She hums a bit. She says a few words, and I try to guess what she wants to express. A tender moment interwoven with sadness. I love this sweet, gentle woman she has become, this funny woman who after one kiss goodbye too many says "that's enough." I lament not having been aware of this woman, not knowing this woman, as a child, a teenager, a young woman, buried as she was under her burdens and pain. So busy trying to be a good mother, a good provider, did she lose her own happy self?

I learn this lesson when Erin is already twenty-one, when her childhood years have slipped away like so many grains of sand through my open fingers. But I am thirty years my mother's junior and Erin is thirty-five years my own. I still have time to shed the judging, teaching, shaping skin of my early mothering and let my daughter know the strong, but gentle, funny woman who is buried beneath my hardened façade. I am learning to let go of pain and fear before my mind does it for me, before my brain erases all I can no longer bear, taking with it all I cherish.

I'm not sure if I actually fall asleep – sleep has not been my friend as I edge my way through menopause – but I relax. I remember the long afternoons napping with baby Erin. I remember that last night in Grayland, Mom's last night in Grayland, when I did not, would not sleep with my mother in her stuffy bedroom. I let the feelings of joy and loss, guilt and regret float over me, through me, and then I just let go.

എ ∞

Another year has melted away like a whisper of snowfall on the wet Seattle streets. It is lull time, those days when the excitement of Christmas has passed, before the New Year's Eve preparations begin. Soon, it will be Mom's second anniversary, the anniversary of her second year in dementia care.

Tom, Erin, and I arrive at Clare Bridge for a holiday visit. Christmas decorations, a bit wilted, a bit tired, still adorn the facility. The routine is the same. We find Mom. She gives us the tour and takes us to her room at the end of Cottage Place hallway. Doreen, a woman of subtle style, has replaced the artificial floral wreath that usually hangs from Mom's door to help her find her room with an equally tacky holiday wreath, resplendent in fake evergreen, plastic holly, and a sparkly red ribbon.

"That's pretty, Nana," Erin says with a look in my direction. That special look she uses to tell me when something is hideous, like when I put together an outfit that just doesn't work.

"My room," Mom says as she opens the door.

"Do you want your flowers here?" Tom asks as he places the large poinsettia on her dresser.

"Good," Mom says. She smiles and hums as she putters around her tiny room.

"We better get a plate to put under that," I say.

This is the pattern: my mother will water the poor plant until it drowns, and then, wilted and straggly, we'll need to throw it out when she's not looking.

"Here's one," Erin says. She pulls a plastic plant tray from the bottom of Mom's closet, a remnant from the last houseplant she had in her room.

We have dressed for this holiday visit and for the meal out we plan to enjoy after the visit with Mom ends. Tom is in slacks, Erin is always beautiful no matter what she wears, and I am wearing a pair of bright red patent leather loafers.

Mom notices my shoes and points to them. "Pretty," she says.

I smile and remember my father, the man who once told me only whores wore red shoes. One of my most defiant, or perhaps disrespectful, moves was the purchase of a pair of red suede heels the year after Dad died. Unable to wear heels much anymore, I now wear red loafers. They always make me smile. And somehow I can't help but think that wherever Dad is now, whatever form he has taken, those shoes make him smile too, if only because my defiance is so little, so late.

"Do you like my shiny red shoes?" I ask my mother.

"Yes," she says. "Pretty."

I open her closet and dig through the hangers until I find a bright red cardigan covered with embroidered reindeer and Christmas trees, even a few tiny bells here and there. "Mom, do you want to wear your Christmas sweater?" I ask.

"Oh yes," she says.

As I help my mother put on the sweater, I get another look from my daughter. Tom only sits in the corner chair silently flipping through a decade-old *National Geographic*.

We wander toward the activity room and spend a few minutes piecing together puzzles, but Mom has no more patience for puzzles. I'm not certain she ever really liked them much. Just something to do. We walk. At the nursery we stop and play with the baby dolls. Tom winds up the mobile of tiny stuffed animals hanging above the crib. Mom hums as she turns the babies onto their sides and tucks the blankets tight around them. We're unsure if she knows they are only plastic and cloth, that they do not have hearts and blood and brains. She hums her contentment, and I smile with the understanding that what she doesn't know no longer matters.

When she's finished, we continue walking the halls. Tom drops behind as Mom, Erin, and I link arms – my mother sandwiched between my daughter and myself. Mom begins to lift her knees and march, her humming a constant companion.

"We're off to see the Wizard," I sing. "The wonderful Wizard of Oz." Erin joins in, then Tom behind us. "A wiz of a wiz if ever there was, the wonderful Wizard of Oz."

We laugh and giggle. Mom hums along, lifting her knees in rhythm, joyous laughter spilling from her. Maybe, just maybe I have found my way home. Home – that place of love and acceptance, peace and understanding. That place in the heart where all is well.

EPILOGUE

VIGIL

THURSDAY, FEBRUARY 21, 2013

TWO YEARS SLIP away. Two years of steady mental and physical decline. Two years of regular visits and increased care.

Now, I stand at my mother's bedside. I lean forward, kiss her cheek, stroke her hair. "Hello, Mom, Sally," I say. "It's me. Arleen. Your daughter. I love you."

Her eyes seem to focus, a flash of something in the pale gray. Recognition? Connection? Love? Then it is gone.

I sit in this tiny room in the dementia care facility to await my mother's passing, desperate for an end to her misery, hoping it doesn't come today on my sister's birthday. I talk nonsense, grade student compositions, write in my notebook. I read aloud first from one book, then another as the hours layer one upon another. My mother no longer eats or drinks or moves. Even her eyes now seem frozen in place. Her small frail body is shutting down. Only her heavy breathing tells me she is still alive.

I am alone with the shadow of the woman who was once my mother, her quiet strength so often misunderstood. For eleven years since my father's death she has been alone. For eleven years she has been lost in the tightening clutches of dementia, the memories of her greatest joys and her most horrific tragedies wiped away with an indiscriminate, cruel stroke of brain malfunction. In these eleven years I have felt closer to my mother than in all the accumulated years prior. An irony. My loss.

Throughout the afternoon my vigil is interrupted only by caregivers shifting my mother's position, teaching me to moisten her lips, offering their words of comfort. By nurses checking her vitals.

The chair is plastic cold, the room too warm. I sit with my mother, this fragile dying woman who was once the vibrant mother of nine, the love of my father's life, and I am awash in memories. As a growing adolescent, I wanted to be like my mother. I wanted to be petite and pretty, with blond curls, tiny feet, perfect eyes. But I continued to grow, tall and gangly, with dark frizz, big feet, and coke-bottle glasses. I am not my mother's daughter. I do not possess her quiet strength and grace, traits I came to appreciate only in these final years as dementia took her from me. But a brief phone conversation with my Aunt Lilly assures me that I have my mother's eyes. "They were hazel," she tells me. With one simple phone call, the disagreement with my sister, Doreen, about the color of our mother's eyes is clarified. Hazel is an eye color that appears both green and blue dependent on light and ambient colors.

I open the drawer in my mother's bedside table to find the hospice journal. The last entry reads: "Sally continues her dying process." My mother has been dying for eleven years. For the first seven of those years she insisted, demanded, fought to stay in the home she and my father shared on a lonely stretch of Pacific beach where the crash of waves lulled her to sleep after she checked and rechecked the doors and windows, after she raised the thermostat to warm her soul, after her tears dampened her lonely pillow. By 2009 it was obvious to everyone from the home healthcare provider to the post mistress and the grocery cashiers that my mother could not continue to live alone, and we moved her into dementia care against her wishes. She adapted and gained weight. She walked the halls humming and smiling. But the disease kept picking away at her brain, stealing bits and pieces, memories and motor skills.

This room where I sit on this plastic chair, softened now with the padded cushion from her idle wheelchair, has been my mother's home for four years. This tiny room and bathroom. A single bed and bedside table. A dresser with a large oval mirror that once belonged to my paternal grandmother. The floor bare for easy mopping, the walls institutional white, the only personal touches are the family photos of faces she's long forgotten. Her husband of fifty years, her nine children and numerous grandchildren, her beloved parents are all strangers.

My mother has not eaten for a week. She is dying as I sit beside her, my notebook open to record the close of her life. My pen moves across this page because I can do nothing more. I can only sit and sooth her occasional tremors with a hand on her shoulder and listen to the shallow breathing of a life at its end. I can only offer comfort with touch, word, and song. *I love you, a bushel and a peck, a bushel and a peck and a hug around the neck.* My father's deep voice fills my head. I struggle to remember the lyrics and sing to my mother in a voice that even I do not want to hear, a voice that is not my father's voice. *Daisy, Daisy give me your answer do. I'm half crazy over the love of you ...*

At dinnertime I am served my mother's meal, the meal she no longer eats. Barley soup, pork roast, mashed potatoes, mixed vegetables. I do not push the lima beans around my plate as I did in childhood. I eat my mother's dinner at her bedside, her red cloth napkin spread across my knees, the chords of Andres Segovia filling the silence between her breaths.

As evening progresses, I must decide whether to stay or go.

"How much time is left?" I ask Nurse Erika when she returns for a 9:00 p.m. check.

"I don't have a crystal ball," she tells me, her voice a caress. She teaches me about mottling, the blotchy skin discoloration caused by decreased blood flow, as she massages lotion into my mother's cold feet. "It's only progressed to her calves," she says. "But I don't have that crystal ball."

I decide to go home.

FRIDAY, FEBRUARY 22, 2013

I DRIVE NORTH knowing my older brother and his wife are already with our mother. Later Doreen and her husband join us. More chairs are pushed into the small room. Mom's breathing is rough. She's now on morphine applied to the inside of her mouth every two hours. The dosage increases as the hours pass. We fill the afternoon with memories and laughter as caregivers change shifts, hospice workers offer comfort, nurses administer medications.

Before Doreen and her husband leave, we play with Mom's wheelchair and talk of my spending the night in it. By 8:30 p.m., Mom and I are alone again, and I am still undecided. I call Tom to give him an update and assure him once again that I want to be alone with Mom, that it might be her last night. I tell him I don't know when I'll be home.

A half hour later Nurse Erika and I talk of Mom's labored breathing. She shows me that the mottling is now up to Mom's thighs. She decides to increase the morphine. When she leaves to get the medication, I notice we've lost the classical radio station that's been our backdrop for the past two days. I fiddle with the dial and land on 88.5 FM, music of the 40s big band era.

"Go dance with Dad," I whisper to my mother. "He's waiting for you. Put on your black velvet top and your taffeta skirt. Go dancing, Mom. We'll be okay. I love you."

Her teeth clack two, three, four times. Her harsh open-mouthed breathing stops.

"She seems too silent," I say as Nurse Erika enters the room.

She places her hands on Mom's chest, a gentle searching for the movements of breath or heartbeat, the signs of life. I am at her side. I reach forward and place the back of my hand on my mother's cheek. She releases one final breath and leaves this world.

Nurse Erika and I look into each other's eyes, grasp each other's arms. "Is she really gone?" I ask.

"She's gone."

I look at the wall clock. 9:25 p.m.

Nurse Erika's stethoscope confirms my mother's passing. "I'll call hospice," she tells me and leaves the room.

I am alone with my mother's body still expecting another rasping breath. My arm on her chest, I swear I feel movement.

The hospice nurse arrives. Another stethoscope check. Another confirmation. "I'll call Neptune Society," she tells me and closes the door softly behind her.

Doreen and her husband return. They'd only just gotten home when I called. I also call Tom, and he arrives as quickly as traffic allows. My eldest sister who's been in flight, ending a vacation early, is soon with us as well. We sit together, talking quietly, saying our silent goodbyes to Mom's departing spirit.

The hospice nurses assure us that it is all right for us to leave, that they will take care of all the arrangements. Still, we sit. Only when they arrive to take our mother's body do we stand to leave. I kiss Mom's forehead for the last time and walk out the door.

My husband wraps his arm around my shoulders and leads me away from the tiny room at the end of Cottage Place. He keys in the code for the last time and helps me into his car.

I speak softly in the deep darkness of the cold February night. "It was a gift," I tell him. "Being with her in her final moments was a gift, and I am so grateful she shared it with me."

ACKNOWLEDGMENTS

Shortly after the conversation with my sisters at the Alki Bakery in early 2005, I was at writing practice. I'd attempted to write of the encounter but found myself struggling for authenticity, for truth. After reading aloud around the table, Robert Ray pulled me aside and encouraged me to write the words as I'd heard them, as I'd felt them. For that encouragement and instruction in the art and craft of writing remembered dialogue, I am grateful.

Mom's Last Move has taken fourteen years to completion. I began jotting notes and scenes in my journal throughout the early years after my father's death in 2002. When *The Thirty-Ninth Victim* was published in 2008, readers asked about my mother and how she was coping with the death of her husband of fifty-four years and the conviction of her youngest daughter's murderer. I knew then I had another story to write. I continued to chronicle my mother's journey and my own while also turning to fiction. By April 2016, three years after my mother's death, I had three published novels, *The Thirty-Ninth Victim* was scheduled for re-release, and *Mom's Last Move* under publishing contract. That's when I received notification that my publisher was going out of business.

After re-releasing the novels and first memoir, I was ready to share this new work.

Fourteen years is a long time to remember all the gracious, generous people who offered encouragement and suggestions, who read and edited manuscript drafts. At the risk of omitting names, I'd like to mention a few of these wonderful souls. Boundless gratitude to my friend and writing partner, Pamela Hobart Carter, with whom I share tea and words each week. You keep me grounded. To my mentor and friend, Jack Remick, who is always available when I reach out, I am forever indebted. To others who read the various drafts of this manuscript as *Mom's Last Move* morphed into the book you hold, I appreciate your insight and honesty. Trust comes hard to me. You have taught me to share my words and to trust my truth: Karen Burns, Veronique Burke, Susan Knox, Gail Kretchmer, and Gouri Sivarajan.

My Sunday morning writing group supports and sustains me. An early excerpt under the working title *Moving Mom* was published in *Sunday Ink: Works by the Uptown Writers* in 2010. Thank you for all you are and all you do: Carol Bolt, Billie Condon, Pamela Hobart Carter, Geri Gale, Randy Hale, Susan Knox, Stacy Lawson, Catherine Sutthoff, and Janet Yoder.

My thanks also to Loretta Matson for another lovely cover and to Adam Bodendieck for interior design and technical assistance.

Finally, I wish to express my love and gratitude to my dear Aunt Lilly Lund for her enduring love, to my beloved mother-in-law Lucy Williams for believing in me, to my daughter, Erin Williams for blessing the publication of this story, and to my rock, Tom Williams, without whom I may never have found my way to the page.

READ ON...

THE THIRTY-NINTH VICTIM

PROLOGUE

STILL A SECRET

I WROTE THIS memoir telling myself I was facing the truth. Yet I kept these pages hidden. No one in my first family knew I was writing. No one knew I completed a yearlong memoir-writing program at the University of Washington. Only my husband and daughter watched me walk through graduation in June 2003.

Our house is small, and my office is the guest bedroom. When guests came to stay – my mother, out-of-town siblings, nieces – I hid all evidence. I locked the beautiful antique oak desk my husband and I found on one of our afternoons of haunting the antique shops of Seattle. There are two cabinets, each with a storybook-shaped, brass-lined keyhole. The key is also ornate brass. In today's world, they're too beautiful to be practical. I used this key to lock away my secrets, to hide my truths.

One bright summer day in late July 2003, almost a year into the project, I was visiting my mother. During our dinner conversation at a local restaurant, Mom said something about how I was more comfortable talking about Maureen and Dad than anyone else in the family. She said it was easy talking with me because I was so open.

When she touched on openness, on honesty, I felt like a fraud. "I haven't been totally open with you this past year. I have a secret I need to tell you."

I saw a shadow cross her gentle face. "Is it okay here? Should we go out to the car?"

"No, no, it's okay. It's not that big of a deal, and you're a tough cookie."

We were both already teary-eyed from talking about Dad and Maureen. She didn't want to make a scene in a public place, and she was truly afraid of what I might tell her.

"I've been writing a memoir about Maureen and myself and what I remember. Let me back up. For the past year…" I paused, hesitated, not sure how to tell her. Then I just plunged forward. "Last September, I signed up for a writing program at the University of Washington because I wanted to write, but I wasn't sure what. Within a month, I knew I needed to write about Maureen. So I'm trying to write."

Mom was very quiet, but she looked relieved. It wasn't a horrible secret. It wasn't terrible, bad news. Not like bad news she'd had to bear in the past.

"I know we're a big family, and everybody's story is different. But I had a unique vantage point as the middle kid. So all I can do is write my story, and Maureen's story as I know it, as I remember it."

"Okay, that's good." She paused. "She came to see you in Mexico."

"Yes. Those are the pieces I'm trying to put together, Mom. The little pieces of memory. But I'm afraid to tell anyone. I was afraid to tell you. Please don't tell anyone yet."

She put her forefinger to her lips and whispered, "I won't tell your secret to anyone."

CHAPTER ONE

CHRYSANTHEMUMS

GARY RIDGWAY MURDERED my baby sister. Now known as the Green River Killer, Ridgway murdered at least forty-eight women during the height of his killing spree from 1982 to 1984. He continued to kill through the 1990s. Today, no one, not even the killer himself, knows the gruesome total. My sister Maureen was the thirty-ninth victim of his slaughter.

My writing mentor insists that to write Maureen's story, I must understand Ridgway. I must see, feel, express this story from all points of view. I must be Gary Ridgway. But I can't do it. I don't want to do it. I can't write about Ridgway, or Ridgway's motives, or Ridgway's point of view about murder, because to do that, to be Ridgway, I have to try to understand why a man kills, what motivates a man to pay for sex, to promise to pay for sex, knowing he'll never pay.

He won't have to pay. The girl will be dead.

On a Thursday in late September 1983, Ridgway left work at Kenworth Truck Company in Renton, Washington, and cruised fourteen miles into Seattle with the intent to kill.

Where did he find my sister? I don't know. No one knows, not even Ridgway. "I killed so many women," he said, "I have a hard time keeping them straight."

They meant nothing to him. They were garbage to him. Maureen was garbage. Not human. Not a girl with family, dreams, potential. Ridgway knew nothing about, cared nothing about these girls, about Maureen.

Where did he kill Maureen? In the canopy on the back of his truck, the police now know. But where was the truck parked? The International District? Under an Interstate 90 overpass? Lower Beacon Hill? Near Seattle University?

All of these areas I knew well, both before and after the murder. As a student at Seattle University in the early 1970s, I worked at Todd Chemical Company on Rainier Avenue. I walked to and from my dorm room in Campion Tower, clutching a small can of mace in my pocket. Always aware of who was in front, beside, behind. Aware of doors, alleys, danger spots. I was a farm girl, just like Maureen, living in the big city for the first time.

Was I born streetwise, and she wasn't? Was I born lucky, and she wasn't?

How can I be Ridgway? How can I understand his motives, his desires, his needs? How can I imagine the thoughts that went through his mind as he cruised for prostitutes? He called it "patrolling." Later, he told the Green River Task Force he was helping the police clean up the streets of Seattle by getting rid of prostitutes. As if they were rats.

The Task Force suspected Ridgway early on, while Maureen was still alive. They questioned him on May 4, 1983, four days after victim twenty-nine, Marie Malvar, disappeared, but they said that they had no hard evidence connecting Ridgway to her disappearance. I have to wonder: how hard did they look before writing him off as a suspect?

They had a chance when Marie Malvar vanished. Following her disappearance, two police detectives stood at Ridgway's door to question him about Marie. Then they left. Marie's body lay in the woods, only a few miles away. Ridgway took detectives to the spot in September 2003, twenty years later.

Victims thirty through forty-eight were still alive the day the police questioned Ridgway about Marie Malvar. Maureen was still alive. It nags me: how hard did they look?

How can I pretend to be the man who stood in his yard chatting with two cops, knowing the body of his most recent victim was still warm in her shallow grave? A good old white boy passing the time. An average Joe. How can I be the man so devoid of human emotion that he passed a lie detector test?

I can't. So I tell my story – mine, not his – and I tell Maureen's story, because she can no longer tell it.

* * *

Maureen was nineteen when Gary Ridgway murdered her. It is impossible to believe, even harder to accept, that my sister got lost in the world of prostitution. For twenty years, there was no proof that she had. But with Ridgway's confession, denial was no longer an option. Denial does not honor Maureen. The truth must be examined and understood. It must be accepted.

Maureen was missing for thirty-one months before her remains were discovered less than ten miles from our family home on Tiger Mountain. On May 2, 1986, a worker at a nearby residence for juvenile delinquents came across some scattered bones in the woods. A skull, a jawbone, a tibia. Dental records proved the unfathomable.

My worst nightmares could not stand up to the horror of reality: Ridgway murdered my baby sister and left her body to decompose in the foothills of the Cascade mountain range. It is beautiful country, not far from Echo Glen Children's Center, where our mother worked as a night nurse. Mom could have known the young man who found her daughter's strewn remains. She could have been working in the infirmary the night Gary Ridgway dumped the body of her youngest child practically at her doorstep.

Even today, Mom relives her fears of working the graveyard shift. "Have I told you about the night it was snowing so hard my car couldn't get up the hill?"

I only smile, unwilling to cut her off by telling her that in the past few years, I've heard her memories so often they've become my own.

"I was on my way to work. You know I worked at Echo Glen, don't you?" She glances at me, and I nod my head. "That night, it was snowing so hard I couldn't get up that big hill, so I just stopped under the I-90 overpass."

I know my line here. "Did you have a blanket or anything in the car?"

"Always," she says. "But I didn't have to wait long. When I didn't show up for my shift, the night watchman came looking for me. He drove out in that horrible snow and picked me up in his big truck."

I smile again as a distant terror washes over her face. "That was really nice of him."

"It just makes me sick to my stomach to think that horrible man was out there killing girls right there where I was parked." Tears fill her eyes. "He could have been out there with her."

My mother doesn't mention Maureen by name, but I know who she's talking about. And we sit together in silence, remembering.

I now know that the date Mom's car refused to face the snowy hill does not actually coincide with Maureen's date of death, but frankly, it doesn't matter. The fear, the pain, and the place associations are what matter to me. For my mother, the memory of her many years of dedicated service at Echo Glen will always be tainted by its proximity to her youngest daughter's long-lost remains.

Prior to the discovery of Maureen's body, I had loved nature. I was a hiker and a backpacker. I wandered the forests of the Pacific Northwest with the abandon of an inquisitive child, and I felt more spiritual peace in the woody, damp undergrowth than I ever felt in any church. Since the discovery of my sister's remains, I cannot even take a walk in a wooded city park without imagining bones in the undergrowth. It's a constant battle I fight with myself. I want to be in the woods. I want to feel that peace, that ease I felt before my youngest sister disappeared, but it has left me.

I finally drove to that spot in the woods only a short time ago. I wanted – no, I needed – to see the spot where my sister's spirit soared, where her spirit left her body, where nature reclaimed her physical remains. I went to the spot where Ridgway dumped my sister's body in search of what? Her soul? My peace?

I'd thought of going since that day in 1986 when I first learned Maureen's remains were found at the junction of Interstate 90 and Highway 18, but I never knew the exact location. I couldn't bring myself to learn it.

Almost twenty years later, I sat in reporter-turned-professor Tomas Guillen's Seattle University office. I asked questions about the investigations he and fellow reporter Carlton Smith had conducted back in the early eighties, when the bodies of the earliest victims were first being pulled from the Green River. Later, they co-authored a book about the murders.

Professor Guillen asked me if I'd visited the site. When I told him no, when I said I wasn't even exactly sure where it was, there was an unspoken question in his eyes I chose to ignore for another year or so. That didn't mean it wasn't a good question.

On a dry, sunny day in Seattle in the summer of 2005, I finally faced my fears, climbed into my car, and headed east on Interstate 90 headed towards Snoqualmie Pass. I'd done my research. I knew where I was headed.

Again, I tried to follow my writing mentor's advice: I tried to be Gary Ridgway, to imagine the thrill of the kill, the body of my sister still warm inside the camper on the back of his pickup truck. I tried to understand why anyone would do what he had done, but I couldn't. Instead, I lost myself in a cassette recording of Ernest Gaines's *A Gathering of Old Men,* and denied my fears. Unlike Ridgway, I felt sick to my stomach. Unlike Ridgway, I stopped when I reached Issaquah.

I was alone. My husband had offered, had insisted on going with me. A girlfriend had promised she'd sit in the car with *Harry Potter* for as long as I needed. I thought about their offers for a long time, but I knew it was a journey I'd begun alone and needed to finish alone. So I said no to both of them and drove alone towards Issaquah, just Ernest Gaines on the tape player and me.

Downtown Seattle to Issaquah is only twenty minutes. It can be two or three times that during rush hour, of course, but I left Seattle in the early afternoon, and the road was clear. I felt compelled to stop at a grocery store off Interstate 90 to buy some flowers. Maureen has no gravesite. I'd never taken her flowers.

As I looked over the wide assortment of bright, fragrant bouquets, I realized I didn't know my sister's favorite flower, or even her favorite color. As children, we gathered armfuls of Shasta daisies and brightly colored foxgloves that grew wild each spring in any cleared spot of land, but I hadn't known Maureen as a young woman. What would she have chosen? My eyes moved from the cut flowers to the potted plants and lighted on a large pot of soft white chrysanthemums, and I was overwhelmed with memories.

I remember nothing of the memorial service itself, only that my mother had adorned the church and altar with dozens of virginal white, potted chrysanthemums. The service was held at Saint Joseph's Catholic Church in Issaquah the summer of 1986, after the Green River Task Force released the skeletal remains of Maureen's body they had recovered from that spot in the wilderness. After dental records had been matched, after forensics had determined an approximate date of death, after cremation of what little remained of my baby sister, after the service, Mom planted the flowers in her garden, where she tended them for the duration of their natural life cycle.

I left the store with a large pot of chrysanthemums, climbed back into my car while wiping tears from my eyes, and continued east on Interstate 90.

On the car seat beside me lay page 105 of the *King County Prosecutor's Summary of Evidence*. It was a dense, gruesome document outlining Ridgway's unspeakable crimes, the evidence that would have been used had the case gone to trial. Because he confessed, he was never tried. He admitted his guilt, leading police to sets of remains, in exchange for his life. The death penalty was taken off the table. The document was released to the public on the Internet, just after Ridgway's confession to forty-eight counts of first-degree murder.

I knew I would never remember the details of Ridgway's description. I couldn't memorize the minutiae. My brain couldn't hold them. So I carried the page with me.

Nearly three years later, on May 2, 1986, an Echo Glen (juvenile detention center) employee was looking for an escapee when he came across some of Maureen's remains. They were found on the west side of Highway 18 at 105th, a short distance south of the intersection of Highway 18 and Interstate 90. A pull-out and utility shed were near the area. Tina Thompson's remains had been found two years earlier on the other side of Highway 18. The Task Force subsequently recovered Maureen's remains, which were spread out over some distance. Some bones were found near a barbed wire fence. (*Superior Court of Washington for King County, State of Washington vs. Gary Leon Ridgway, Prosecutor's Summary of the Evidence, p. 105*)

Some ten minutes later, I exited Interstate 90 onto Highway 18. The spot I was looking for had to be just off the interstate, on the right side of the highway. I stopped at the first pull-out. There was no utility shed and no barbed wire fence, only a chained metal gate blocking access to a narrow, one-lane road into the wilderness. An old logging road, perhaps. The road went straight for a ways and then curved to the right.

I parked by the gate and got out, my notebook and pen in hand. My shield against pain. I felt the old, familiar cloak of distance and denial engulf me; I was a child again.

I didn't allow myself the luxury of emotion. I stayed near the car, not venturing past the gate or onto the dusty, dry trails heading off on opposite sides of the pull-out into the thick forest of cedar and fir.

There was minimal undergrowth near the highway, but I could see it grew denser as I left the roadside. The loud roar of non-stop Thursday afternoon traffic filled my senses, huge semis barreling past me, shaking the earth under my feet. New traffic. Traffic that didn't exist when Ridgway chose this spot, twenty years before. The area was littered with garbage. A Miller Genuine Draft twelve-pack box, a crushed Franz Old-Fashioned Donut box, a discarded CD. I didn't venture deep enough into the woods to see the title.

It felt like I was in the right place, but a green Washington state road sign hanging across Highway 18 told me I was wrong. "SE 104th St.," it read. *The King County Prosecutor's Summary of Evidence* said 105th.

I climbed back into my car and headed south on Highway 18 in search of 105th. A little over a quarter of a mile from the Interstate 90 intersection, I found another pull-out, but it was unmarked. I had no idea if it was 105th, but it felt wrong. It was too far from the Interstate 90 intersection and too well used. Frustrated, I made a U-turn and headed back to 104th.

I pulled off the road to the east of Highway 18, just across the highway from where I'd stopped a few minutes before. On this side of the highway, 104th was a small, paved road that headed off into a rural residential area. I coasted to a stop and tried to figure out what to do next.

I was parked in a large, open area next to 104th. Another smaller dirt road went off into the woods in a different direction. There were large piles dirt and gravel, zig-zagged with the telltale tire marks of BMX bikes and motorcycles. As I sat staring into space, a young man drove past on a dirt bike, and I jumped out of my car to stop him. "Is there a 105th around here somewhere?" I asked the dark glasses and helmet.

"Not that I know of." It turned out he was a local firefighter, and he lived up the road, so I figured he knew what he was talking about. He asked me what I was looking for, so I showed him the *Summary of Evidence* and said I was doing some research. We talked a bit about the case, and then I thanked him for his help and watched the dust settle as he sped up 104th.

I climbed back into the car and reread page 105 slowly, carefully: "...the west side of Highway 18 at 105th, a short distance south of the intersection of Highway 18 and Interstate 90." What was I missing? My eyes dropped to the bottom of the page. "Norm Maleng, Prosecuting Attorney." An address followed, and a phone number.

I dialed the number from my cell phone at exactly 4:27 p.m. and got a recorded message telling me that the office closed at 4:30 p.m.

I stayed on the line. I listened to the phone tree offerings and waited. I felt the seconds ticking away, knowing I had less than three minutes to reach someone before they went home for the evening. A receptionist answered. After I explained who and where I was, she asked me to hold while she tried to find someone who might be able to help me.

I felt like I was on hold forever, fear climbing my spine. The realization of where I was and what I was doing finally hit me. I began to tremble. I reminded myself that I wasn't alone. The young firefighter on the dirt bike was just up the road.

"Ms. Williams?" It was a man's voice.

"Yes. Arleen Williams."

"Hello. I understand you have some questions about your sister, about Maureen. Let me introduce myself. I'm Sean O'Donnell. I was one of the prosecutors on the Ridgway case. How can I help you?"

"Thank you for taking my call, Mr. O'Donnell." My voice was shaking. I limited my words. "I'm sitting in my parked car on

Highway 18 and 104th. I'm trying to find 105th, the spot where Ridgway left Maureen's body." My voice cracked. "There is no 105th."

He stalled for a minute or two, telling me how the document on the web didn't provide accurate details. It was deliberately vague because it was for public consumption. They were concerned, he said, about possible desecration of the sites.

"I don't think it's vague," I said. "I think it's wrong."

He asked if he could call me right back. He needed to look up the facts. The case had closed over a year before, and it was an enormous file. I didn't expect him to remember every detail.

True to his word, Mr. O'Donnell returned my call in less than the promised ten minutes. He said the error was just a typo: 105th on page 105. A typo!

Again, I wondered about the judicial system that allowed Ridgway to kill, to avoid capture for so many years. But I said nothing. I wanted to know whatever this man could tell me about my sister's death. I was again a child, desperate for information, but afraid to ask.

Referring to his notes, Mr. O'Donnell explained that Maureen's skull was found thirty yards off the end of the 104th pull-out on the opposite side of Highway 18 from where I still sat in my parked car. I heard the hesitation in his voice. He asked me if I was alone.

"It's okay," I told him. "I need to know."

He explained that the skeletal remains of three victims were found in the same area. In addition to the skull, other bones that were later identified as part of Maureen's scattered skeleton were also found, some as close as fifty feet from the highway. He was kind. He was gentle. He didn't want to tell me more than I could stomach. Again, I told him I wanted to know.

From thirty yards to fifty feet, he said.

I'm no good at math, but as I sat in my car staring at the pull-out on the opposite side of Highway 18, I could see the magnitude of the area he was describing. Yards and feet are quite different units of measurement. Somewhere in that space, my sister's decomposing body had lain for three years, exposed to nature's mercy. Her bones were spread apart by animals, both wild and domestic, as they sought nourishment from her body.

I wasn't just imagining this; I knew. The young man under the motorcycle helmet told me one of his neighbor's dogs had found a bone. Thinking it might be human, the neighbor had turned it over to the police, and his suspicions had been confirmed. The young man wasn't being cruel or insensitive. He just didn't know who I was, or the pain he was causing. And I had no way of knowing whether that bone was part of Maureen or one of the other two victims Ridgway left in the area.

I thanked Mr. O'Donnell for his help and ended the call. As I sat in my car, staring across the highway, I watched a red Subaru Forester stop at the pull-out. The driver, a heavy-set, middle-aged woman, unloaded four or five dogs of varying shapes and sizes. The woman was playing with her dogs and seemed in no hurry to leave. After another five minutes or so, I realized I could be waiting a very long time if I wanted to have the place to myself. I crossed Highway 18 and parked next to her.

Maybe it was her friendly smile, or maybe it was the reassuring presence of another living human being that gave me the courage to walk around that chained gate and up to the first bend in the logging road. Pacing it out, it felt like about thirty yards.

The air changed, becoming damper and mustier, as I distanced myself from the highway. The undergrowth deepened with salal, fern, and blackberry. Vines and thick grass encroached on the edges of the narrow road. It seemed like the kind of place an unwary hiker could pick up a bad case of poison oak or nettle stings, if she wasn't careful.

I walked just beyond the bend, just beyond sight of the highway, the cars, the woman and her dogs. It was as far as I could go. With each step deeper into the woods, my legs grew heavier. I didn't want to be alone in those woods, alone on the spot of earth where Maureen's young body had lain, consumed by the ravages of nature. I could feel the worms and maggots. I could smell the decay. And I wanted to turn and run.

I made myself stay. I stood still and quieted my breathing. I whispered my sister's name, but she wasn't there. I knew it was not the place to leave the beautiful white chrysanthemum.

I didn't feel her presence the way I often do when I walk the Pacific beach in front of the last home my father built, the home where my mother still lives. Perhaps that was unsurprising: the beach is washed with the waters of the Pacific Ocean, into which my parents released Maureen's ashes from the stern of Dad's small fishing boat. In this place, I only felt a deep, evil sadness and an urgent desire to get the hell out of there.

Being there reminded me of Morrie Schwartz. Not long before, I had used Mitch Albom's *Tuesdays with Morrie* as a text in a college course I was teaching. It's the story of an elderly man, Morrie Schwartz, who is dying of Lou Gehrig's disease. Morrie called himself lucky, because he had time to prepare for death, and because he knew he would die surrounded by love.

My sister didn't have time to prepare for death. She didn't even have time to learn how to live. Ridgway robbed her of that time. Unlike Morrie Schwartz, Maureen died in violence and hatred. Perhaps it was this very contrast that drew me to Albom's book. It wasn't that it helped me come to terms with my sister's death, but rather it allowed me, it gave me permission, to again cherish my own life.

I retraced my steps as quickly as possible, said goodbye to the woman and her dogs, and got back in my car. I kept my head down, my eyes guarded. To her, I was probably just another woman who needed to stretch her legs or take a quick pee in the woods.

I decided not to return to Seattle the same way I'd come. Instead, I headed south on Highway 18, knowing I'd reach the turn-off to the Issaquah-Hobart Road within six or seven miles. I knew the area. I rode horseback there even before Highway 18 was cut through the wilderness. As I drove, I clocked the distance to the driveway entrance of the last house Dad built in Issaquah on Tiger Mountain Road, the house where Mom and Dad were living when Maureen disappeared. Nine miles. Nine point two miles, to be exact. Hiking distance.

I drove the twenty-mile-per-hour curves of Tiger Mountain Road, the blinding sun filtering through the dense canopy of alder, cedar, and fir. I thought about another icy night when my mother had car trouble. She slid off the edge of one of those curves and ended up in the hospital. My old riding grounds had turned out to be a dangerous place.

When I reached the four-way stop in downtown Issaquah, I turned left, thinking I'd go into the new library and do some writing. Instead, I kept driving. Almost without volition, I headed up the hill in search of Saint Joseph's Catholic Church, where Maureen's memorial service was held in 1986. It was the church where the nine of us kids were baptized, confirmed, and indoctrinated during Monday evening catechism classes and regular Catholic Youth Organization meetings. I could have found my way there drunk and blindfolded from anywhere in the state.

But I couldn't find the church I remembered, the church that had been such a big part of my teenage years. Instead, I found a church so completely remodeled I no longer recognized it from either the outside or the inside. Gone was the long central aisle leading to the altar, lined by rows of pews. Now, there was a circular seating arrangement with a central altar. Staring at this new configuration, I wondered whether the priest would have seemed so all-powerful to me in my youth had I seen him surrounded by the congregation. The dark wooden pews felt familiar, but the crucifix that once hung over the altar seemed homeless, disoriented, off center on a far wall, the wall that used to stand behind the altar.

Had it been like this for Maureen's memorial service?

I didn't think so, but I couldn't be certain. I don't remember the memorial service, the words that were spoken, or the songs that were sung. Only the white chrysanthemums Mom had chosen to decorate the altar.

I left the potted chrysanthemum there in the church. I set it just inside the front door on the base of an ornate marble font of holy water, near the four original pillars that remained of the church I remembered.

CPSIA information can be obtained
at www.ICGtesting.com
Printed in the USA
FSHW011653061118
53592FS

9 781730 764233